Fishing in New Mexico

Fishing

UNIVERSITY OF NEW MEXICO PRESS
ALBUQUERQUE

Ti Piper

Library of Congress Cataloging-in-Publication Data

Piper, Ti, 1952–
  Fishing in New Mexico.

  (Coyote books)
  1. Fishing—New Mexico—Guide-books.   I. Title.
  II. Series: Coyote books (Albuquerque, N.M.)
  SH527.P57 1989   799.1′1′09789   88-33746

ISBN 0-8263-1138-5 (pbk.)

Maps by Mark Taylor

Contents

Preface

In 1956 Jess T. (Pop) Reid, a gentleman angler, wrote a book titled *Fishing in New Mexico*. When the University of New Mexico Press published the book, I was four years old and living a thousand miles to the north, catching sunfish, suckers, and small northern pike from Minnehaha Creek. Almost thirty years later, and now a husband and father, I found an autographed copy of this little paperback, and it became my goal to write an up-to-date version of *Fishing in New Mexico*. After driving thousands of miles, fishing hundreds of lakes and streams, and engaging in dozens of phone calls, interviews, and revisions, the book—four years in the making—was completed.

With the book finished, I could go fishing without tape recorder, notebook, camera, or sketchpad. I could show my daughter the wild roses and the wild brown trout in the Pecos, or share a sunset at a secret high-country lake in the headwaters of the Red River. I could shiver in the cold predawn calm of Elephant Butte as little threadfin shad explode out of the water (while a school of white bass—or maybe stripers—corral the baitfish for breakfast). Now I could catch brook trout, seven-inch imports from New England, in the high country of the Gila Wilderness. Now I could cast a shallow-running seven-inch Rapala far out into the blackness of midnight, hoping once again to catch the power of a huge Conchas Lake walleye. I do so enjoy the anticipation, the action, and the memories of fishing in New Mexico.

This book is the collective wisdom of hundreds of anglers and dozens of professional resource managers. Read the chapter on your favorite fishing water and compare it with your own experiences, or check out the chapter on a lake or stream where you've never been. Get excited about angling in Nuevo México and then go fishing!

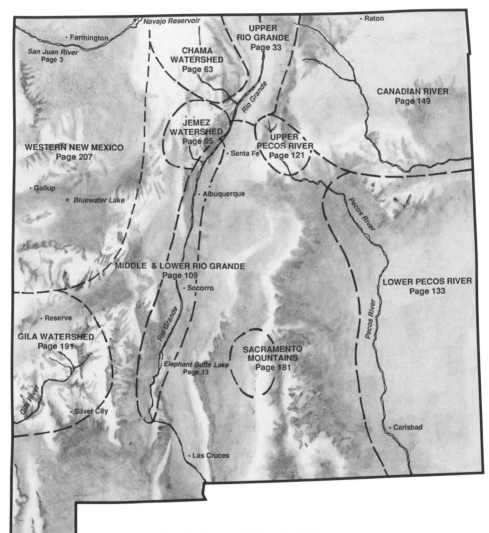

Navajo Reservoir

• Raton

• Farmington

UPPER RIO GRANDE
Page 33

San Juan River
Page 3

CHAMA WATERSHED
Page 63

CANADIAN RIVER
Page 149

Rio Grande

JEMEZ WATERSHED
Page 95

WESTERN NEW MEXICO
Page 207

UPPER PECOS RIVER
Page 121

• Santa Fe

• Gallup

○ Bluewater Lake

• Albuquerque

Pecos River

MIDDLE & LOWER RIO GRANDE
Page 109

• Socorro

LOWER PECOS RIVER
Page 133

Pecos River

• Reserve

GILA WATERSHED
Page 191

Rio Grande

SACRAMENTO MOUNTAINS
Page 181

Elephant Butte Lake
Page 13

Gila River

• Silver City

• Carlsbad

• Las Cruces

FISHING IN NEW MEXICO

Introduction

This book presents information for anglers interested in exploring New Mexico's major and minor fishing waters. Specific information is given for each lake or stream, including location, size, flow, depth, shoreline description, road access, fish species, specific angling techniques, camping and boating facilities, and handicapped accessibility, as well as a year-round fishing report for each area.

The main body of the book details almost two hundred public, private, and Indian reservation fishing waters. Each chapter represents a major water, drainage, or geographic area. A state map gives general locations. Specific details are provided in the five watershed maps and in the two site maps, one on the San Juan River and the other on Elephant Butte Reservoir. Included is a description of the sportfish found in New Mexico, a look at the New Mexico Department of Game and Fish, and a rundown of current boating and historic fishing regulations. In the back of the book is a list of nearly every fishable water in the state with a brief description of each.

In the main table of contents, New Mexico's watersheds are separated into chapters. Each heading includes a list of waters covered in that chapter. By turning to the first page of any chapter, you will find a detailed table of contents with page numbers for that area's individual lakes and rivers.

The book begins with two of New Mexico's best angling waters, the San Juan River and Elephant Butte Reservoir. Then the upper Rio Grande and all its tributaries are described, from the Rio Grande Gorge south to the Santa Clara Indian waters. Next come the complete Chama and Jemez watersheds, followed by Cochiti and then south to Caballo Reservoir. The Pecos River is surveyed from high-country trout fishing downstream through Sumner Lake and ending at the Texas border. The Canadian River drainage is treated the same way, from the trout fishing at Eagle Nest down to the warmwater fishing in the Conchas and Ute reservoirs. Next comes the Sacramento Mountains in south-central New Mexico, including Bonito Lake and all of the Mescalero Apache waters. Farther west is the trout, bass, and catfish angling in the Gila country, where elk and turkey roam the high desert wilderness. Last is the western side of New Mexico, from Quemado Lake north through Bluewater, ending at Navajo Lake State Park.

Although it is home to sand dunes, rattlesnakes, and cactus, New Mexico also contains more than a thousand miles of fishable creeks, streams, and rivers, as well as as almost a quarter-million surface acres of lakes and reservoirs. New Mexico has abundant recreational fishing opportunities. World-class trophy trout fishing is found in the fabled San Juan River—where the average rainbow is seventeen inches long! The excellent black bass fishing at Elephant Butte Reservoir makes this one of the ten best largemouth bass fisheries in the United States. Wild streams full of cutthroat flow out of the Sangre de Cristo Mountains in northern New Mexico, while fantastic spring walleye fishing is available in the big eastern New Mexico reservoirs. You can catch three-to-a-pound crappie with a cane pole, or hook a thirty-pound striped bass with saltwater gear. With a four-wheel-drive vehicle or a backpack you can make a trek into the Gila Wilderness, or enjoy a family picnic and fishing outing less than thirty feet from the pavement. New Mexico offers a lifetime of angling experiences.

What information do you need to enjoy fishing in New Mexico? When and where do you fish; how do you get there; what bait, lures, or flies should you bring; what angling secrets are recommended by the local people; what is the best time of year for your type of fishing; how does the Department of Game and Fish manage the water; is it stocked, and what are the species of fish to be found there? Are there bathroom facilities, shade trees, drinking water, recreational-vehicle hookups, crowded weekends, special regulations? Do you need a four-wheel-drive vehicle to get there? When does the ice melt from the lake, or when does the runoff reach its peak in the stream? Are there rattlesnakes or wildflowers, or both? Where is the nearest tackle shop, gas station, or convenience store? When do the stonefly, caddis, and mayfly hatches reach their peak? What size and color are the baitfish? Are there any crayfish? What type of wind, rain, or snow storms can you expect? What is the fishing like for the four seasons of the year? These questions and more are answered in this book.

Details for each lake and stream were gathered from visits to all of the major and many of the minor fishing waters; from interviews with local anglers, fishing guides, and local tackle-shop owners; and from discussions with the professionals at the New Mexico Department of Game and Fish, the U.S. Fish and Wildlife Service, the Carson, Santa Fe, Cibola, and Gila national forests, the New Mexico Division of State Parks and Recreation, the Bureau of Reclamation, the Bureau of Land Management, the U.S. Army Corps of Engineers, and the Interstate Stream Commission, as well as fisheries managers at the many fee-fishing areas (on both private lands and Indian lands). The main body of the book was reviewed by fishery biologists from the New Mexico Department of Game and Fish. The author, however, is responsible for the book's accuracy.

Fishing is, after all, fun. And if catching fish is an important part of your angling trips, you must present the right lure at the right place and at the right time. It is the purpose of this book to offer the information that will make your fishing in New Mexico the most enjoyable experience possible.

PART ONE

New Mexico Fishing Waters

CHAPTER ONE

The San Juan River and Elephant Butte Reservoir

THE SAN JUAN RIVER

The San Juan is the best river in New Mexico for consistent catches of trophy-size rainbow trout. The water is cold, typically forty-two to forty-four degrees all year long. There are few places where one can safely wade across this big river. Flows run from 500 cubic feet per second (cfs) to 5,000 cfs. There are big pools, long runs, and miles of shallow side-channels; and all are loaded with trout.

Located below Navajo Dam in northwestern New Mexico, much of this tailwater fishery is managed with special regulations. Currently, the three and three-quarter miles (the Quality Waters) of the San Juan below Navajo Dam are restricted to angling with barbless flies or barbless artificial lures, with no bait fishing allowed. The quarter-mile just below the dam is catch and release only; that is, no fish may be kept. The remaining three and one-half miles of the quality waters have a one-trout, twenty-inch-minimum bag limit (two in possession). If you catch and choose to keep a trophy fish, you must immediately leave this portion of the river. After putting your twenty inch plus fish on ice you can go to the catch-and-release area below the dam; or you can go below the special regulation area and resume fishing under normal regulations.

This complicated set of rules has produced superb trout fishing in the cold water coming out of Navajo Reservoir. The average trout caught in the San Juan Quality Waters is seventeen inches long! The catch rate on the San Juan is above the state average. In the Quality Waters you can sit on a rock and eat lunch, surrounded by a hundred feeding fish all rising in clear water to the almost daily midge hatch. Further downstream you can fish late in the evening with a big elk hair caddis dry fly and catch seventeen-inch brown trout. You can use a spinning rod and cast a bubble-fly rig, or use a pencil sinker and a red nymph and catch a dozen fish before lunch. You can cast lures or big leach flies. You can go to the regular regulation

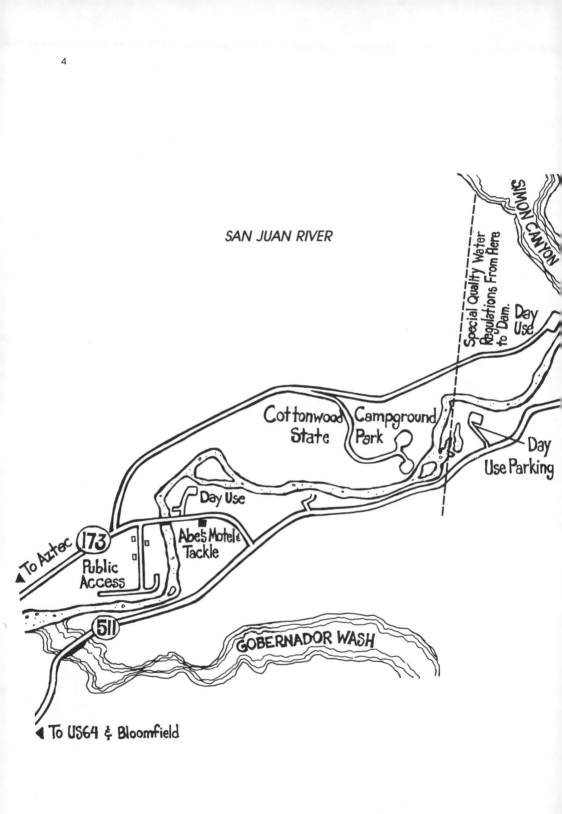

SAN JUAN RIVER

SIMON CANYON

Special Quality Water Regulations From Here to Dam.

Day Use

Cottonwood Campground State Park

Day Use Parking

Day Use

To Aztec 173

Public Access

Abe's Motel & Tackle

511

GOBERNADOR WASH

◀ To US64 & Bloomfield

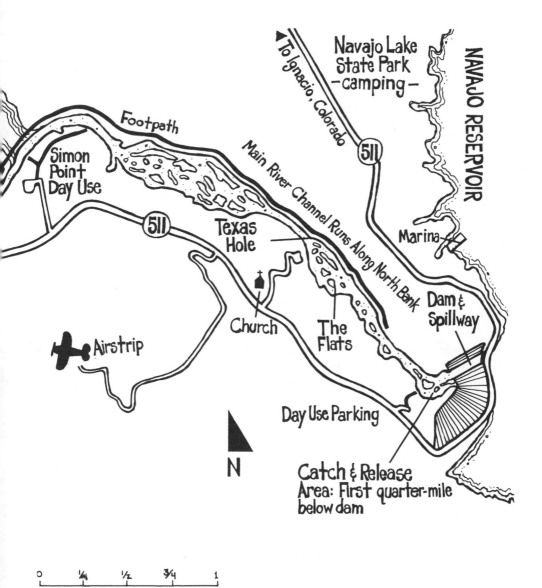

section and use lures, flies, or worms to catch and keep eight pan size rainbows; or you can go up near the dam and release every fish you catch.

In 1966 the Department of Game and Fish put special regulations on the one mile of river just below the dam. Before the dam was built, the San Juan was warm and muddy; after the dam was completed, the river flowed cool and clear. Knowing that these new conditions were excellent trout habitat, New Mexico fisheries managers convinced the State Game Commission to approve a special set of rules; artificial lures or flies only (no bait-fishing) with a bag limit of six trout over twelve inches. By 1971 the special regulation section had increased to two and three-quarter miles and the bag limit was reduced to four fish with a fifteen inch minimum size. In 1973 an eleven-pound, ten ounce rainbow—then the state record—was caught in the San Juan Quality Waters on a dry fly.

Electroshock studies demonstrated that the San Juan could produce even better trophy fishing and in 1979 the limit was changed again, to two fish at sixteen inches, with the upper quarter-mile restricted to catch and release only. In 1983 regulations again changed to one fish at eighteen inches. Electroshock statistics showed still more room available for larger fish and the bag limit was reduced to one fish at twenty inches. In 1985 the State Game Commission applied the special rules to an additional mile of water. Almost four miles of the San Juan River are now loaded with big rainbow trout ranging in size from sixteen to twenty-six inches and from two pounds to ten pounds. That's what makes the San Juan River one of the best spots for trophy trout fishing in the lower forty-eight states.

Since these restrictive regulations were established, more and more anglers have been coming to the San Juan for its great trout fishing. While mostly rainbows are caught, catches also include Snake River cutthroats and brown trout. Special techniques have evolved in fishing the San Juan, and knowing the way to catch its trophy trout is important.

The first tackle innovation on the river was the San Juan Special. Based on a small aquatic worm that lives in the water moss, this fly can be as simple as wrapping fluorescent red or orange floss on a barbless hook. Another technique is to tie a thin two-inch strip of leather to the hook, leaving both ends free to move around in the water. Anglers also discovered the effectiveness of the egg fly, which is nothing more than yellow, red, orange, or green yarn bunched together, tied on a hook, and then trimmed to look like a trout egg.

These styles of flies are fished deep, right on the bottom, through the runs and deeper pools of the San Juan. Fly fishermen use splitshot, while spinning rod anglers use pencil sinkers. Both techniques allow the angler

A twenty-two-inch rainbow caught and released from the San Juan River just below Navajo Dam at sunrise using a #10 Royal Wulff parachute dry fly.

to cast upstream and then wait to detect the trout's subtle strike. And "subtle" is the right word, since the trout often just mouth the fly. It is difficult for the fishermen to maintain the right feel with the fly. Some fly-rod anglers use strike indicators, little bits of brightly colored adhesive foam stuck on their leader; this acts like a small bobber, and if the strike indicator pauses or makes any unnatural movement, you strike. Spinning-rod fishermen must retrieve at just the right speed. If retrieved too fast the fly is pulled up from the bottom; too slow and the strike goes undetected.

Rapalas, Panther Martins, Flatfish and other popular lures catch fish, and sometimes big fish. But the lure fisherman is a rare sight on the Quality Waters. Lures imitate minnows, but there are few minnows in the river's quality section. And because of the amount of moss in this river, the lure caster will spend a good deal of time in removing this green stuff from the barbless treble hooks. A good lure fisherman will have no trouble in catching trout, but most fish are caught on flies, bits of fuzz, fur, and feather which imitate the aquatic bugs that make up the major portion of the food supply in the San Juan.

The leech fly is also popular with fishermen catching San Juan trout. These are weighted flies tied on large (No. 4) hooks, with plenty of black marabou feathers to imitate the slinky swimming motion of a leech. The fly is cast across the current and allowed to drift downstream. Most of the strikes are solid and come after the fly has finished its swing around the angler. Fishing with a leech fly is most effective when the sun is off the water, on cloudy days, or at dawn or dusk.

Midges—little bugs that look like small mosquitoes—are a staple food for San Juan trout. Midge pupae live in the moss, hatching by the billions in the summer time. The rainbows eat the pupa as it floats to the surface; rise to the pupa as it struggles to hatch; or sip clumps of the little midges as they float downstream. Standard pupa imitations are tiny (No. 18–22) hooks, wrapped with just a hint of dubbing and finished with a bit of fluff near the eye of the hook. A No. 16 or No. 18 hook, tied Palmer style with hackle (Griffins Gnat), imitates a clump of the hatched midges.

Midge fishing requires accuracy and timing. Dozens of real midges come right down their feeding lanes and the rainbow trout have no need to swim a foot or two to take a caster's fly. This type of fishing is done in shallow water with a fly-rod, a floating line, and a long, light leader. In sight-casting to a trout that is rising to midges, the fly must float naturally over the feeding rainbow at just the time it is going to rise. Once the fish is hooked, the maximum amount of pressure must be applied that the terminal tackle can bear. The idea is to get the fish in and carefully released before it is completely exhausted.

The San Juan also supports a good number of mayfly and caddis hatches. When the fish are not rising, a No. 16 nymph fished deep with splitshot is effective. Hatches of small mayflies (baetis) are common in the summer. Most of the caddis live in the warmer water further downstream and offer great summer-evening hatches. Larger dry flies, like a No. 12 Royal Wulff, are effective when floated over the slightly deeper pockets found in the shallow runs.

Access Points on the San Juan

Access is from U.S. Highway 64, twelve miles east of Bloomfield. Turn north at the marked turnoff (S.R. [State Route] 511) to Navajo Lake State

San Juan River

Fly-fishing in the quality waters of the San Juan River. (Courtesy of Mark Taylor)

Park; S.R. 511 follows the river to the public fishing areas. The turnoff at the Sportsman Inn, paved S.R. 173, is the first place where the angler must make a decision. If you turn here you drive down the hill toward the river, with Abe's Tackle Shop and Motel on your left. This is a good place to stop for snacks, tackle, a motel room, and the latest fishing information.

Just past Abe's is the Aztec Bridge. Before reaching the bridge on the north side there is a paved place to pull off that has good parking and a fishing pier for the handicapped. You can stop here to fish or walk upstream. This part of the river is not under special regulations (bait-fishing is allowed), and it is characterized by big pools, big riffles, and big runs. This day use area, with no camping allowed, is stocked with catchable rainbows. Browns and cutthroats, occasionally big ones, are also caught. If you cross the Aztec Bridge, turn south on a gravel road, and drive downhill past some houses, you end up at a sandy parking area right next to the river. This lower part of the San Juan offers good lure- and bait-fishing as well as wonderful summer evening caddis and mayfly hatches.

If you cross the bridge and take the marked gravel road to the north, you are heading toward the day use and camping areas of the state park. The gravel roads are maintained. Cottonwood Campground, the first turnoff, is an improved fee area with outhouses, paved roads, drinking water, and forty-eight assigned camping spots. Pan-size trout are stocked near the

San Juan River

campground. The special regulation area starts at the upstream end of Cottonwood. A mile past Cottonwood, the road ends at the Simon Canyon Day Use Area. The mile of river between Cottonwood and Simon Canyon is lightly fished. Here, the San Juan is contained in its natural river channel with no wadeable flats. Unless the fish are rising, this is a place to fish deep, with spiltshot, lures, sinking fly-lines, or pencil sinkers. A trail leads upstream, all the way to the dam.

If you backtrack to the Aztec Bridge and Abe's Tackle Shop, staying on S.R. 511 and continuing past the Sportsman Inn, you are driving along the south side of the river. Just across from the Cottonwood Campground the San Juan flows next to the road, two paved day-use parking areas provide good access to the river.

The next place to pull off is the paved road leading to the Simon Point Day Use Area. This is an unimproved parking area overlooking the river. Trails lead down to some excellent fishing. This part of the river, some of it wadeable, receives less angling pressure than the upstream areas.

Continuing on toward Navajo Dam, an old church marks the paved turnoff to the Texas Hole, the most famous landmark on the San Juan River. The road leads to a large fishermen's parking lot next to the river. The Texas Hole is a large and wide pool, two hundred yards across and six hundred yards long. This should be the first stop for the newcomer to the San Juan. Not only can you get an earful of the latest fishing information, but as crowded as the parking lot may be, you can hike and wade upstream or downstream and find your own private fishing spot. There are outhouses in this day-use area, but overnight parking is prohibited.

The Texas Hole gathers the river from the main channel on the northern side as well as from the acres of flats and side-channels on the southern side. The main pool of the Texas Hole's deep waters is a popular spot for spinning-rod anglers casting bubble-fly or pencil-sinker nymph rigs. In addition to handicapped-access fishing piers, there is decent bank-fishing available for those angling without waders. A hike downstream will reach some good fishing, but the wading is difficult.

Just upstream from the Texas Hole is the Cattail (or Kiddy) Pool. This is the most fished spot on the entire San Juan River. The Cattail Pool is a long and gentle run with a nice riffle at its head. This normally wadeable water is usually full of feeding rainbow trout. Upstream from the pool is about a mile of similar water, known as The Flats. Many anglers park at the Texas Hole parking lot and wade upstream until they find a side-channel to their liking.

The last designated parking spot is just below the dam, past offices of

The San Juan River is New Mexico's best trophy trout water.

the Bureau of Reclamation. A ten-minute hike down from the parking lot puts you at the big pool below the settling pond of the outlet works. You can wade through moderate flows to the island separating the outlet-works settling pond from the spillway settling pond. During high flows you should wade the edges downstream to safer water. The catch-and-release area runs one-quarter mile downstream, from the dam to a large steel cable crossing the river. Here, all fish caught must be released. The area around the cable is also a very popular (and usually wadeable) fishing spot.

Water Flows

Water flows on the San Juan range from a low of 500 cfs to a high of 5,600 cfs. The best fishing (as measured by catch rates) occurs when the water flows are between 1,500 and 2,000 cfs. Flows over 2,500 cfs make most of the flats difficult to wade, while much of the river becomes dangerous in flows over 3,000 cfs. During high flows, the trout and the safe fishing are found in the backwaters.

Water temperatures ranging from 39°F to 45°F throughout the year provide prime conditions for growing big trout as well as for producing hypothermia in the wading angler. Most fishermen, even in summer, get out of the water at least once every half-hour. If you find yourself shivering, get out immediately. Quite a few embarrassed fishermen have needed help getting to shore when they realized that the cold had sucked the strength from their legs.

Reasonable flows, a minimum of turbidity, and cold water are the mainstays of trout production on the San Juan. Flows are controlled by the Bureau of Reclamation to meet the needs of downstream users. Turbidity—how clear the water is—is determined by the clarity of the water at the inlet tube on the reservoir side of Navajo Dam. In some years a layer of cold, muddy water will be trapped (by a thermocline) in the reservoir, at the same depth as the inlet works. This turbid water then flows into the river. Fish will still be caught, but you won't be sight-casting to rising trout.

The San Juan has received national acclaim for its trophy rainbow trout fishing, and a number of guide businesses now accommodate visiting anglers. Most guides operate both wade and float trips. These professional fishermen have the expertise to lead you to big rainbow trout almost any day of the year. Their brochures can be found in all of the local tackle shops.

Fishing the San Juan can easily turn into an all-day affair. Bring along a lunch, something to drink, and a handful of high-energy candy bars to replace the calories lost when fishing in this 42°F water. Many anglers swear by their neoprene waders, a type of insulated chest wader which helps to keep out the cold. A wading staff is another helpful tool on the San Juan, a river full of slippery rocks; a stable staff can aid a tired angler in getting back safely to the parking lot.

The Angling Year on the San Juan River

Spring.   Flows can be high as the Bureau of Reclamation lowers the reservoir to handle the runoff. Wade safely and don't fight the high water. The trout will be in the easily waded backwater areas. San Juan Specials and egg flies fool the trout, while lures work fine in the deeper runs. The midges start hatching in May, when the days grow longer and the air temperature warms.

Summer.   Afternoon showers can bring high winds that blow the midges into the surface film, making for fabulous fishing. The midge hatch is in full swing every day. Hatches of No. 16–18 baetis mayflies can fill the Texas

Hole. Deerflies, dragonflies, and damselflies mean action for those casting larger dry flies. As the flows drop (and the main channel becomes more accessible), spoons, lures, and weighted nymphs work well. Don't let a full parking lot scare you—plenty of fishable water is available. There is an excellent evening rise to caddis and mayflies in the regular waters up and down from the Aztec Bridge.

Fall.   During these cooler days there is still plenty of surface action for the fly fisherman. Black leech flies are deadly when the sky is overcast. Midges still hatch in force. Explore the Simon Point Day Use Area with lures or with weighted woolybuggers, and watch for the evening rise.

Winter.   Midges are still strong until January, but the surface rises are few after January. The toughest months are February, March, April, and May. Try San Juan Specials fished slow and deep, and use leech patterns on stormy days.

Current fishing reports and flow-rate information for the San Juan River are found in the Albuquerque newspapers' weekly fishing reports and on the Department of Game and Fish's tape-recorded fishing report. Abe's Tackle Shop, located right next to the river, collects daily information from fishermen. The tackle shops in Albuquerque, Santa Fe, Durango, Bloomfield, Aztec, and Farmington also keep track of river conditions. The best information is from the man or woman fishing upstream who keeps hooking rainbows while you just can't buy a strike. Wade up and ask about their technique, then use it to catch (and carefully release) trout from the San Juan, New Mexico's only world-class trout stream.

ELEPHANT BUTTE RESERVOIR

Elephant Butte Reservoir is the biggest Chihuahuan desert bass pond in New Mexico. Located between Albuquerque and El Paso along I–25, the Butte holds the best all-around bass fishing in New Mexico—largemouth, smallmouth, and striped bass, as well as white bass. Bass from ten inches to thirty pounds can be caught on any day of the year. Other sportfish include crappie, walleye, catfish, and even a few trout. Gizzard and threadfin shad are the important baitfish. Find the shad and, especially for the white bass, you've found the action.

Elephant Butte is an irrigation impoundment on the Rio Grande, just upstream from Truth or Consequences. The reservoir started to fill back in 1916, when the Bureau of Reclamation put the finishing touches on the huge concrete dam. In 1970 the lake was around ten thousand acres, but

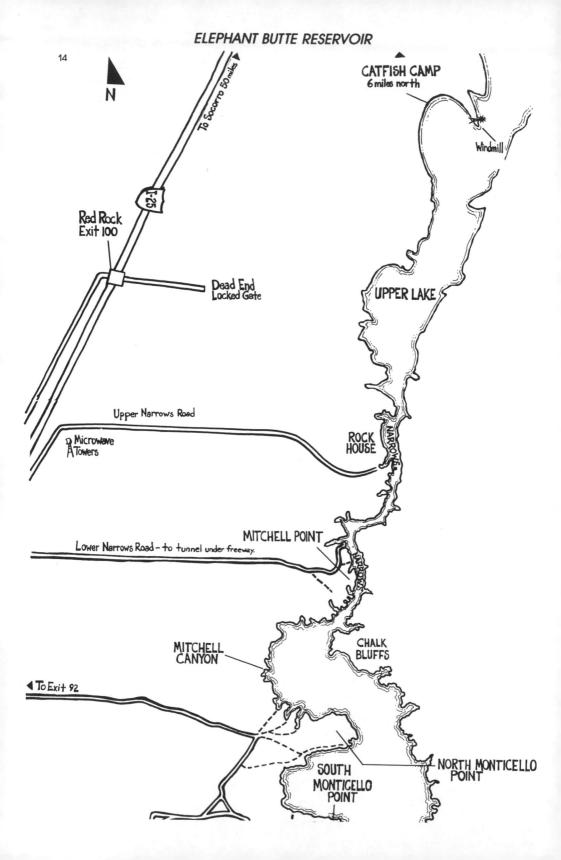

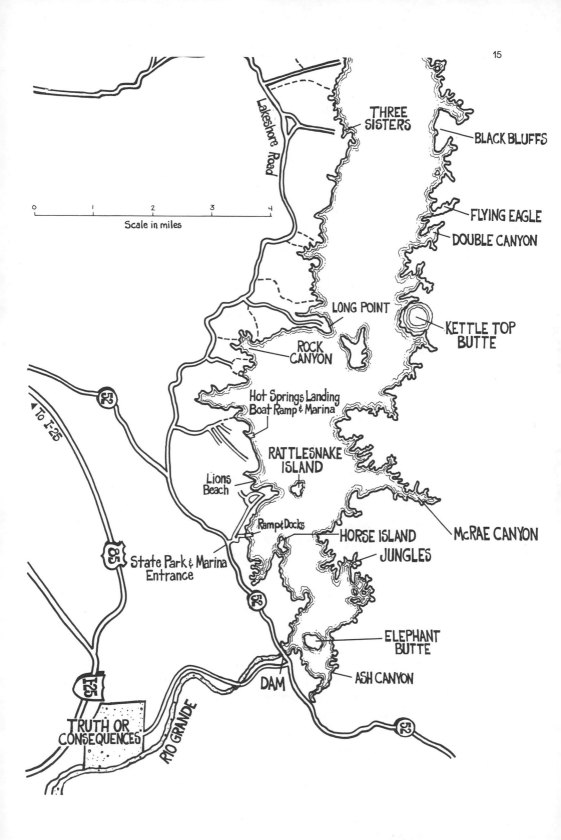

heavy northern snowpacks in the 1980s have extended Butte to its maximum of 40,000 acres. The result has been an explosion in sportfishing, particularly bass fishing, at Elephant Butte.

This reservoir is currently considered one of the top ten largemouth bass fisheries in the United States, with more than a million people visiting the state park every year. During the Memorial Day weekend it becomes New Mexico's third largest city. One-third of the boating done in New Mexico takes place at Elephant Butte. Bass fishing tournaments—some national and many regional—are held here all year long. In other words, Elephant Butte can be a very busy place.

The lake is over twenty miles long when it is full, and it varies from one-quarter mile to three miles wide. There are two developed state park areas; three marinas; excellent boat ramps; recreational-vehicle hookups and improved campgrounds; motels; miles of pick-your-own-spot, dirt-road camping areas; rattlesnakes; gulls; catfish; quail; walleyes; crappie; shad; giant carp; and very few shade trees.

The shoreline angler expecting to equal the weekly fishing report will often be disappointed. Most of the sportfish follow the baitfish; if the baitfish are within casting distance of the shore, then bank fishermen catch fish. But since that's not always the case, summer midday fishing can be tough. Minnows are arguably the best bait for the bank fisherman, but they are not a guarantee. It is more important to find the right location than to quibble about bait or lure selection. If catching fish is important and you are not getting any strikes, then move to a different type of shoreline. In general, the size, varied structure, and fish habits found at Elephant Butte work in favor of the angler with a boat.

Death by drowning is the first thing to consider when boating on Elephant Butte. Think of this lake as a huge wind tunnel on the floor of the Rio Grande Valley. Spring winds blowing down the valley build tremendous waves, and summer thunderstorms turn quiet August afternoons into a mad rush for a safe shoreline. Waves have reached a height of eight feet. Inexperienced folks will lose control of their boats in two- to three-foot swells. Boats can easily be swamped in three- or four-foot waves. Five-foot waves are merciless. Every year people drown while boating at Elephant Butte. Don't drink while boating. Pay attention to the weather, know your abilities, and get off the lake before the waves grow dangerous.

At the present, near full-water level, Elephant Butte is actually two lakes connected by a narrow canyon called the Narrows. The lower lake once ended about twelve miles above the dam; then, as recently as 1975, water levels expanded the lake to a twenty-mile length. Now, with a half-dozen

Elephant Butte Reservoir

Mark Taylor, *Albuquerque Tribune* outdoor writer, fishing for largemouth bass on the east side of the Upper Lake of Elephant Butte.

strong runoff years during the first half of the 1980s, a boat can go a full twenty miles from the dam through the lower lake, through the Narrows, into and through the upper lake, and ending where the Rio Grande enters the reservoir.

The fishing in the upper lake was discovered in 1984. Reputedly, a tournament bass fisherman looked at a topographical map and identified what he considered to be the remains of an oxbow lake in the upper lake. He smashed and bashed his boat through the flooded cottonwood trees, salt cedar, mesquite brush, and willows. It was like fishing in a southern Georgia swamp, but without the moss. He caught enough bigmouth bass to win the tournament, and his discovery was soon public knowledge. There is limited road access to the upper lake, but those with boats have excellent bass fishing from March to mid-August.

This upper lake is only one-fifth the size and much younger and shallower than the lower lake. The submerged brush and shrubs, which have not yet disintegrated, act as food farms, as grocery stores, and as a nursery for yearling fish. The Rio Grande drops much of its silt load in the upper lake,

Elephant Butte Reservoir

and this sediment provides an incredible supply of nutrients. Sunlight, water, and nutrients are the start of Elephant Butte's food chain. These are all strong reasons why the upper lake can offer very good fishing.

Fifty degrees is the minimum for good catches in the upper lake, and such temperatures are reached in March. At sixty degrees the bass angler can switch to topwater baits, with excellent up-lake fishing continuing until about mid-June. As water temperatures climb in midsummer the catching grows more difficult. In September the water cools and largemouth catching is easier. But colder temperatures arrive in November and during January and February the upper lake is almost deserted. The few anglers persisting during these months are pursuing trophy largemouth, and though catches will be few and far between, this is the time to hunt seriously for big fish.

There is access to the ponded water at the uppermost end of the upper lake on dirt roads east from I–25 at the San Marcial exit (Exit 124). This is not access to the open water of the upper lake, nor is it access for those pulling boats on trailers. Heading east from the overpass, the road turns to gravel, then turns south where the road divides. The road follows the Low Flow Conveyance Channel and eventually disappears into the channels, mudflats, marsh, and ponds at the north end of Elephant Butte Reservoir, a favorite area for early spring catfishing on bait with rod and reel. There is also a good run of white bass in the conveyance channel, usually in May. As water levels drop, the fish and the fishing disappears. Before you try the angling at San Marcial you should check with Albuquerque bait shops for up-to-date fishing information. At high water levels the Bureau of Reclamation often closes the gravel road. This area is sometimes called Milligan Gulch.

Access to the open water of the upper lake is by boat. It requires nearly an hour-long ride with a sixty-horsepower motor at full throttle to travel from the launch ramps near the dam to the middle of the upper lake. This means that a round trip to the Windmill—a landmark in the upper lake— and back is beyond the gas range of most boats (about thirty gallons). There are no floating gas stations on this end of the lake, so you should take with you all necessary gasoline and food and supplies.

For those trailering boats the Catfish Camp state park campground affords access to the upper lake. Take Exit 107, go south on the east frontage road for 2.5 miles, and then east on 8 miles of gravel road. This is the northernmost state park campground and is known for its litter and weekend crowds. Fishing the area's submerged brush with jigs or trolling shallow running crankbaits in the deeper water of the upper lake produces good

Elephant Butte Reservoir

Tournament fisherman and guide Dale Wagey about to release a largemouth bass at Elephant Butte.

catches of smallmouth, largemouth, walleye, white bass, and crappie for the early summer angler based out of Catfish Camp.

The state park Rock House area (an abandoned rock house) is the only accessible spot on the south end of the upper lake. Because of its location in the deep water of the Narrows and just south of the shallow water of the upper lake, this may well be the best spot for the boatless angler after springtime white bass. It also has an unimproved boat launching area (a four-wheel-drive vehicle normally is not necessary), which is important for the small boat owner who wants to fish the upper lake. Even though the Rock House location is unimproved (chemical toilets only) it is the most popular spot other than the paved-road state park areas, and it is very crowded on weekends. Keep in mind that this is rattlesnake country.

To get to the Rock House from Albuquerque, get off I–25 at Exit 100 (Red Rock Exit) and head south for several miles on the westside frontage road. Turn and go under the freeway at the first tunnel, then head north on the eastside frontage road. At the site of a high microwave tower the road veers east, reaching the Rock House about seven miles later on a gravel road. If traveling from the south, take the Mitchell Point Exit (Exit

92) and head north on the westside frontage road to reach the microwave towers.

The upper lake will continue to offer great fishing only if Elephant Butte stays near its full capacity. After three or four dry years, the upper lake will gradually turn into more of a swamp than a great warmwater fishing lake.

The Narrows

The Narrows is the old Rio Grande river channel connecting the upper and lower lakes. This canyon is less then a quarter-mile wide and about four miles long. At full throttle it's about a thirty-minute (twelve-mile) boat ride from the state park boat ramp to the lower end of the Narrows. The current running through the Narrows is not the kind you notice while drifting in a boat, but it's a subtle continuous current that attracts the baitfish; and baitfish attract the sportfish.

Catches here are good throughout the year. In fact, the Narrows is the outstanding spot for catching white bass in the entire lake. Most anglers get decent action by trolling lures. Electronic sonar will often show the whites to be deeper than a normal lure's depth. The key to fishing most of the Narrows is to get your lure where the fish are, and that often means using a deep water technique.

Mitchell Point is at the south end of the Narrows, and you can get there by taking the Mitchell exit off I–25 (Exit 92). Head north on the westside frontage road for a few miles, then go under the freeway at the first tunnel and head east. The unimproved boat launching area at Mitchell occasionally requires a four-wheel-drive vehicle for safe launching and trailering. This unimproved area is very popular in the summer.

Elephant Butte Lake

Following the upper lake, which is a wide shallow spot in the Rio Grande, and the Narrows, a deep river canyon, we finally reach the lake that started bass fishing in New Mexico—the lower, or main Elephant Butte Reservoir. Below the Narrows, from Mitchell Point south, the Butte widens. The old river bed curves around North Monticello Point and heads toward the Chalk Bluffs. Below the Bluffs, Elephant Butte really starts to open up.

The lower lake is much more stable than the upper lake. The main lake has a much slower and smaller change in water temperature. The upper lake acts as a sediment trap, and thus the lower lake has clearer water. The lower lake is bigger and deeper. Neither lake ever freezes over. These contrasts make for differences in both the fish and the fishing. Smallmouth bass are more abundant in the southern half of the lower lake. Spring largemouth catches are better in the submerged trees in the upper lake. Walleye are more prevalent in the lower lake, and striper action is consistently better in the southern half.

The main entrance to Elephant Butte Lake is off I–25 at Exit 83. The paved road, S.R. 52, goes past a handful of convenience stores and gas stations. There is a marked turnoff to the Old Hot Springs Marina. This is not the main boating facility at the Butte, but if you take the turn you can drive north for a dozen miles. The road, which changes to maintained gravel, is known as Lakeshore Drive. It skirts the lakeshore, leading to the lake's westside landmarks: Cedar Canyon; Rock Canyon; Three Sisters; North and South Monticello points; and Monticello Bay with its recreational-vehicle park and convenience store. Lakeshore Drive is the boatless angler's only access to the great fishing and unimproved camping on the west side of Elephant Butte Lake. This gravel road eventually turns west and meets the freeway at Exit 92, Mitchell Point Exit.

If you do not take the Old Hot Springs turnoff, but continue driving south on S.R. 52, you will pass through the developed area of Elephant Butte, with its jumble of boat storage and repair shops, a motel, post office, restaurants, vacation cabins, gas stations, stores, trailer parks, and residential neighborhoods. The entrance to Elephant Butte Marina and the state park is next.

Elephant Butte Marina is the state's largest: it includes a full-service facility with a tackle shop, a convenience store, marine equipment, boat rentals, a gasoline dock, fishing information, fish-cleaning stations, and a snack bar. There is an excellent paved boat ramp with parking and toilet facilities. The marina and tackle shop and the boat-ramp parking lot are the best sources for up-to-date fishing information, especially at dusk, when most boaters are pulling in.

Elephant Butte State Park operates, two full-service, fee-use campgrounds with hot showers, shelters, recreational vehicle hookups, a dump station, and drinking water. The Lions Beach facility is next to the Elephant Butte Marina. The Damsite facility, near the dam, is a smaller and older full-service state park facility with the welcome benefit of shade trees; it also has a marina.

Elephant Butte Reservoir

A Texas rigged plastic critter was used to catch this largemouth bass at Elephant Butte.

Fishing the Main Lake

Much of the south end of Elephant Butte is characterized by deep, clear water. The south end is reached by boating from the state park boat ramp due east across the lake to the Jungles, and then south to Ash Canyon and the dam. Here you'll find good walleye, largemouth, smallmouth, crappie and striper fishing. With clear water and rocky cover, you often need to use techniques that get your lure deep. Use jigs, deep-diving crankbaits, downriggers, jigging spoons, or weight-forward spinners.

Ash Canyon is as far south as you can go in Elephant Butte Lake. The canyon is right next to the Damsite facility. Its steep sides make for difficult shore-fishing but the walk down can be worth the effort. Incidentally, striped bass ruin more tackle here than in any other other spot accessible to the boatless angler.

The Jungles is a prime area for largemouth, and the most consistent walleye producer in Elephant Butte. This large area of shallow water lies two miles north of Ash Canyon on the east side. Trolling the edge between the shallows of the Jungles and the deeper waters of the main lake is often very productive.

McRae Canyon is a no-wake area just north of the Jungles. McRae is heavily fished, and for good reason—it's an excellent place to cast a lure any time of the year. Located in the southern part of the lower lake, it has plenty of deep clear water; but it also contains reeds, shallows, drop-offs, and little islands. In other words, you can find here just about any type of structure you want. Fifty boats can fish this canyon bay without bumping into each other. If you're new to Elephant Butte and have a boat and operator capable of handling that day's weather, try McRae. It is *the most consistent* area on the entire lake for productive fishing. As for tournament fishing, thousands of dollars have been won in this section of very fine black bass water.

The next landmarks north of McRae are the deep-water canyons of Kettletop, Double Canyon, Flying Eagle, and Black Bluff. All contain a variety of sloping shorelines, and are excellent places to catch largemouth bass during the spring spawn. Many people come to know these canyons quite intimately when high winds force them to spend the night in their protected coves. Fishing in these eastside areas is good throughout the year, with a special emphasis on white bass catches in the spring. Angling below the Black Bluffs is known for its crappie action.

The most northern stop on the east side of Elephant Butte is at the Chalk Bluffs. These light colored cliffs, with steep drop-offs and plenty of underwater shelves, provide good places for winter fishing. The bluffs are located next to the old river channel coming out of the Narrows, which makes for great deep-water angling.

Much of the east side of Elephant Butte Lake is characterized by many side-canyons with steep walls leading directly down to deep water. There is no good road access to the east side. The west side, however, has a gently sloping shoreline leading gradually to deeper water. The west side is characterized by sandy beaches, shallow brush-filled coves, good gravel-access roads, carp, spring crappie fishing, excellent unimproved camping areas, and some of the best autumn fishing on the lake. Rock Canyon, Long Point, Willow Canyon, Cedar Canyon, Three Sisters, and Monticello Canyon are all landmarks on the west side. Rock Canyon is a deep-water exception to the shallow-water rule, it offers good autumn bass fishing.

Lakeshore Drive gives the boatless or small-boat angler access to these westside areas. The shorebound fisherman should look for spots where shallow and deeper water meet, such as Long Point, Three Sisters Point, and North and South Monticello points. In these good fishing spots you can camp anywhere. There is a convenience store with gas, tackle, propane, minnows, and recreational vehicle hookups between the two Monticello points. Canoes or small boats are appropriate on the west side of Elephant Butte as long as you stay near the shore and out of the main lake. Even on a glassy-smooth day, the wind can build two-foot swells in less than ten minutes. So be careful and stay alive.

Big and Little Fish at Elephant Butte

Striped bass, ten to forty pound ocean imports, can be fought and landed with eight pound test line and an ordinary rod and reel. Sharp hooks, good knots, a decent drag, and a bit of luck are more important than hundred-dollar tackle. Once you learn how to use an electronic-sonar unit and discover how effective it is to jig a one-ounce, swivel-rigged, white bucktail over the deeply submerged cottonwood trees, you'll switch to a stout boat rod, seventeen-pound test, and a reel that can handle a thirty-pound fish when the drag is set at five pounds. If a big striper, weighing say twenty-three pounds, is the catch of a lifetime, keep that fish and have it mounted. But if you've learned where to look for these huge sportfish, consider using stout tackle and getting the fish quickly to the boat, and then release them. Striped bass have not been shown to reproduce successfully in Elephant Butte.

If you find an area that consistently has pieces of dead six-inch baitfish (gizzard shad) floating on top, you've located a striper feeding ground. Only rarely will you see stripers attacking shad against the surface, something for which other striper lakes are famous. When you find a school of white bass, cast a white bucktail jig and let it sink beneath the whites. Stripers often cruise under the school, eating the threadfin shad stunned by the white bass.

Shad

Shad, which are not a sportfish, are the prevalent baitfish in Elephant Butte. From March to November, if you can find a school of shad you have found the sportfish. When bass bunch and herd a school of shad, the surface erupts with the baitfish leaping into the air.

Threadfin shad grow to four inches in length, and can spawn more than once each year. A small black dot on their shoulder gives threadfin shad their name. Shad eat plankton, and Elephant Butte bass definitely eat the shad. If wind and wave action blow plankton against the north shore of a bay, that's where the shad will be. And where the shad are, the white bass will be.

Any lure that has the shad's colors of a dark top and a pearly white bottom will be good for casting in Elephant Butte. A white marabou lead-head jig is the cheapest and often the most effective. Many people choose the white and black plastic shad imitation (Mr. Twister style) on a leadhead hook. The shad colored Model A Bomber is the most popular crankbait on Elephant Butte.

Landmarks at Elephant Butte

Upper Lake.   Windmill, Bird's Roost, Catfish Camp. This shallow Rio Grande inlet, with submerged brush and trees, is a fishable lake only when the water level is near full. The largemouth fishing is superb from March through mid-August, with trophy chances in February. There is dirt-road access to the lake's extreme upper end with no trailered boat launching. Catfish Camp has an unimproved boat ramp and fee camping. You can fish for crappie, carp, catfish, white bass, smallmouth, walleye, stripers, and largemouth.

Narrows.   Rock House, Mitchell Point. This deep water canyon, cut by the Rio Grande, connects the upper lake to the lower lake, always has a subtle current, and is an excellent year-round area to troll for white bass. It is the best white bass spot in the lake, but often requires deep water techniques. There is road access at Rock House and Mitchell Point. In this rock wall canyon with its submerged shelves and deep water you can fish for stripers, white bass, crappie, walleye, and largemouth.

Lower Lake, north end.   Chalk Bluffs, Tom's Rock, North and South Monticello Point, Mitchell Point. Here you can find any kind of structure you want, from shallow to deep, sandy shores to canyon walls, from sub-merged cottonwood trees to underwater shelves. There is good winter fishing at Chalk Bluffs, and a gravel road and bank access to the west side, but no road on the east side. Here, you can fish for white bass, crappie, largemouth, catfish, and stripers.

Lower Lake, east side.   Black Bluff Canyon, Flying Eagle Canyon, Double Canyon, Kettle Top Butte. There is no road access to these steep walled canyons, where you can find largemouth bass, good crappie, decent walleye and striper fishing.

Lower Lake, open water and midlake islands.   Long Island, Rattlesnake Island, Horse Island, Elephant Butte Island. Here are walleye and small-

Elephant Butte Reservoir

White bass offer great fishing and good eating. These imports reproduce rapidly, and the forty-fish limit on white bass affects their numbers less than do natural conditions.

mouth bass as well as stripers, white bass, and largemouth bass. Fishing is good around the islands, but a sonar unit is needed for productive open-water fishing. This is dangerous water for small boats when the wind comes up.

Lower Lake, west side.   Monticello Canyon, Three Sisters, Cedar Canyon, Willow Canyon, Long Point Canyon and Island, Rock Canyon, Old Hot Springs Marina. Very good autumn fishing is found in the westside canyons, with good crappie in the spring. An excellent gravel road provides access to a dozen unimproved spots for launching small boats. There is a convenience store at Monticello Bay.

Lower Lake, south end.   State Park Boat Ramp, Dam, Dirt Dam, Ash Canyon, McRae Canyon, Damsite Marina. In the deep and clear water are smallmouth bass, walleye, largemouth, and white bass; it is also good for stripers. McRae Canyon has perhaps the best fishing on the entire lake. A developed area on the west side, where state park headquarters are located, has recreational vehicle hookups and camping. There is good fishing below the dam when flows are moderate, especially in April.

Elephant Butte Fishing Report

January is a slow month for fishermen at Elephant Butte. Short days and cold water shut down much of the food chain. Most of the sportfish are in deep water. When fish are lethargic and deep, the most productive technique is deep water jigging with natural bait. The south end of the Narrows is the best place to start, but any spot with a deep vertical structure can produce good catches. Put your minnow or jig thirty to forty feet deep. Crappie will be the main catch, but you may fool a walleye, largemouth, or a striper. A mild winter can make the black bass catchable in shallower water, but rarely in January. While walleyes will hit slab spoons in deep water around Kettletop, the white bass will stay hidden until the water warms. Catfishing is always good.

A cold February continues the January slowdown. But a warm spell will wake the sportfish, and surprisingly, a crankbait can produce largemouth bass. The norm will still be deep-water jigging with minnows, and the south end of the Narrows is still a good place to start. Walleye, crappie, black bass, or an occasional striper will strike a minnow, jig, or slab spoon. Catfishing will be good at the north end of the upper lake. Still, no white bass are seen or caught.

In March the spring winds start to blow, the afternoons grow warm, and the white bass emerge from hiding. The crappie begin feeding at shallower depths, largemouth strike at minnow imitations and at plastic worms, and the walleye and smallmouth bass grow active. There is good white bass and largemouth fishing in the low-flow conveyance channel above the upper lake, and in the south end of the lower lake at Ash Canyon, McRae, and the Jungles. Stripers will be caught in Ash Canyon and along the dirt dam and by late March the black bass will be in shallow water. Flipping will be productive, especially in the upper lake where the water first warms.

Better striper action arrives in April and Ash Canyon and the Dirt Dam are good places to begin. The Chalk Bluffs will be a favorite place for the crappie angler and a good starting location for the white bass fisherman. A strong afternoon wind will often be dangerous. Black bass fishing is good in the upper lake as well as at the north end of the main lake. Catfishing will still be good.

In May, when the south end warms, the sportfish are being caught in shallower water, and there's good flipping action for largemouth. Crappie action is still improving, with good largemouth, excellent walleye, and decent crappie fishing in both McRae Canyon and the Jungles. White bass are being caught in the main lake, with the best action at the north end. Good crappie fishing is found near the Marina. Although the upper lake may slow down a bit by the end of May, this is one of the best months to fish at Elephant Butte.

June is a fine month for warm-weather fishing. Catches of black and white bass and crappie are good in the north end and south to the dam. The whites are going deeper at midday, but they still offer plenty of good action, especially in the morning and evening. Topwater lures create strong strikes from black bass both early and late in the day. Now, with summer here, the upper lake is still good but the catching is definitely slowing.

On the July Fourth weekend Elephant Butte State Park is the third largest city in New Mexico. If you enjoy the company of just a few other anglers, don't fish at Elephant Butte on the Fourth of July; it's a circus. The best fishing is often at night. Shore-fishing is decent off rocky points, but best with bait. The upper lake is difficult. White bass are very catchable if you jig deep water. July is the worst of the summer months for easy fishing, but July at Elephant Butte is still better then most other New Mexico bass lakes. Catfishing is still good.

It's still hot in August, but the fishing improves. Casting mid-depth lures is productive for black bass, especially in the Narrows. There's some top-water action in the morning and evening, mostly in the south end. Day fishing in the south end is good with plastic worms. Very good striper action, maybe the best of the year, is found by jigging in deep water around Kettletop. White bass fishing is good at night around the Marina. Overall, August is better than July for fishermen.

In September fishing is superb everywhere. Striper action is still good around Kettletop. The white bass are back in medium to shallow water, mostly on the west side. Largemouth fishing is excellent in the upper lake, the west side of the main lake, and at the south end. Topwater lures offer exciting fishing for blacks in heavy brush. Consistent walleye catches are found in the Jungles. This is one of the best two months to fish at Elephant Butte.

October is a changeover month. As the days grow shorter the white bass go to deeper water, but fishing for whites is still good in the south end. Black Bluff is the place to find walleyes and crappie. Though there is little

A white bass from Elephant Butte can usually be caught using a lure that imitates threadfin shad.

top water action for black bass, flipping produces good strikes in the upper lake. Striper catches are not consistent, but they are still best around Kettletop and in Ash Canyon. When autumn brings its cooler temperatures, the food chain slows down and so does the fishing.

November finds the sportfish heading for deeper water. The white bass are twenty feet deep in late afternoon and down to forty-five feet in the morning and evening. Walleye fishing is still quite good in McRae and the Jungles. Fewer but larger black bass are caught, with the smaller blacks already holding in deeper water. Crappie fishing is good, as usual, at Black Bluff. Cold weather really slows down the fishing.

Fishing December's cooler water means getting your lure deep, from thirty to sixty feet with minnow, jig, or slab spoon. Warm and sunny days will pull the bass up in the ten- to twenty-foot depths, especially in the upper lake. The crappie are still available in deep water, just over brush, at the south end of the Narrows. Fishing is good around the marina, so try using patience and bait.

Elephant Butte Reservoir

Fishing below Elephant Butte Dam on the Rio Grande

The Rio Grande below Elephant Butte Dam holds walleye, rainbows (both little stockers and big river trout), browns, striped bass, white bass, catfish, suckers, carp, threadfin and gizzard shad. Although fishermen catch large sportfish on this part of the Rio Grande, the catch rates are low. Anglers get few strikes, but those fish they do catch are big. Five to ten pound rainbow trout, ten to thirty pound striped bass, and five to fifteen pound walleye have been caught.

The river just below the dam is on Bureau of Reclamation land and is posted (and fenced) "No Trespassing." A quarter-mile below the dam the river is open to public fishing. This area is part of Elephant Butte State Park. The roads are paved, and bathrooms, shaded picnic tables, and drinking water are provided in this fee area. Fishing in the state park area is fairly good during moderate to strong flows, and is poor at low flows.

A paved road follows the river downstream from the dam and crosses the river at a bridge near the end of the state park. A dirt road turns off the pavement just before the bridge and also follows the river downstream. Regardless of flow rates, this stretch of the Rio Grande at and below the bridge offers good angling opportunities in the deeper runs, riffles, and pools.

The next easy access is at the Cuchillo Creek bridge. Follow the paved road downstream toward Truth or Consequences and you'll get to Cuchillo Creek. Cuchillo is an intermittent creek but it meets the Rio Grande at a large pool. There's a good parking area. Both the pool and this part of the Rio Grande have given exciting moments to lucky anglers. A quarter-mile downstream from Cuchillo there are a pair of gravel, manmade "riffles." Good catches have been made below these structures.

The Rio Grande continues downstream, through Truth or Consequences, and into the mudflats at the head of Caballo Lake. Fishing can be good (or bad) in this entire stretch. Water releases out of Elephant Butte Dam are the limiting factor for fish and fishermen on this part of the river.

Years of continuous heavy snowpacks in the upper Rio Grande watershed puts Elephant Butte Reservoir near its highest elevation. When this happens, releases are kept near maximum during the spring and summer. Exceptional years finds water still being released at strong flowrates right through winter.

Compare this high flow scenario with what happens in years when the mountains to the north get moderate to low snowpacks. The release gates on Elephant Butte dam will be opened just enough to provide the required amount of summer irrigation water. In winter the gates are almost completely shut and the Rio Grande flows very low and quite clear.

Fish and fishermen must deal with the results. In extremely high flows, typical in the spring, angling is decent with bait in the back flows and eddies near the shoreline. At moderate flows the lure, fly, and bait fishers all have reasonable success in the runs, pools, and just below the riffles. At low flows the anglers must find the deeper runs and pools which still hold fish.

Those after stripers get their best hookups before sunup. Many of these fishermen use very stout tackle, salt-water spinning reels loaded with seventeen pound test line and capable of casting heavy, seven inch lures. Big nets are needed as these stripers can range from twenty to forty pounds. In the predawn darkness these fish are easier to hook, but not necessarily easier to land.

White bass, walleye, and large trout are caught on large, lead-head jigs holding plastic shad imitations. Small, stocked rainbows are caught using salmon eggs, corn, or worms.

Fishing for all species is often better in the spring when these fish, especially the whites, the walleye, and the stripers, move up-river from Caballo Reservoir. Caballo acts as a downstream "ocean," the fish move upstream for their springtime spawning maneuvers.

Strong water flows throughout the winter months means good habitat and growth for these Rio Grande sportfish. Low winter flows shuts off the supply of water and the baitfish (threadfin shad) needed to produce trophy-size catches. Check the weekly fishing report in the Albuquerque newspapers and in the recorded Game and Fish fishing report. Rio Grande fishing is either good for large fish or poor for all species. Check out the fishing reports before you go.

CHAPTER TWO

Upper Rio Grande and Tributaries

RIO GRANDE GORGE

The Rio Grande Gorge is famous for its big trout and equally famous for its long switchback trails leading to the river. The gorge is a deep, forty-eight-mile-long canyon running from the Colorado border south to Pilar, New Mexico. To cast a line in the Rio Grande requires a healthy walk down the steep, six hundred foot rim; but the effort is worth the perspiration, for this river grows big fish. The lure angler will catch trout and be surprised with the big northern pike. The fly-rod fisherman casting for trout will occasionally pull in a dace or chub. The bait-caster takes a chance for carp, suckers, northern pike, catfish, and trout. Rainbows, browns, cutbows (hybrids) and a few cutthroat naturally reproduce in the river. The New Mexico Department of Game and Fish helps by stocking thousands of brown trout fry both above and downstream from the Red River confluence.

During the spring runoff the water is high and muddy, the wind brisk, and the angling often impossible; you're more likely to hook a two hundred pound kayaker than a trout. The river clears after the high-country snow disappears. The fishing starts somewhere between May and July and continues until the next year's runoff. Summer fishing is best early and late in the day, when the sun is off the water. The long summer evenings invite cutbait catfishing in the long, quiet pools. Even on warm winter days the trout will be feeding. In autumn, which is definitely the best time to hike into the Rio Grande Gorge, you'll hear the geese honking high overhead as they fly downstream to their winter pasture. The cottonwoods match the spawning colors of the big browns and these fall-season trout are on the move, defending their territory during the spawning urge and eager to strike at the fisherman's lure.

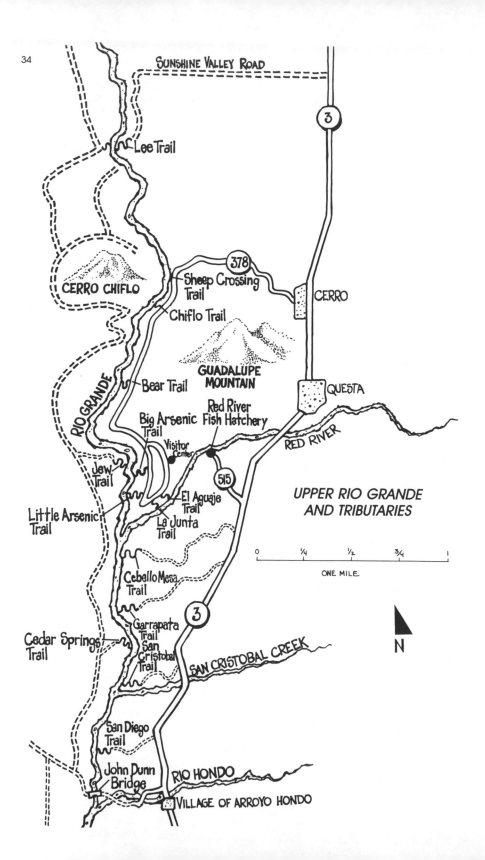

SUNSHINE VALLEY ROAD

3

Lee Trail

378

Sheep Crossing Trail

CERRO CHIFLO

Chiflo Trail

CERRO

GUADALUPE MOUNTAIN

RIO GRANDE

Bear Trail

Red River Fish Hatchery

Big Arsenic Trail

QUESTA

Visitor Center

RED RIVER

Jew Trail

515

El Aguaje Trail

Little Arsenic Trail

La Junta Trail

UPPER RIO GRANDE AND TRIBUTARIES

0   ¼   ½   ¾   1

ONE MILE.

Cebello Mesa Trail

3

Garrapata Trail

Cedar Springs Trail

San Cristobal Trail

SAN CRISTOBAL CREEK

N

San Diego Trail

John Dunn Bridge

RIO HONDO

VILLAGE OF ARROYO HONDO

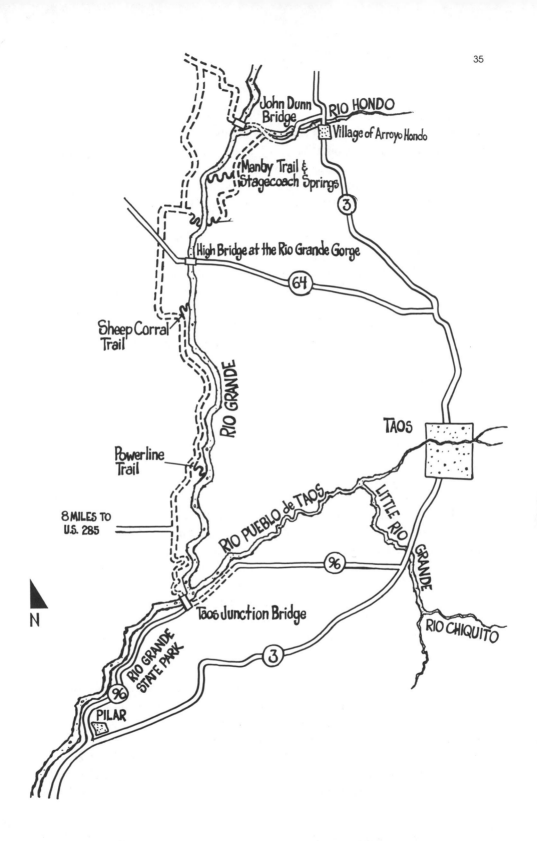

Rio Grande Gorge

From the Colorado border south to Lee's Rapid the Rio Grande does not support a very good fishery. Low-water levels raise water temperatures too high for a large trout population. Access is difficult and fishing is a matter of chance. A guided float trip from Colorado's Lobato Bridge down to Lee's Rapid is an exciting way to get wet while seeing this northern part of the river. The better fishing starts near the Bureau of Land Management's Wild River Recreation Area camping sites near Questa. Here are tributaries and springs, an abundance of water that turns the Rio Grande into an excellent trout fishery. Two tributaries, the Red River and the Rio Hondo, harbor good spawning beds and serve as nurseries for the trout fry. This part of the river grows large fish. Ten-pound German browns have been caught and released by fisheries biologists in the lower Red River area. Three-pound trout, prize catches by local anglers, are found by hiking down the mile-long trails in the recreation area. Remember that this is high desert country: pack a canteen—with water!—respect the rattle of the local snakes, and don't sit on the cactus.

The John Dunn Bridge is the only way to get to the bottom of the gorge without a hike. Follow State Highway 3 north from Taos and turn west at the village of Arroyo Hondo, just north of the little river. Drive the three mile dirt road along the Rio Hondo to its confluence with the Rio Grande at the John Dunn Bridge. If this is your first trip here, make it when the road is dry. Park your car at the bridge, hide your valuables, lock your car, and start fishing. Wheelchair fishermen take note: This is your only spot for fishing the gorge. Fish downstream or upstream on either side. There are big pools, good riffles, wild fish, and stocked rainbow trout. If you like fishing alone then walk for 20 minutes before casting. This is a well-used spot.

There are dozens of trails leading from the rim down to the river. Some are well marked and maintained by the Bureau of Land Management, while others are rough paths known only to the longtime gorge hiker. A few of these trails require the agility of a mountain goat. For easy access, the John Dunn Bridge is the only road to the river between Colorado and the Taos Junction Bridge near Pilar.

Except for warm winter days, trout fishing in the Rio Grande Gorge is best when the sun is off the water. Overcast days with a light wind are perfect. Overnight camping on the bottom is the best way to see this wild river wake to a new day. Ospreys and eagles share a morning's fishing. Many of the local fishermen hike down in the afternoon to catch the evening's fishing. You will need a good flashlight for the tired walk out. Your favorite bait will work anytime, sunk into a deep pool or cast upstream to work the drift. If you start catching suckers, then cast to slightly faster water. The lure-caster, like the fly fisherman, must find the fish, so keep trying different types of water and different lure weights. Once you get a strike, take the hint and cast to similar water.

Fish the structure of the streambed. Gigantic river rocks have been falling into the Rio Grande for eons, and each one offers a home to a big brown or rainbow trout. Cast upstream and let your lure work the front, the side, and the backwater pockets of these boulders. Try the head and tail areas in the big pools, fishing deep through the long runs. During high water, fish the holding spots at the very edge of the river; the trout don't like to fight the mainstream current any more than you would. Take a fat inventory of differently weighted lures and remember a spare reel (although you won't need the spare reel because nothing ever breaks, of course, when you're a two-hour hike and a one-hour drive from the nearest tackle shop). Small lures work better in shallow water, while the heavyweights get down fast in the deep pools and fast runs.

The fly fisherman must hope for the rise while fishing the nymph. Cover the pocket water with a big, weighted nymph (No. 10 peacock or No. 12 white caddis pupa). In November the browns are busy spawning but you can trigger their attack reflex with a streamer or bucktail. Autumn through early spring brings the snowfly, a tiny midge that the trout may rise to all day long. Look for warm, sunny days; cast only to rising fish; and use a long, fine leader. In May a No. 16 tan caddis hatches by the millions. Depending on the runoff and the Colorado irrigation drawdown, this can be the best dry fly action all year—or the worst.

Except for the John Dunn Bridge area, there are no hatchery trucks stocking nine-inch rainbow trout into this part of the Rio Grande. Instead, here are wild trout in a wild river. Even the few stocked fry that live to catchable size are survivors, because for two years they have escaped the jaws of the northern pike, the hungry trout, and the sharp dive of the osprey. Regardless of your fishing style, you must change your technique if you aren't getting strikes: keep trying different kinds of water and consider your first strike as a clue to the type of water the trout are holding in.

Hiring a fishing guide for the Rio Grande is the closest thing to a guarantee for the fisherman. A good guide knows the back roads, the trails, and the spots likely to be successful for your type of fishing. He knows where the trout lie throughout the changing seasons, and he can locate fish for you even as conditions change throughout the day. Good guides are well known at the local tackle shops, so check them out before you put your money

Rio Grande Gorge

Jump fishing trout in the deep canyon of the Rio Hondo upstream from the John Dunn Bridge. Taylor Streit, Taos Fly Shop owner and guide, keeps a tight line on a feisty brown trout.

down. The cost of hiring a guide can be worth the pleasure of good fishing—especially if you are new to the Rio Grande Gorge.

The three bridges crossing the river in the gorge connect to a maze of dirt roads on the west rim. Depending on conditions, theses roads can lead to adventurous angling or to an exercise in freeing yourself from the mire. North from Taos Junction Bridge is the steep Powerline Trail, with great spinning-rod water at the bottom. Driving across the John Dunn Bridge gives access to Jew Trail and the often great fly-rod water at Cedar Springs. North–south dirt roads on the west side of the Rio Grande High Bridge lead to McCraken and Sheep Corral trailheads. These dirt roads and trails, unmarked and not maintained, are not for the family station wagon; a sturdy, high-clearance pickup or a four-wheel-drive vehicle is recommended. The back roads on both rims lead to many great fishing spots but they are a long distance from a tow truck. Be prepared by taking extra water, food, and blankets.

The Sangre de Cristo Mountains parallel the gorge to the east, rising tall to meet the winter storms and catching the snow for next year's runoff.

The Rio Costilla, Red River, the Rio Hondo, San Cristobal Creek, and the Rio Pueblo de Taos all have their headwaters in these mountains. Much of the Rio Costilla, which is on National Forest land or on state-leased property, offers the finest cutthroat fishing in New Mexico. Access is off S.R. 3 at the town of Costilla (see the separate section on the Rio Costilla). Good paved-road access to the Red River, at the Red River Hatchery, offers good fishing as well as a trail all the way to the Red River's confluence with the Rio Grande; but this route involves a long, switchback hike to the better fishing in the lower Red River Box. Better access to the lower Red River is from the El Aguaja Campground in the Bureau of Land Management's Recreation Area. This section above the confluence is famous for its autumn run of big brown trout. For a private fishing day, take the hike into the San Cristobal Creek confluence, a quiet cottonwood spot explored by few anglers. The lower Rio Hondo is heavily fished because it parallels the Arroyo Hondo–John Dunn Bridge road; and here an autumn angler can watch the browns leap small waterfalls on their upstream spawning run. The lower Rio Pueblo de Taos offers paved access but difficult fishing. Upstream from the Taos Junction Bridge, the Rio Pueblo de Taos tumbles over boulders and gouges pockets of deep, swift water. The trail is rough and wading is dangerous. Fish with lead on your leader, so that your hook sinks deep in these fast pools.

The Spanish Conquistadors named this wild river *El Rio Grande de Norte*, the great river of the north. Respect the name of this river and the canyon it made. As you hike down to this grand river, keep your mind on the trout and your eyes on the trail; this is no place to twist an ankle.

Getting there is half the fun on the Rio Grande. There are good fishing trails on the west rim, but the nearest gas station is many rough miles away. A dry, bumpy drive to a new hotspot can turn into a forced campout if the clear morning sky becomes an afternoon gullywasher, so inform others of your schedule and destination. Plan your fishing trip carefully, and be prepared for early- and late-season snow, spring winds, and summer thunderstorms. A good day in the gorge will net you three nice rainbows, a sunburned neck, one ten-inch and two sixteen-inch browns (plus one that got away), and a chill on the hike back out.

People have been fishing here for thousands of years. In 1968, the U.S. Congress included this part of the Rio Grande in our nation's Wild and Scenic Rivers Act. In fact, the Rio Grande was the first river to come under the protection of the act. The Rio Grande Gorge is truly one of New Mexico's wild and scenic places.

Rio Grande Gorge Access

Sites marked with a double asterisk (**) are in the Bureau of Land Management Rio Grande Wild and Scenic River Recreation Area, just north of Questa. This is an improved area with paved roads, camping, drinking water, outhouses, bathrooms, a visitor center, and marked trailheads leading down to the river.

Costilla Creek.   Twelve miles north of Questa, turn west at "Top of the World Farms" dirt road, then travel three miles west to reach the trail.

Lee Trail.   Nine miles north of Questa take the "Sunshine Valley" dirt road; travel west six miles to the rim and a fair trail.

Sheep Crossing.   Two miles north of Questa, follow paved S.R. 378, beginning at the Cerro turnoff, two miles from Cerro.**

Chiflo.   Take S.R. 378 three miles from Cerro to reach a half-mile trail.**

Bear Crossing.   Five miles from Cerro on S.R. 378, a one-mile trail leads to the river, its rugged shoreline, and tough fishing.**

Big Arsenic.   Almost nine miles from Cerro on S.R. 378, this is an excellent two-mile trail, with no "arsenic" in the springs.**

Little Arsenic.   Nine and one-half miles from Cerro on S.R. 378, this is an excellent one-mile trail.**

La Junta.   Ten miles from Cerro on S.R. 378, this a poor one mile trail.**

El Aguaje.   Ten and one-half miles from Cerro on S.R. 378, this good three-quarter-mile trail offers good access to the Red River confluence.**

Jew Trail.   Travel nine miles of dirt road, north of John Dunn Bridge on the west side of the river, to reach a fair trail.

Cebolla Mesa.   Four miles south of Questa then travel three miles west to the rim on a marked dirt road. The campground provides good access to the Red River confluence via a one-mile trail.

Garrapata Canyon.   Travel four and one-half miles south of Questa, then three miles west to the rim via a jeep road, to reach a fair trail leading to the river.

Cedar Springs.   Five miles north of Arroyo Hondo, travel west one mile on a dirt road to trail on east side (this access usually closed off by private land), or north from John Dunn Bridge on west rim for five and one-eighth miles on a dirt road to an old mining trail leading down to the river.

San Cristobal Creek.   Two miles west of San Cristobal Village, take a unmarked dirt road to the rim and the trail.

San Diego.   Two miles north of Arroyo Hondo, travel west two miles on a dirt road to reach the trail.

John Dunn Bridge.   Travel the gravel road from Arroyo Hondo three miles west, the road leads right to the river.

Manby Hot Springs (Stagecoach Springs).   One and a half miles west of Arroyo Hondo, travel south two and one-half miles on a dirt road to a half-mile trail.

Rio Grande High Bridge.   About three miles north of Taos on S.R. 378, then west on U.S. 64 to the bridge, no trails at bridge.

McCraken (Raven).   From the west side of the Rio Grande High Bridge, travel north one mile on a dirt road to reach a good half-mile trail.

Sheep Corral.   Go south one and one-half miles on a dirt road from the west side of the Rio Grande High Bridge to reach a fair three-quarter-mile trail.

Powerline.   Drive up the west rim from Taos Junction Bridge, then travel north four miles on a dirt road to high voltage lines, and take a steep three-quarter-mile trail to the river.

Taos Junction Bridge.   Exit S.R. 68 at Pilar, about ten miles south of Taos, then drive the paved road through the state park to the bridge.

RIO DE LOS PINOS

Rio de los Pinos is a trout stream starting near Cumbres Pass, upstream from Trujillo Meadows Reservoir in southern Colorado. Before it heads south to enter New Mexico, the little mountain river passes beneath the tracks of the wood-powered Cumbres and Toltec Scenic Railroad. You can fish Los Pinos in Colorado by taking the steam-powered locomotive (or a gravel road) to the town of Osier and then hiking down to the river. You might arrange to have the train drop you off in the morning and pick you up the next afternoon. Wild brown trout are the quarry; elk, deer, and mountain jays will be your only companions.

A few miles downstream from Osier, Los Pinos enters New Mexico on Carson National Forest land. Access to the upper section is by backpacking down from the railroad tracks. Adventurous anglers will find six- to ten-inch stream-bred brown trout. Call the Toltec and Cumbres Scenic Railroad in Chama, New Mexico, or Antonito, Colorado, for ticket information.

The river then moves into six miles of private land. The Carson National Forest map shows access through this land on Forest Route 284. Call the ranger station in Tres Piedras for current access information. Most fishermen are interested in the section below this private land.

Rio de los Pinos

The public Rio de los Pinos Wildlife and Fishing Area is reached by driving north on U.S. 285 from Española, through Tres Piedras and into Colorado, and by turning west on the unmarked paved road just before Colorado State Route 17 at Antonito. That turnoff is right next to the only gas station on the west side of U.S. 285, across from the cafe and just before the railroad tracks. Follow the paved road as it meanders to the little village of Ortiz. Turn west on the gravel road, which follows along the north bank of the Rio de los Pinos, to reach the marked public fishing area.

The Department of Game and Fish bought this property in 1953 to provide public fishing on this mostly private stream. There are outhouses and picnic tables, but no drinking water or trash barrels. The sign at the no-fee camping area asks fishermen to pack out what you bring in. In June the dirt and gravel access road is passable, and the hatchery truck arrives with its first load of catchable-size rainbows. The stocked trout can be found in the deeper runs and pools, in any spot where you can't see the bottom.

If you drive further upstream you come to another bridge. This is Forest Route 87A—with four-wheel-drive recommended—which leads south to the trout lakes at Lagunitas and Laguna Larga national forest campgrounds. Don't cross the bridge if you want to fish Los Pinos. Continue west on the north side of the stream, where there are more campgrounds. Farther upstream you enter well-marked private property.

Casting for trout in the Rio de los Pinos is an angler's delight. An easy cast across the stream will put your hook in the trees on the other side. Hip-waders will keep your knees dry, and you can cross Los Pinos almost anywhere. Once in the morning and once in the afternoon, you'll hear the steam whistle of the wood-fired locomotive. Deer, raccoon, and occasionally elk leave their footprints in the river bank; and the trout, mostly stocked rainbows and a few wild browns, feed all day long in this quiet little river.

Light tackle is the key to catching the sportfish in Los Pinos. The fly-rod is superb at presenting flies or bait to these hungry trout. Another good choice is a lightweight spinning rod set with splitshot and a wet fly. Very small lures or worms cast on four pound test line will also fool the trout. The active fisherman, working upstream and casting to likely holding spots, will catch more trout than those who choose to sit back and drown salmon eggs. Both types of anglers, however, will enjoy fishing Los Pinos.

The fly fisherman will find a good hatch of stoneflies in May and into June. A late runoff will keep the roads closed and the river unfishable. By June there are dependable hatches of small mayflies and caddis. A No. 16 or 18 dry fly or nymph will catch trout all day long. Spin fishermen who see rising fish should tie on a casting bubble and a No. 12 wet fly.

Lagunitas and Laguna Larga

A female mayfly laying eggs on a car top.

The campgrounds are sometimes crowded, but a short walk will take you to an unfished portion of the stream. Stretches of Los Pinos some distance from the campgrounds will occasionally produce a few wild browns. Unless you see rising fish, walk right by the areas that are wide and shallow. Trout, whether wild or stocked, prefer to lie in water that can hide them from above. There are very few classic pools in Los Pinos. Look for runs that are one to three feet deep, for that's where the trout are.

While the family car will do just fine when the roads are dry, a pickup or four-wheel-drive vehicle is recommended. Summer showers are common and can turn portions of the gravel access road into an impassable mush. Handicapped fishing access is possible in one or two spots where the road is right next to Los Pinos.

LAGUNITAS AND LAGUNA LARGA LAKES

Lagunitas (little lakes) and Laguna Larga (large lake) are two little fishing spots in the northern reaches of the Carson National Forest. Both are east of San Antonio Mountain, ten miles south of the Colorado border and about seventy miles north of Española on U.S. 285.

Lagunitas and Laguna Larga

Laguna Larga

Laguna Larga is closest to the pavement and right in the middle of antelope country. This is open rangeland with only a few distant trees. Between summer rain showers this countryside is hot, brown, and dusty. It is gorgeous and green in the spring, cool and crisp in autumn. Winterkill is not a problem in this pond and springtime fishing for holdover rainbows is decent as soon as the roads clear. In June the stocking truck drops off about six hundred catchable-size rainbow trout. That makes early summer the best time for fishing this fifteen-acre natural pond. A hot July and August with limited rainfall will hurt the fishing at Laguna Larga. A thick algae bloom is to be expected as there is no constant supply of fresh water. If it doesn't rain, the fishing suffers.

Laguna Larga is about fifteen miles off the pavement, has an unimproved, no-fee campground with a few outhouses and no drinking water. The road is impassable in wet weather and rough but usually passable in dry weather.

Lagunitas Campground

Lagunitas Campground is about thirty miles off the pavement. This improved no-fee camping area has drinking water, bathrooms, and picnic tables. The road is bladed a few times each year and though it does get rough, this Forest Service road (at least in summer) is passable when dry. Figure an hour's drive from pavement to campground. Little Hondas, Escorts, and Toyotas bring in anglers all summer long. A four-wheel-drive vehicle, however, is a definite asset as a big thunderstorm will make the road impassable for a day or two.

Lagunitas sits in the foothills just east of the Brazos Ridge. Firs and spruce surround the little lakes. Fed by seeps and springs and stocked in June with about 2,000 catchable-size rainbows, Lagunitas offers good late-spring angling, good hot weather fishing, and good autumn catches. Because there is rarely a winterkill, you might even catch some of the self-reproducing brook trout or hook into a fat fourteen inch holdover rainbow. The top two lakes contain trout, the others do not. Fly-fishing is good, especially early and late on summer days. Grasshoppers are the best natural bait. Worms and salmon eggs also produce. Lures, even tiny ones, do not bring many strikes. The kids will enjoy the beavers, the chipmunks, and the fresh air views of the distant mountains.

The drive into these two fishing areas starts at the marked Forest Service road (F.R. 87), about ten miles north of Tres Piedras. Turn west and after eleven miles you'll get to the Laguna Larga cutoff (F.R. 78). Laguna Larga is only three miles in on F.R. 78, but the road can be rough. To get to Lagunitas, continue west on F.R. 87. Gradually you will leave the antelope rangeland, drive through the ponderosa landscape, and finally reach the tall trees which surround Lagunitas Campground. Four to five miles before the campground you'll pass the Los Pinos cutoff (F.R. 87A) and the Beaver Creek jeep trail (F.R. 572). The first leads to the great fishing on the Los Pinos (see the chapter on the Los Pinos) and the second leads to some great walk-in brook trout fishing on Beaver Creek.

Stop in at the Tres Piedras Ranger Station for up-to-date road conditions and to buy a Carson National Forest Map. Handicapped access is reasonable at both Lagunitas and Laguna Larga. Be prepared, big summer thundershowers can cut off the access road for days. A quick look at the Carson National Forest map will show you that it is only an hour's hike from the Lagunitas area to the fishing in the upper Brazos Meadows on the Tierra Amarilla Land Grant. Don't even consider sneaking into the land grant. You'd be trespassing on posted, very private property. If you want to fish a good small trout stream than head over to little Beaver Creek or the larger Rio de los Pinos.

FISHING THE UPPER RIO GRANDE TRIBUTARIES

There are dozens of good trout streams on the west side of the Sangre de Cristo Mountains, little rivers which tumble down to feed the mighty Rio Grande. We'll cover these streams from north to south, starting with the Rio Costilla, New Mexico's newest public-access trout stream; but first, a word about chasing the runoff.

On an average year, April is too soon to fish the west slope tributaries. These streams harbor few quiet pools; the snow-melt tumbles over two thousand feet from the headwaters down to the Rio Grande, and until the runoff quiets, you are better off fishing somewhere else. Wait until May before venturing forth (check the weekly fishing reports in the Albuquerque newspapers). Summer thundershowers can muck up a day's fishing, but that is no problem: if one stream is high and muddy from a summer rainstorm (or too low from a lack of summer rain), then just jump in your car and go to a different drainage.

RIO COSTILLA

The Costilla's two headwater creeks start on the Vermejo Ranch and are collected at Costilla Reservoir (see Chapter Eight for information on the great fishing on the Vermejo property). Just below the reservoir, the Costilla is on the new 100,000 acre Valle Vidal addition to Carson National Forest, and you'll need to buy a ten dollar Wildlife Habitat Improvement Stamp to fish this section. Get your stamp from any Department of Game and Fish office or check to see if your local tackle shop sells them. The fishing season on the Valle Vidal is from July 1 to December 31.

Below the Valle Vidal, the Costilla flows on Rio Costilla Cooperative Livestock Association (RCCLA) property, but the Department of Game and Fish leased public fishing rights from the RCCLA for the five miles of river just below the Valle Vidal boundary. This area is open for fishing throughout the year; the good fishing starts in June, slows down at the end of October, and quits in late November. The river below the state lease section is fishable with a permit purchased from the RCCLA office in Costilla. You will still need a state fishing license.

Access to all of the Rio Costilla is off S.R. 3 at Costilla, about forty miles north of Taos and just a mile south of the Colorado border. There are gas stations, convenience stores, and a restaraunt in Costilla. Drive east on S.R. 196 through Costilla and you'll soon be driving along the river.

Continue east through the village of Amalia, past the turnoff to the Rio Costilla Ski Area, and where the wide river valley shrinks to a narrow rock canyon you will see signs marking the beginning of the public access area. The lower 2.8 miles of this stretch are stocked with catchable-size rainbows and normal regulations apply. But upstream from the confluence of Latir Creek, the Costilla is managed as a wild cutthroat fishery. Signs state the regulations: lure- or fly-fishing only, no bait allowed, with a two-fish bag limit.

The same regulations (fly or lure only, with a two-fish bag limit), hold on the Valle Vidal. Studies by state and federal fisheries managers show a good population of naturally reproducing cutthroat trout. Actually, these are cutthroat hybrids: the native Rio Grande cutthroats have crossed with stocked rainbows to produce the present population. Regardless of their genetics, these cutthroats offer great trout fishing. The Rio Costilla is the best cutthroat stream in New Mexico.

In the no-bait section, spin fishermen should use small lures, splitshot, and a selection of wet flies and nymphs. Rio Grande King wet flies and gold ribbed hare's ear nymphs are two excellent choices for casting with a lightweight spinning rod. Use four-pound test line and just enough splitshot so that you can cast the flies. Fly fishermen should bring their favorite nymph and dry-fly patterns (don't forget some No. 14 elk hair caddis dry flies). Caddis, midges, and mayflies are abundant in the Rio Costilla. The Costilla is a small river and hip waders are adequate to fish this little north-country stream.

The river has a good strong flow throughout the summer because water releases are controlled from the upstream Costilla Reservoir for downstream irrigation needs. While many of New Mexico's streams can be too low for good mid-summer fishing, the Costilla produces excellent angling through the dog days of summer. Fishing is best during the weekend as that is when the RCCLA stops releasing water from its upstream dam, but weekday fishing is still very good. Water releases are usually shut off at the end of September. October and November fishing is still good on the Costilla below the confluence of little Comanche Creek. The best map of this great cutthroat stream is available from your closest national forest office, ask for the Valle Vidal Unit map.

Fee camping is available on a private campground near the state lease section as well as much farther upstream on the few public campgrounds in the Valle Vidal. No camping is allowed on the state lease section. Remember to buy a user stamp for fishing on the Valle Vidal.

Downstream from the public waters, the Costilla heads north into Colorado and then dips back into New Mexico before dropping into the Rio Grande Gorge. Few other than whitewater enthusiasts have seen the confluence. There are some nice fish caught here, but only occasionally. Fishing is best in the fall when the browns are spawning.

An added plus for those who drive into the Valle Vidal is the fishing available at Shuree Lakes, right off Forest Road 1950. One of these big ponds is reserved for children under twelve years of age. The lakes are regulated with a bag limit of two fish over fifteen inches and tackle is lures or flies only. All three of these small lakes are stocked with oversized rainbow trout and occasionally with Rio Grande cutthroat hybrids. Spin fishermen can cast lures, but these anglers seem to get more hits with a black wooly worm and a casting bubble. Fly fishermen should bring along black wooly-buggers and elk hair caddis dry flies. The larger of these ponds is perfect for canoe or float tube fishing. This larger pond is also closest to the parking area and, with help from an able-bodied friend, is accessible to handicapped anglers.

It is a long drive to Shuree Ponds (four to five hours from Albuquerque).

You have to have a fishing license and a ten dollar Valle Vidal stamp for each adult angler. There is no camping allowed around the lakes. These are good reasons to fish Shuree Ponds. The drive from the town of Costilla is a beautiful, one-hour cruise on a good gravel road which brings you right into the middle of the 100,000 acre Valle Vidal wilderness. And nine of the ten dollars you paid for your Valle Vidal stamp goes right back into habitat improvement on the Valle Vidal. And camping is available, just not around the lakes. And best of all, the fish are big.

LATIR LAKES

The other trout lakes in this part of the Costilla watershed are the Latirs. These natural jewels are stair-stepped down the steep sides of Latir Peak. In the 1950s these high mountain lakes were nationally known for their huge cutthroat. The state record came out of the Latirs in 1981. Caught on a Mepps in-line spinner, it weighed ten pounds, two ounces, and was over two feet long. A permit from the Rio Costilla Cooperative Livestock Association (RCCLA) is necessary to fish the Latirs. The RCCLA office is in Costilla.

Even if the jeep trail to the lower lakes is open, it is at least a two-hour hike to the upper lakes. There are nine lakes, each set in a natural basin and all connected by Latir Creek. Latir Lake Number Nine sits under Latir Peak at an elevation of almost 12,000 feet. Access is usually possible in early June.

The fishing is tough in these small clear lakes. Fly fishermen should bring scud patterns, midge flies, big dries, woolybuggers, and large, peacock-bodied flies. Salmon eggs, corn, and worms rarely produce fish, bait fishermen should try grasshoppers. Spin fishermen should bring casting bubbles and some wooly worms. The key to good hookups seems to be to retrieve the wooly worms very slowly. If you try the Latirs, ask the RCCLA folks (when you buy your permit) which of the lakes are producing good catches of cutthroats. These lakes were "fished-out" in the early 1980s but are now under a management plan and will soon recover their former stature as producers of big cutthroats.

RED RIVER

The watershed south of the Costilla is collected by the main stem and the tributaries of the Red River. Fishing on the Red River can be divided

Red River

Downstream from the Red River Hatchery, the Red River flows through a deep canyon on its way to the Rio Grande. Plenty of browns, cutbows, and rainbows live in this unstocked river.

into three sections: the headwaters above the town of Red River; the stretch from Red River town downstream to Questa; and the lower run from the Red River Hatchery down to the Rio Grande. Each of these sections offers a very different kind of trout fishing.

The headwaters of the Red River are just a couple miles east of the Taos Ski Valley. Reached by paved road (S.R. 150) heading south from the town of Red River, the Red River breaks into a half-dozen forks and feeder creeks. This is small stream fishing for small wild trout: rainbows, brookies, and cutthroats. Goose Lake is in this area, a stocked five-acre mountain trout pond reached by trail or jeep road. Goose Lake is located at an elevation of almost twelve thousand feet, and, if you can get there, offers good mid- to late-summer rainbow trout and cutthroat fishing. Middle Fork Lake (of the Red River), also accessible by jeep, is one of New Mexico's better high mountain lakes and is stocked with cutthroat fry. Lost Lake and Horseshoe Lake, both at the headwaters of the East Fork, are the other two headwater lakes; and both are stocked with cutthroat fry.

The middle section of the Red River is heavily stocked and heavily fished.

Centered around the river, the river canyon, the town of Red River, and the surrounding Sangre de Cristo Mountains, this is a vacation corridor with all types of facilities. There are private campgrounds and summer cabins, improved national forest campgrounds, and full-service motels and recreational vehicle parks—all accessible on paved S.R. 38 between Red River and Questa. This is a very busy place in the summertime, especially on weekends. Two ponds near the river, Fawn Lakes and Eagle Rock Lake, are stocked with catchable-size rainbows. Both are located in the national forest campgrounds which bear their names.

The lower section of the Red River is an unstocked wild trout stream feeding the Rio Grande. An easy access point is the Red River Hatchery. The paved turnoff is two and one-half miles south of Questa. Facilities at the hatchery include paved parking, bathrooms, and a self-guided tour. There is a pond stocked with rainbow trout reserved for anglers under age 12, age 65 or or over, and for the handicapped. Upsteam from the hatchery fishing is productive, but most people cross the footbridge and head downstream. The Red River is nearly doubled in size by the springs in this area, and though there are no catchables stocked, fishing can be good. In the fall, winter, and early spring, large browns and cutthroat-rainbow hybrids (cutbows) are found in this stream. The pools and runs in the half-mile below the hatchery get a lot of fishing pressure. Consider hiking downstream before wetting a line, or fish and hike upstream from the confluence with the Rio Grande. Both fly fishermen and bait fishermen should bring along plenty of splitshot. This is a swiftly moving stream with an abundance of deep runs.

CABRESTO LAKE AND CREEK

Cabresto Lake is tucked high in the mountains north of Taos. The road is rough and rocky, the lake is not stocked, and big trout are rare. But the mountain beauty and the wild cutthroat and brook trout are strong attractions for the visiting angler. This fifteen-acre irrigation impoundment is fed by Cabresto Creek Lake Fork, one of Cabresto Creek's main tributaries. The dam smooths out the wild spring runoff for summer use by farmers living downstream.

Cabresto Lake is located within Carson National Forest. The best access is from the village of Questa, twenty miles north of Taos. From Questa, turn toward Red River on S.R. 38. A few hundred yards east, turn north on Forest Route 134. The turnoff is marked with a "Cabresto Lake" sign.

After a mile and a half of pavement, the road turns to maintained gravel and Forest Route 134 follows Cabresto Creek into the national forest. The little stream is heavily stocked with catchable-size rainbow trout, and summer fishing is good. On this and other little mountain streams, cast your bait upstream and let the current bring your worm into fish-holding pockets. There is some private property along Cabresto Creek, but plenty of public angling access.

After about three miles of two-lane maintained gravel on Forest Route 134, take a marked turnoff (Forest Route 134A) north toward Cabresto Lake. The road is quite steep, very rocky, one lane wide, and about twenty minutes long. First-timers should use a pickup or four-wheel-drive vehicle; experienced off-roaders can usually get by with a Volkswagen Beetle and good tires. This road is on a south hillside and snow is usually gone by April. Dirt is such a scarce commodity on this rocky road that mud is rarely a problem, even during a thundershower.

Fifteen acres doesn't make for a very big lake, but steep hillsides give this brook-trout pond good depth, and there is rarely a winterkill. Iceout begins in late April, and by mid-May the spring sun has awakened the lake. Fishing is excellent, as brook trout and cutthroat feed after a long winter's siesta.

The prime trout food in Cabresto is a little freshwater shrimp. Fly fishermen should fish a No. 16 scud pattern in deep water, just out from the mudflats in the inlet area. A light spin-casting outfit loaded with four-pound test can do wonders with a worm; add just enough splitshot to give weight for casting. If the trout are rising to bugs on the lake's surface, use a small gray-hackle peacock and a casting bubble.

Irrigation drawdowns vie with summer rains to determine the level of this high mountain lake. The steep sides of Cabresto mean very little surface acreage is lost when water is extracted for irrigation. Expect daily afternoon August thunderstorms at this 9,200-foot elevation. While a bright sunny day will make for difficult fishing, rain showers can wake up Cabresto's trout for a midday feed. Dawn and dusk are the preferred times for summer angling.

Although a canoe or float tube is fun on such a personal-size lake, it's unnecessary for catching trout. Both deep and shallow water is fishable by the shore-bound angler. A trail leads around the willow thicket above the inlet area to Cabresto's feeder creek, Lake Fork Creek. This little stream holds wild little cutthroats, rainbow trout, and brookies. The creek below the dam holds trout but is almost never fished.

Autumn, like spring, offers the angler excellent midday fishing without the summertime crowds. The brookies spawn in the fall, and a scud or small wooly worm pattern fished around the inlet area is a favored technique. Catching and keeping a bunch of six- to ten-inch wild brook trout for a fresh fish dinner will not harm the trout population at Cabresto. These self-reproducing fish will maintain their own natural level.

Free camping is allowed on the level ground where the access road reaches a dead end. Outhouses, but no drinking water, are provided. Vacationers from Memorial Day to Labor Day know the way to Cabresto, so it does get crowded. Local people like to fish the lake in May and again in mid-September. They know the fishing is better before and after the summer vacation season.

RIO HONDO

The Rio Hondo drains the west side of the mountains that hide the Taos Ski Area. Driving north out of Taos, follow the signs to the ski area along a road paralleling the Rio Hondo from the village of Arroyo Seco upstream through the Carson National Forest. The swift little river is stocked near each of the five improved national forest campgrounds. There are few pools. Fishing for rainbows or cutthroats is best done with bait or weighted nymphs. Fish the pocket water behind the rocks, and fish deep through the runs. A few wild cutthroats are found away from the campground areas. Fly fishermen should bring some No. 14 high floating dry flies for good midsummer angling. The small headwater creeks which form the main Rio Hondo are strictly cutthroat waters. Williams Lake, located at the head of Lake Fork Creek (south by trail from Twining) is a ten-acre, unstocked, but good cutthroat lake.

The lower Hondo enters the Rio Grande west of Arroyo Hondo at the John Dunn Bridge. This stretch offers good fishing late in the year for spawning browns. Access is about eight miles north of Taos at Arroyo Hondo. Turn west just north of the bridge over the Rio Hondo, the gravel road follows the river to its confluence with the Rio Grande.

RIO PUEBLO DE TAOS

The Rio Pueblo de Taos is a strong little river flowing through the edge of Taos. It collects the waters from the mountains of the Taos Pueblo Indian Reservation. With its headwaters at the sacred Blue Lake, the Rio Pueblo de Taos is not open to public fishing on Indian lands. Taos Creek (Rio

Fernando de Taos) enters the Rio Pueblo de Taos on the east side of Taos. Just west of town, U.S. 64 follows Taos Creek uphill toward Eagle Nest Lake. This is a small creek in summer, and stocked with rainbows at the half-dozen national forest camping spots. Taos Creek and the campgrounds are next to a busy two-lane highway.

LITTLE RIO GRANDE

The Little Rio Grande (also called the Rio Grande del Rancho) is the last feeder stream to the Rio Pueblo de Taos. Most of the Little Rio Grande is in the Carson National Forest. Access is south from Ranchos de Taos on S.R. 3. Following the stream, you can see where it is stocked by looking for the few access points for the hatchery truck. The Little Rio Grande breaks neatly into three headwater creeks, with each accessible on dirt forest roads. Rio Chiquito, the first to be reached (and the smallest), is brushy on the lower end, but more open upstream, and it contains plenty of small brown trout. Pot Creek, the second of the three, has some good beaver pond fishing. The last little feeder creek, which is still called the Little Rio Grande, is larger than the other two. All three have extensive populations of wily and wild brown trout. The dirt access roads get difficult, if not impossible, after big summer rainstorms. Gin-clear water makes the fishing tough. Fish like a raccoon: be sneaky. If the wild browns see you, move up to the next spot, they are rarely caught when spooked.

The Rio Pueblo de Taos, from Taos downstream to its confluence with the Rio Grande, contains some of the best (and toughest) brown trout fishing in New Mexico. If you meander through the hustle of summertime in Taos, you might find yourself on the west end of town, near the new sewage plant, downstream from where the Little Rio Grande and Taos Creek empty into the Rio Pueblo de Taos. This is the access to the upper portion of the Rio Pueblo de Taos canyon.

Access to the middle section of the Rio Pueblo de Taos canyon is on dirt and gravel jeep trails heading north from S.R. 96, a paved road which turns off S.R. 68 south of Ranchos de Taos. The river is in a steep-walled canyon, and there are no easy trails leading into some of the toughest and best brown trout fishing in the state. The upper part of this stretch is characterized by a continuous series of long pools. The riffle at the head of each pool is the tail riffle of the next pool. This area offers some very good dry fly-fishing in late summer. The lower stretch is a series of deep runs winding around big river rocks. Fishing here is best done with a considerable amount of lead to get your wooly worm or real worm deep, where the browns are hiding. Although this river is not stocked and access is tough, the angling can be terrific. The Rio Pueblo de Taos enters into the Rio Grande at the upstream end of the Rio Grande Gorge State Park. S.R. 96 continues into the state park where there is easy access to the lower end of the Rio Pueblo de Taos.

RIO EMBUDO

The Embudo's confluence with the Rio Grande is just west of Dixon and Embudo, where S.R. 75 takes off from S.R. 68. The confluence and the lower end of the Embudo is on private land. The Embudo is sometimes stocked with catchable-size rainbow trout where it goes under the highway (S.R. 68). North of the village of Embudo, the Rio Embudo enters a canyon (embudo is the Spanish word for "funnel"), which is on Bureau of Land Management land. Access to Embudo Canyon is on a dirt and gravel road heading upstream, which is located just before the bridge north of town. Embudo Canyon is not stocked, has no easy access, and is rarely fished for its wild browns, cutthroats, and occasional rainbow trout.

If you cross the Embudo and stay on the paved road (S.R. 75), you will be driving out of the river valley and climbing the hills to the high country of Picuris Pueblo and the village of Peñasco. This is where the Embudo is formed, at the confluence of the Santa Barbara and Peñasco Rivers. At the marked turnoff, you can drive to Picuris Plaza, buy a tribal fishing license, and fish in the stocked four-acre trout pond at the plaza. Fishing is not allowed on the streams which are on Picuris lands.

RIO SANTA BARBARA

State Route 75 enters the village of Peñasco and turns north in town; but if you continue without turning, the paved road becomes maintained gravel and follows the Rio Santa Barbara to the Santa Barbara campgrounds. Stocked with rainbows near the campgrounds, this stream is a wild cutthroat fishery for as far upstream as you care to hike and wade. The upper Santa Barbara is an excellent midsummer trout-fishing stream.

The Santa Barbara is a cutthroat stream nine thousand feet above sea level in a northern New Mexican mountain valley. The Santa Barbara flows out of a healthy watershed, and clears quickly after a summer thunder-

Rio Santa Barbara

The Santa Barbara, one of New Mexico's best wild cutthroat streams. On this and other mountain streams, use a bit of split shot if you are fishing wet flies or salmon eggs. Dry flies need to be fully hackled to float in this fast water.

shower. The stream's three forks, which drain the north side of the Pecos Wilderness, are all prime cutthroat habitat. The forks meet and form the main Santa Barbara two miles upstream from the campground.

Much of the Santa Barbara, especially upstream from the Santa Barbara Campground, has a fairly high gradient, which means that the stream rushes down the valley with little chance to slow and form pools. This little river is a series of riffles and runs. The food chain works in the riffles, with the sun shining into shallow and highly oxygenated water. The trout hold in the runs, below the riffles. The fisherman should cast his hook in the riffle and let the current wash it down through the run. Use enough splitshot to get your bait or fly near the bottom. If you are not hanging up on the bottom, then put on another splitshot.

Grasshoppers and beetles make great natural bait. Salmon eggs and worms also produce. The key is to present the bait where the trout are holding.

Rio Santa Barbara

The cutthroat will hold right below the biggest obstruction in the stream. There are miniature waterfalls all along the Santa Barbara, with a trout in the little pocket at the base of each one.

Trout streams typically have a big spring runoff that drops off to low water levels in the summer, which makes for hot water temperatures and lousy fishing. But such is not the case with the Santa Barbara. The Fourth of July finds the Santa Barbara running medium high and clear. This is a north-slope stream with a late runoff. The water levels drop by mid-July, but the water stays cool. August is a perfect time to fish the Santa Barbara with flies, bait, or small lures. The forest floor is bright with flowers, the trees full of green, and the hatchery truck has filled the campground stream with catchable-size rainbows. Stream-bred cutthroats can be found after just a short walk upstream.

The fly fishermen enjoy this stream with weighted nymphs in the spring and with dry flies from July through October. Stonefly hatches come off from May to the beginning of July. After the water drops, the caddis and mayfly bring the trout to the surface. A warm afternoon in November can deliver good fishing, but autumn days are short, and this north-slope stream shuts down quickly for winter.

The national forest campgrounds are open from May through October. Hodges is an unimproved, no-fee camping area located just within the entrance to the national forest. This section is heavily fished and heavily stocked. Stretches of the stream here are enclosed within a tunnel of green. A canopy of trees shades the water and makes casting almost impossible. But you can wade downstream, letting the current pull your hook into all the likely looking spots.

Upstream from Hodges the road parallels the riverbank, but winds up the hillside and away from the stream. Then the road cuts back down and crosses the stream. From this bridge upstream to the next campground, the road again runs away from the stream. These two stretches of the Santa Barbara receive very little fishing pressure. It's not more than a five-minute walk from the road, but that is enough to keep out most anglers.

The gravel road ends at Santa Barbara campground, an improved (with a fee) camping area with paved roads, drinking water, horse corrals, outhouses, picnic tables, and reasonable access for the handicapped angler. This campground is the main trailhead into the north side of the Pecos Wilderness. Campers, fishermen, horseback riders, and backpackers make this a busy spot from Memorial Day to Labor Day.

The campground area is stocked and anglers fish this area hard. But just upstream, past the last bit of pavement and where the little tributary called

Jicarita Creek enters, the cutthroat fishing starts. These wild fish, mostly six to twelve inches in size, leap clear of the whitewater when hooked.

Just up from the campground, canyon walls close in on the Santa Barbara. You can wade and walk up the stream as far as your legs will take you. If you wish to fish the wilderness waters upstream, don't hike up the stream bank, but take Forest Trail 24. This maintained trail parallels the little river seventy yards up the canyon walls.

In less than two miles you will reach the confluence of the Middle and West forks of the Santa Barbara. The canyon walls open up, and at this point you face a great problem. From here you can fish downstream on the main river; or you can fish up either of the forks; or you can take a sun-drenched catnap in this almost private meadow. Straight south, five miles away, is Chimayosos and Truchas peaks.

The Middle Fork is one of the finest little cutthroat streams in New Mexico. The West Fork, which also offers good fishing, is one of the prettiest spots in New Mexico. The elevation at the confluence is about 9,400 feet. The ridges on the skyline run over 11,000 feet, and the peaks are all over 12,000 feet. There is good fishing in these upper forks, but be prepared: it can snow in the middle of July and summer thunderstorms are common.

The Pecos Wilderness Area starts a mile upstream from the Santa Barbara campground. Permits are no longer required for people camping in the wilderness area. Maps are available at national forest area offices in Peñasco, Las Vegas, and Santa Fe.

Downstream from the national forest campgrounds, the Santa Barbara River is on private property. The river flows through Peñasco where it joins the Rio Pueblo to form Embudo Creek, and the Embudo joins the Rio Grande.

RIO PUEBLO

If you turn north in Peñasco and follow S.R. 75, the road brings you to S.R. 3. Follow S.R. 3 southeast and you're paralleling the Rio Pueblo on national forest property. The river is heavily stocked near the public camp-grounds and fishing is good from May to November with bait, lure, or fly. Sipapu Ski Area offers summertime lodging for vacationing anglers. Further upstream, La Junta Creek, a major tributary to the Rio Pueblo, is also stocked with catchable-size rainbows. A good gravel road, Forest Route 76, follows along the creek. The Rio Pueblo and La Junta Creek are major summer recreation areas.

Rio Pueblo

Purchase a Carson and a Valle Vidal National Forest map from your local forest service office. These maps offer some of the best information for summer fishing in our northern trout streams. And don't forget to be on the lookout for grasshoppers, these free baits (or a good grasshopper fly) are great for fooling vacation-time trout in the rushing streams of the Sangre de Cristo Mountains.

SANTA CRUZ LAKE

Santa Cruz is a 120-acre canyon lake with hundred-foot depths at the dam and acres of muddy shallows at the inlet. The fishing is for stocked rainbow trout and wild browns, but white suckers will occasionally compete for your hook. There is fine bank-fishing around the entire lake, and good wading water near the boat ramp. Santa Cruz Lake once closed for the winter, but beginning in 1987 the lake was opened for year-round use. For safety reasons ice fishing is not allowed, however, good fishing is possible on nearly any winter day when the surface is free of ice.

Fishing is reasonably good just as soon as the shore is clear of ice, usually in March. Catch rates increase through spring and early summer, and the fishing stays good until the hot summer sun forces the trout down to cooler and more oxygenated water. Summer angling is best from dawn until around 9:00 A.M. ; you have to fish deep during the day to find the holding level of the trout. Or you can fish in the evening from a boat and light a lantern when it gets dark; the rainbow trout and the bats will flock to the minnows and bugs attracted by the light. Catch the rainbows and enjoy the bats. In autumn the cottonwoods turn yellow, the brown trout suddenly become catchable, and the summer crowds disappear.

Two- to four-pound trout are the big fish in Santa Cruz. Many of these have been caught, cleaned, and found to be full of crawfish; and leeches are another fine trout food living in these waters. These are two good reasons why many of the best lures and flies for this lake are black. Wooly worms, black Marabou streamers, and black bucktail Mepps are favorites. Trolling a Renigade or Warden's Worry also does the job. Fly fishermen should bring some No. 12 black-ant dry flies. Calm evenings usually bring on a midge rise.

Santa Cruz is a perfect lake for boat-fishing. The lake has a no-wake regulation, and on calm days a canoe does nicely. If you are new to boating this lake, the area around the inlet stream is the best spot to begin. Rocky points offer good casting spots on the east shoreline, while a steep canyon wall drops straight down the west side of Santa Cruz. There are evening rises for the fly fisherman, shady beaches for the relaxed bait-caster, and a variety of bottom structure for those trolling lures.

Access is easy. Head north from the Santa Fe city limits on U.S. 285 for nine miles, and turn east on S.R. 4 at Pojoaque. Follow Highway 4 for eleven miles to the marked Santa Cruz exit. Don't be misled by the Highway 520 turnoff; stay on Highway 4. You'll see a sign pointing to a dirt-road turnoff that leads to a scenic overlook of the lake. This is a nice picnic area with a half-mile trail leading down to the west shoreline. You'll drive through the little village of Cundiyo and then pass over the Rio Medio, the little stream that feeds Santa Cruz Lake. Then, it is two miles further to the marked entrance to the lake.

The main entrance road to Santa Cruz Lake is narrow and paved. The Bureau of Land Management operates fee campsites with drinking water and outhouses. A private concession stand has snacks, boat rentals, tackle, and daily fishing tips. A fee is charged for launching a boat (this may change in the future). The Santa Cruz River below the dam has some trout fishing.

NAMBE FALLS LAKE

Three or four times a month the park ranger at Nambe Falls Recreation Area retells the story of Nambe Falls to a carload of lost tourists looking for the road to Chimayo. This good-size little lake is still unknown to most New Mexicans. The ranger calls it the secret of Nambe Pueblo. The inlet and outlet streams are off-limits to the fisherman, but this blue-water, sixty-acre lake offers medium-size rainbow trout along with a sprinkling of wild cutthroats and an occasional lunker. These waters are stocked by Nambe Pueblo for the angler who pays a daily fee (about $5.00) for the privilege of casting for trout in this foothill lake.

The Bureau of Reclamation built the dam on the Rio Nambe for downstream Indian irrigation needs. The dam is located above Nambe Falls. Yearly irrigation drawdowns peak during August, and during dry years the water level can really drop, but the lake can still offer good fishing. Nambe Lake is deep enough for the trout to survive the winter's freeze.

The quality of this beautiful fishery is measured not only in its scenery, but in its lack of noisy beer parties. The foothills of the Sangre de Cristo Mountains reach down to the waters of Nambe Reservoir—blue water reflecting blue sky, and all surrounded by the hillside forest. The daily fishing fee keeps all but the serious outdoors aficionado off the lake. Boating is

Nambe Falls Lake

Nambe Reservoir (Nambe Falls Lake) on the Nambe Pueblo Recreation Area. A tribal permit is required on this quiet trout-fishing lake located twenty miles north of Santa Fe.

limited to rowboats less than fourteen feet long or to canoes; motors are not allowed.

While park rangers keep a close watch on the visitors to Nambe Falls Recreation Area, the rules are simple to follow: no firearms, no live bait, one rod per person, no fires on the shoreline, driving allowed only on the established roads, and no littering. The many trout available to the angler, the daily fee, the good gravel roads—these all combine to make Nambe a special place to fish. This lake can be a trip saver, especially if your excursion to Santa Cruz Lake is interrupted by a boisterous weekend crowd.

The inlet stream to Nambe Lake is fishable for about 100 yards above its entrance to the lake. Pueblo rules specify no fishing above this well-marked point. Fishing below the dam is also prohibited. A good gravel road goes almost completely around the lake, and a good boat ramp is located on the northwestern shoreline. The boat ramp, the inlet area, and the south side of the dam provide favorite spots for bank-fishing. Small, light-colored lures match the minnows in the lake, and Mepps style lures attract fish when cast into deeper water off the many rocky points. Combining a fly-rod with a canoe allows the fly fisherman to reach the daily rises. If you have trouble matching the midge hatch, try a small streamer. Worms, salmon eggs, corn, and cheese all catch fish in Nambe Reservoir; keep changing the location of your cast to find the level the trout are feeding in. Typical of most trout lakes, Nambe's best fishing is in the spring and fall.

User fees are collected at the guardhouse where the paved road turns to gravel. Fee camping is available at the lake and below the dam (be sure to visit Nambe Falls). The recreation area is open from March to the end of November. Wheelchair access is good at the boat ramp or at the inlet.

Nambe Falls Recreation Area is found by driving north from Santa Fe about twelve miles to the N.M. 4 turnoff. Turn east (not west to Los Alamos) on N.M. 4 in Pojoaque. Drive slowly along N.M. 4, and take the well-marked Nambe Falls turnoff. The paved road heads east toward the foothills. While obeying the speed limit signs, continue until the pavement ends at the ranger station. There are picnic tables, outhouses, and shelters on the south side and the inlet areas. Weekends can get crowded in the summertime. Trophy-size trout are rare in this lake, but plenty of the stocked catchables grow to good size, and the views are wonderful. As the sun starts to slide down the western sky the coyotes will sing their evening vespers, and this lake at the end of the road—Nambe Lake—becomes the secret of Nambe Pueblo.

SANTA CLARA LAKES

Located south of Española and west of the Rio Grande, the Santa Clara lakes are a series of small, stocked trout ponds. Owned and operated by Santa Clara Pueblo, this fee area (for camping, picnicking, and fishing) is a quiet retreat in a mountain canyon, complete with tall trees, wildflowers, trout, chipmunks, and hummingbirds. The fishing is for catchable-size rainbows in each of the four little lakes and in the feeder creek. Bait and flies produce the most catches, but lures do work in the larger of the lakes.

Access is on a paved road off State Route 30, about two miles south of Española on the west side of the Rio Grande. The turnoff is marked with a large sign. Though the pavement turns to gravel at the entrance gate (where the fees are collected), the road is driveable even after a strong rain. Camping areas, outhouses, garbage cans, picnic tables, and the gravel road are all maintained. Most people stop at the first or second lake, but a few drive the extra ten minutes it takes to get to the upper lakes.

Santa Clara Lakes

The setting is a steep-walled canyon holding a little creek with large trees blocking the view to the sky. Ancient townhouses—the Puye cliff dwellings—can be visited near the entrance. This is safe place to bring the kids, to see the ruins, to do a little fishing, and to enjoy the out-of-doors in a controlled area.

The Chama Watershed

CHAMA RIVER OVERVIEW

The Rio Chama enters our state from Colorado as a lively little trout stream. It ends its journey 120 miles later, just above Española, where it drops a big load of silt and water into the Rio Grande. Between these two extremes lies more than two thousand square miles of watershed. There are tiny headwater creeks coming out of small mountain trout lakes, and huge main-stem reservoirs behind massive dams. The fishing ranges from the mixed warmwater and coldwater species in the southern Abiquiu Reservoir to the strictly coldwater fishery in the middle and northern reaches.

U.S. Highway 84 runs right up the middle of the Chama watershed. Starting just north of Española, U.S. 84 parallels the river upstream to Abiquiu Dam, the first good fishing spot. Angling below the dam is only marginal for browns, rainbow trout, and catfish. The flow is usually murky and the river here is big. The exception is in winter, when low and clear flows make this a good spot for cold-weather fishing.

Above the dam, Abiquiu Reservoir fills a wide desert canyon with a great warmwater lake. Smallmouth, largemouth, crappie, walleye, perch, and catfish are the favorite catch. The river above Abiquiu is too murky for sportfishing, so it's best to return to U.S. 84 and head north.

Canjilon village is about twenty miles north of Abiquiu and leads in to the Canjilon lakes—a handful of small trout lakes set against the south-eastern hillsides of Canjilon Mountain. Native cutthroat and stocked rainbow trout are the quarry. Just up the road from the Canjilon turnoff is Forest Route 125, leading to Nutrias (Trout) Lakes, another set of small high mountain lakes, which are also visited by the hatchery truck. Tierra Amarilla is the next stop north on U.S. 84; the decision to be made here is which way to turn.

East from Tierra Amarilla on U.S. 64 is Hopewell Lake, home to brook

63

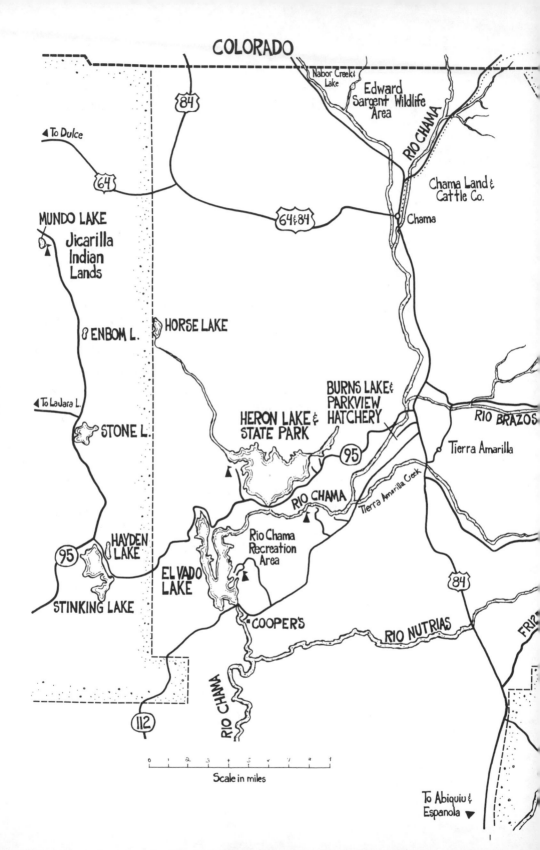

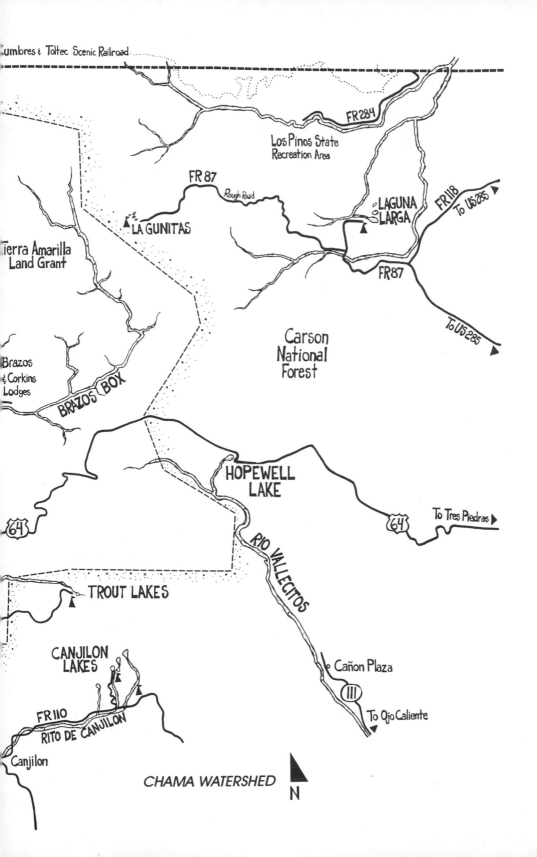

trout and stocked rainbows, and headwaters to Vallecito Creek. The terrain and easy access at Hopewell makes for great summer family fishing trips.

The Brazos River crosses the highway just north of Tierra Amarilla. There's good fishing for browns and stocked rainbow trout on this stream; all of it is private and much of it is open to public fishing. Two lodges cater to the Brazos fisherman at the end of S.R. 512.

To the west of Tierra Amarilla, S.R. 112 leads near the Parkview Hatchery. Burns Canyon Lake, which is the old brood pond at the hatchery, is a fine little trout pond. S.R. 112 continues west toward El Vado Dam and, below it, the Chama River.

In 1946 the largest brown trout caught in New Mexico came out of the Chama River below El Vado Dam. This stretch of river is still one of our most productive spots for bait-, lure-, or fly-fishing. Access is easiest through the Cooper family's El Vado Ranch. Fishing is good both upstream toward the dam and for about five miles downstream. As you hike downstream, you will notice that the river gradually loses its appeal to trout, changing to a silty desert river.

Above the dam is El Vado Lake State Park. This lake holds kokanee, browns, lake trout, and rainbows in its 3,500 surface acres. Big brown trout are the prize catch but kokanee and stocked rainbow trout are the mainstays. One of the better spots at El Vado is where the Chama River enters the lake.

The Chama above El Vado runs through the state-owned Rio Chama Wildlife and Fishing Area. This twelve-mile section of the Chama River is walk-in fishing at its best. Access is via dirt roads heading north from S.R. 112. The river here is wild, for there are no upstream dams to staunch the flow. In spring the runoff is master and the Chama caters more to whitewater rafters than to fishermen. Just after the runoff subsides, the bait and lure anglers show up. Next the fly fishermen appear, right on time to catch the early summer insect hatches. Good midsummer fishing on the Chama depends on the water level. If the high country gets steady moisture, the river will offer good catches right through the dog days of summer. Late fall is when the browns begin to spawn. Early winter finds the kokanee running up from El Vado.

This part of the Chama is a glorious place to be in autumn. Tall canyon walls guide the wind past golden cottonwoods and the river carries yellow leaves downstream. The fisherman walks the shoreline, casting as he goes.

A major part of the water in the Chama watershed comes from Heron Lake. Heron, which is not part of the Rio Chama, was formed by building a dam on Willow Creek, just north of the Chama River and El Vado Reservoir. Most of the water in Heron comes from Colorado, on the other side of the Continental Divide; it is pumped over the divide through a series of tunnels, and dumped into Willow Creek in New Mexico. Willow Creek feeds Heron Reservoir, and Heron feeds the Chama just above El Vado. This is a most confusing start to the great fishing in Heron Reservoir.

Lake trout are the big prey in Heron. Kokanee salmon are the normal catch but rainbow trout are also caught. This five thousand acre reservoir is regulated as a no-wake lake. The no-wake rule makes this big lake a quiet place for sailers and for anglers. Access is just north of Tierra Amarilla on S.R. 95.

Highway 84 follows the Chama River north of Tierra Amarilla but the river here is on posted land. To fish the river go north on U.S. 84 to Chama town. There's good fishing east of U.S. 84 on small tributaries to the Chama flowing through land owned by the private Chama Land and Cattle Company, which offers good angling for guests at its sportsman's lodge.

The town of Chama has its namesake river running north–south, through the middle of town. All of the land is private and some of the river is posted. The Department of Game and Fish has a public fishing easement just south of town. Look for the department's access sign on the west side of U.S. 84. This heavily used spot is stocked with catchable-size rainbows. Better angling is found north of town, where the river is on the eastern edge of the Edward Sargent Fish and Wildlife Management Area. Park where Highway 17 crosses the Chama River, just north of town, and you can fish upstream through six miles of brown trout water.

The Rio Chamita runs through the western side of the Sargent area. This unstocked creek is full of wild little cutthroats, browns, and rainbow trout. Nabor Creek and its small reservoir feed the Chamita and hold native Rio Grande cutthroats. Access to the Chamita is on a dirt road from the north end of Chama. Access to the Nabor is by trail from the dirt road.

Above the Sargent area the Chama tumbles into New Mexico on private land operated by the Lobo Lodge. Here the Rio Chama is a small headwater river, and lodge guests cast for wild browns and stocked rainbows.

To the west of the Rio Chama is the Jicarilla Apache Indian Reservation. Fishermen enjoy camping and fishing in the many stocked lakes. This is fee-fishing for stocked rainbow, brown, and cutthroat trout, and for channel catfish. Access is on paved and improved gravel roads. Dulce, the reservation town, offers a Best Western motel, restaurants, gas stations, and grocery stores.

Chama River Overview

Northeast Area Fisheries manager Jack Kelly with a nice catfish netted during a fish population study at Abiquiu Lake.

The entire Chama watershed gives New Mexico a year-round fishery: south in the winter and spring, north in the summer and fall. The following chapters provide details on the Chama's great fishing.

ABIQUIU RESERVOIR

Abiquiu Dam is a sediment- and flood-control dam located on the Chama River, thirty miles northwest of Española. Throughout the 1970s this reservoir was a marginal catfish, kokanee, and rainbow trout lake. Bass and crappie were stocked in the 1980s and then, from above-average snowpacks, the water levels rose, greatly increasing the size and stature of Abiquiu. Catch rates were once below average, but higher water levels and the explosion of the smallmouth and crappie populations have made this a popular place to cast a line. And recently, perch and walleye were stocked.

Dramatic water level changes are a fact of life at Abiquiu. In July your favorite fishing spot could be ten feet underwater. A half-year later that same spot could be high and dry, fifty feet from the lake.

The types of fish in Abiquiu Reservoir read like a who's who in New

Mexico fishing. Existing fish include carp, suckers, brown trout, minnows, chubs, and dace. Fish stocked in these waters include kokanee salmon, bluegill, smallmouth and largemouth bass, crappie, catfish, bullheads, walleye, perch, and rainbow trout. Rainbows and kokanee are occasionally caught but are no longer stocked in Abiquiu. Most fishermen now go after the crappie and smallmouth bass. Catfish, largemouth, and kokanee also show in creel census checks and state fisheries managers are hoping the combination of perch and walleye will add to the good angling at Abiquiu.

By mid-April the crappie are just awakening to their spawning urge. Very quickly, in May or June, the crappie run explodes. Stringers full of these panfish are common. Smallmouth bass strike minnow imitations cast among the sunken brush and rocky shorelines. Good crappie, smallmouth and largemouth catches continue through July and into August.

September and October are crossover months at Abiquiu, and catches of all species are good. Kokanee salmon and a few trout are caught trolling lures. Anglers with bass boats are in the coves, searching the structure for largemouth. October is the start of low discharge flows below the dam. Trout and catfish anglers fish this part of the Rio Chama until April, when the high flows start.

The best fishing at Abiquiu occurs during the spring crappie run. Anglers looking to fill their stringers with the forty-fish daily limit should bring a fillet knife and an ice chest. Crappie make their yearly spawning run in shallow water, which is easily accessible to the bank fisherman. The most popular spot is the long bay just south of the parking lot at the main boat ramp. Although everyone will catch a few crappie, a majority of the fish will concentrate on a few choice spots. Look for a flat bottom in two to five feet of water. If you experience no strike within ten minutes, move to a different spot. Once located, a prime spot will yield consistent hookups.

Live minnows, the classic bait for crappie fishing, are unnecessary. Crappie strike at anything threatening their spawning turf. Yellow, lead head crappie jigs are cheap, and they work just as well as the more expensive rigs. The crappie run peaks in May or June, just as the spring runoff is raising the water level. But there is one critter you need to watch out for during springtime fishing at Abiquiu. Warm weather and the rising water levels force the local rattlesnakes to higher ground, where you might just be walking.

While the spring crappie catch is great for filling a big fish fry, anglers after the "fightin'est fish there is" are concentrating on the smallmouth bass. Drift along the shoreline, casting both parallel and toward the lakeshore. Roostertail or Panther Martin–style spinners, plastic curley tail grubs on a

Abiquiu Reservoir

Standing is Dominic Domenici, fishing for smallmouth bass at Abiquiu. Dominic's father owns and operates Charlie's Sporting Goods in Albuquerque.

lead-head jig hook, or small chartreuse spinner baits are all good smallmouth lures.

Access to Abiquiu is off paved State Route 96, thirty miles northwest of Española on U.S. 84. The turnoff is marked. A general store with gas and tackle is located on U.S. 84, seven miles south of the turnoff. Recreation facilities are run by the U.S. Army Corps of Engineers.

The headquarters for most fishermen is the Cerrito picnicking area, which has a large parking lot, picnic tables, outhouses, a good boat ramp, and reasonable access for the boatless angler. Handicapped access, with help from a friend, is also possible. Camping is allowed here, but there is no designated campground.

Cerrito has a big problem with high water levels. Water storage during spring runoff often raises the lake high enough to put the Cerrito area, including the boat ramp, completely under water—which can happen in late June. The access road to Cerrito will be closed to vehicles, but boaters can use the ramp in the Riana campground. Riana is an improved campground (a fee area) with shaded picnic tables, water, grills, a dump station, and bathrooms.

If you pass by the Cerrito and Riana turnoffs, S.R. 96 continues past the Corps of Engineers Project Office and goes right over the dam. A service road goes down the dam face, giving access to the Rio Chama below the dam. A half-mile past the dam is a rocky access road leading down to the Canones Creek inlet arm. This is a good spot to try for Abiquiu's catfish. Check out the road before you drive it; it's steep, rough, and sometimes closed to vehicular traffic. S.R. 96 continues toward Cuba, a fifty-mile drive.

Boating is the only way to fish most of Abiquiu's shoreline. The middle and upper shores are on private property, and the public lands around the campgrounds are tough to cover on foot. Canoes and cartop boats are okay if you pay close attention to the weather; the potential exists for a strong wind funneling through this canyon lake. Watch the two wind-warning lights; one is on the island by the boat ramp, while the other is near the top of the dam.

A good powerboat is excellent for reaching the bays up the Rio Chama arm. These are prime spots for largemouth fishing. The Chama River brings much debris into Abiquiu. Be careful of high-speed runs, especially if you're heading up the lake during the spring runoff. You take the chance of running over a big piece of driftwood—with the throttle wide open. The Canones Creek arm, near the dam, is open to boaters as a no-wake area. Boats are not allowed within five hundred feet of the dam.

The future of Abiquiu is unclear. The reservoir was not known as a good fishery until the crappie and smallmouth populations exploded. The U.S. Army Corps of Engineers has requested a dramatic increase in water storage. Surface areas between one thousand and five thousand acres were once considered normal for the reservoir. The size may rise to between eight thousand and fourteen thousand acres. Many anglers are now enjoying the crappie and smallmouth bass explosion, and future anglers may enjoy the walleye-perch combination. This high desert lake has many angling secrets still waiting to be explored.

CANJILON LAKES

It's hard to beat the Canjilon lakes for a family fishing trip. The destination is five small trout lakes tucked around the southeast slope of Canjilon Mountain, south and east from Tierra Amarilla. A paved road meanders up

Canjilon Lakes

This big catfish got stuck trying for an easy lunch on a crappie caught in a Game and Fish survey net at Abiquiu Lake.

the hillside, past the lakes and the two improved Carson National Forest campgrounds—all surrounded by pine forests mixed in with rocks, rose bushes, creeks, and bogs. The Canjilon lakes have good fishing just as soon as the hatchery truck makes its first springtime visit. Winterkill of trout is a problem because severe winters can freeze these shallow lakes solid.

Canjilon lakes are no secret to New Mexico's anglers. The campgrounds have clean outhouses, drinking water, picnic tables, nice tent sites, and all the roads in the campground are paved. It is a *very* busy place during the prime summer weekends. When the parking lots look full, these lakes can still offer good trout fishing. Since most of the fishing occurs close to the parking areas, a ten- or twenty-minute walk will turn the entire backside of one of these lakes into your own private trout pond. There is great morning and evening fishing in the shallows. Hot summer afternoons are meant for shady naps—or for finding deep spots or feeder-creek inlets where these trout find the colder water they prefer. An added plus are the few wild cutthroats inhabiting the lakes with strong feeder creeks.

Water coming out of the lakes feeds Canjilon Creek; you follow the creek on the access road leading in from the highway. The creek supports some rainbow trout as well as a wild trout population of cutthroats and a few browns.

Paved roads, nice outhouses, and plenty of hatchery-raised rainbows make this a great family fishing spot. To get there, you turn off U.S. Highway 84 at the Canjilon village turnoff (fifteen miles south of Tierra Amarilla or thirteen miles north of the Ghost Ranch Visitor Center). Stop at the Canjilon Ranger Station, located on the west end of town, to check on road conditions. Although the campground roads are paved, the seven miles of access road (Forest Route 559) are not, and after a harsh summer rain the last two miles can be difficult. The campsites in this very popular campground are often full on summer weekends, but even if they are, you can still enjoy the day's fishing and then drive back down Highway 84 (head ten miles south) to the Echo Amphitheater Campground. Late-season anglers should take note that late fall snowstorms can be fierce. Enjoy the autumn fishing, but consider camping at the lower-elevation Echo Amphitheater Campground. The Canjilon Lakes Campground is open from June to September, but fishing is legal throughout the year. Wheelchair access is best at the first parking area. The village of Canjilon has a gas station and a small general store.

NUTRIAS (TROUT) LAKES

The Trout lakes live up to their name. The only problem with the fishing is getting there. Some maps call them the Nutrias lakes because they are located at the headwaters of Nutrias Creek. Wild cutthroats, stocked rainbows, and brook trout can be caught in these waters. What you catch depends on the winter freeze, the work of the beavers, and the stocking schedule. A bad winter iceover can kill all the fish in the lakes. The upstream beaver dams compete with the runoff, and the outcome determines how many cutthroats and brook trout make it down the feeder creeks to the lakes. You can depend on the hatchery truck for thousands of catchable-size rainbow trout, but the number of wild fish varies each year.

The main lake, located at the end of the only access road, is a good spot for a cup of coffee and a stretch because the forty-five-minute drive is on a bumpy, twisty, ten-mile, one-lane, and barely improved dirt road. To reach the largest of the lakes, which is uphill from the main lake, walk across the dam on the north end of the main lake and head uphill on the trail. This is great fly-rod water. Upstream from the largest lake is a series of beaver ponds, which are good in some years and washed out in other years. Two smaller ponds are located two hundred yards down the main road from the parking area. Turn north on a side road to reach these little ponds.

These lakes are a series of hidden trout ponds, and, except on midsummer weekends, the rough road keeps them from being overpopulated with anglers. The lack of human noise brings out the sounds of the trees and the rustle of the forest. Summer afternoon fishing is often spotty; most mountain trout lie low when the hot sun is directly overhead. Fishing is best in the morning and evening, in the shade, or anytime clouds hide the sun.

Your first stop on the way to the Trout lakes should be the Canjilon Ranger Station in the village of Canjilon. Conditions on the forest road change throughout the year, from seven inches of mud to dry and recently graded. Road access to the lakes is off Highway 84, about fourteen miles south of Tierra Amarilla (exactly two miles north of the Canjilon turnoff). Turn east on Forest Road 125 (it is marked) and drive for about ten miles. The road deadends at the main lake, where there are five camping sites (with good wheelchair access), with picnic tables but with no drinking water or outhouses. The Trout lakes offer fine New Mexico trout fishing—as long as you don't get stuck on the only road out.

HOPEWELL LAKE

Hopewell Lake is one of the only easily accessible places in New Mexico where you can fish for the colorful brook trout. This high country lake is located right off a paved highway, has no-fee camping areas, and is stocked with rainbows throughout the warmer months. Highway traffic is light in this classic northern New Mexico valley, complete with a little stream. In 1951, Placer Creek was dammed to form Hopewell Lake, which is about fifteen hundred feet long, four hundred feet wide, and covers about fifteen surface acres. Much of the inlet area is shallow and swampy. The deeper water is in the top third of the lake near the dam, which is where the better fishing is found. This is a great lake for both the fly fisherman and the bait-caster. Normally caught here are the stocked rainbow trout; the naturally reproducing brookies seem wary enough to escape the hooks of most anglers.

Winter fishing at Hopewell is left to the snowmobilers. The highway is often closed by the winter storms—but that's no surprise for a northern New Mexico lake located 9,800 feet above sea level. Once spring opens the road and the ice melts from Hopewell, the brook trout fishing begins. These trout prefer the colder water of springtime and are fun to catch before the warmer summer weather chases them back to deeper water. The winter iceover doesn't kill the leftover rainbows; they also go on a spring feed, fattening up after a cold season of dormancy. Insect life is lush, with midges, dragonflies, caddis, grasshoppers, and mayflies providing the prime trout food. A fly-rod or a casting bubble spinning rig will work for both brook and rainbow trout; and bait-fishing from the bank picks up after the hatchery truck arrives.

Summer midday fishing requires finding the holding level of the trout. The surface, the shallows, and the deepest areas will not have the oxygen that the trout need. Find the correct level by casting to different depths and searching for strikes until you find the right spot. Summer is short at this elevation, and autumn brings the trout back to surface feeding. Waders or float tubes are not needed for a casual afternoon or evening of casting a fly. Rises will fill the upper two-thirds of the lake, and bank casting with a fly-rod is no problem: there's plenty of room for your back cast. A small boat is an asset when fishing for the brookies. A canoe gives quiet access to the thin strip of deeper water in the middle of the lake. Boating is limited to electric trolling motors or oars.

Family fishing is excellent at Hopewell. The trail around the dam is safe; the kids can feed the ducks and the chipmunks when they get bored with fishing, and they can catch grasshoppers for bait while you continue to cast. The shore around the dam, when dry, is wheelchair accessible, though some assistance may be needed. There is no fee for camping, and picnic tables and outhouses are provided; but no drinking water is available. Hopewell Lake is about sixteen miles from Tres Piedras on U.S. Highway 64, between Tierra Amarilla and Tres Piedras. This paved road is closed by the highway department during bad winter weather; the snowstorms determine the actual dates, but it is often closed by December. Big snows can keep it closed until spring, but in dry winters it is open all year. Roadgraders clear it in the spring, usually before mid-April.

THE RIO CHAMA BELOW EL VADO DAM

The easiest access to the great fishing below El Vado Dam is through Cooper's El Vado Ranch. Take S.R. 112 west from Tierra Amarilla and turn off the pavement a mile before the dam, at Cooper's well-marked gravel road entrance. There is a small fee for parking. The Cooper family has

Rio Chama below El Vado Dam

Results from an electro-shocking survey by the U.S. Fish and Wildlife Service on the Chama below El Vado Dam. After weighing, measuring, and a check for spawning condition, this nice brown trout (and many more) was released.

been watching this river pass through its seasonal changes for more than forty years.

Stop in at their little convenience store and tackle shop for the latest fishing information. Look above the candy bars and you'll see a state record hanging on the wall: twenty pounds of brown trout. It was caught in 1946, on this part of the Chama, using a live chub for bait. The Coopers operate a fee campground and rent housekeeping cottages.

Early spring fishing begins just as the ice melts on the lake above the dam. Watch the weekly fishing reports in both Albuquerque daily newspapers for this pre-runoff fishing. The runoff peaks from mid-May to mid-June, and high water levels can make fishing poor. But once the flows drop, from summer through midwinter, the Chama becomes one of New Mexico's most consistent producers of twelve- to seventeen-inch rainbow trout. Kokanee run up from Abiquiu in the fall, and there are still many big browns in this part of the Chama. A sixteen-pound brown was caught below the dam in 1986.

Flows in this part of the river run from an easy 50 cfs to a runoff peak of over 4,000 cfs. Coopers is also a popular launching spot for rafting and canoeing, usually when the flow is over 1,000 cfs. Periods of low flow are good for the angler wearing waders and casting lures or flies. Medium to heavy flows, 1,000–2,000 cfs, are good for all styles of fishing. Flows over 2,000 cfs favor the bankside bait fisherman.

If you want to fish upstream, a footbridge near the parking area gives access to the west side of the river. It's a mile upstream to the dam. Downstream access is good on the east side for about a half-mile. A four-mile hike and wade downriver will put you at the inlet of Nutrias Creek, a good area to fish anytime. Pack a lunch and make it a day-long fishing trip. There are plenty of chubs, suckers, and catfish in the quiet pools, a lot of browns and rainbows in the faster water, and maybe a few giant trout in the deep slow runs.

This river runs for thirty miles between El Vado Dam and Abiquiu Reservoir. For the first five miles the Chama is an excellent trout river, especially favored by New Mexico fishermen. The lower twenty miles are too silty for trout. The Chama is a canoeist's delight, but the angler should stay in the upper reaches.

EL VADO LAKE

El Vado is New Mexico's only major reservoir with a large and high quality trout stream as its inlet. The Rio Chama flows into El Vado, and the inlet area is one of the premier places to catch trout on this three-thousand-acre irrigation reservoir. Set in a northern New Mexico river valley southwest of Tierra Amarilla, El Vado Lake holds rainbow trout, kokanee salmon, sunfish, carp, lake trout, suckers, and brown trout. Though there are more suckers than trout, the sportfishing is just fine. Many of New Mexico's best trout lakes, such as Bluewater and Eagle Nest, have lots of suckers and still offer great trout fishing.

El Vado Dam was built in 1935 to control irrigation water for the Middle Rio Grande Conservancy District. The Bureau of Reclamation now operates the dam for all downstream water users. In dry years the reservoir was once prone to dramatic drawdowns. But the addition of Heron Reservoir, which feeds the Chama River just upstream of El Vado Lake, has helped to stabilize water levels. The Department of Game and Fish concentrates its El Vado management program on rainbow trout and kokanee salmon. About 200,000 kokanee fry and 200,000 rainbow trout fingerlings are annually stocked in El Vado.

El Vado Lake

A two-thousand-acre, full-service state park sits along the northeast shoreline of El Vado Lake. The park has paved and maintained gravel roads, bathrooms and outhouses, drinking water, a small marina, a good concrete boat ramp, a gravel airstrip, dozens of improved camping spots with shaded picnic tables, and overflow areas for pick-your-own-spot camping. The lake is open to water-skiing and swimming.

There are three public access points to El Vado Lake. The state park access is off S.R. 112, about twelve miles west from Tierra Amarilla. Take the gravel road north (marked with state park access signs), pass the airstrip, and the road ends at the state park on the middle of the east shoreline. This is a reasonably good, maintained gravel road. If you continue past the state park turnoff and stay on paved S.R. 112, passing first the large convenience store operated by El Vado Lakes RV Resort and then the access to Cooper's El Vado Ranch (see the previous section on the Rio Chama below El Vado Dam), you end up at El Vado Dam. Here, there is a motel, restaurant, and convenience store. Dirt and gravel roads on both sides of the dam provide access for the shore fisherman and for those with cartop boats. The route to the north end of El Vado is on S.R. 95, which is paved from Tierra Amarilla to Heron Dam. At Heron Dam the road turns to dirt and gravel, skirting the north shore of El Vado. This road was once impassable in wet weather, but recent improvements have made it a good gravel road. A new boat ramp and parking facility have been built on this north end of El Vado. Except during winter and during the spring runoff, this road gives the fisherman access to some great trout fishing near the Chama River inlet and on the peninsula. There is a dirt road along the west shoreline linking the dam area with the north end, but this road is rough.

A variety of shorelines are available to the angler at El Vado Lake. A two-mile-long peninsula (called the "Peninsula") divides the upper two-thirds of El Vado into two long narrow bays. The upper westside bay receives water from creeks flowing out of Stinking Lake and Stone Lake on the Jicarilla Apache Indian Reservation. The upper eastside bay, the inlet for the Rio Chama, is one of the most consistent fishing areas on the lake. Both bays are characterized by a shallow sloping shoreline. The western shoreline of the main lake, which cuts sharply down to the waterline, is a good place to troll. Hargroves Point is a notable fishermen's landmark in the middle of the west side. The middle of the east shoreline is state park territory. Shale Point is about a half-mile north of C-Loop. C-Loop is a good bay for bank-fishing or trolling, and is located next to the "C-Loop" camping area in the state park. At the southern end, where the dam is, El

Vado is divided into two bays by a peninsula called South Point. The tip of South Point is a favored area for bank fishermen, but its roads are impassable in wet weather. El Vado Lake is about a mile and a half wide and four miles long from north to south. The water is rarely clear.

What about the fishing year at El Vado Lake? December, January, and February oversee the ebb and flow of winter at El Vado. Until the lake starts to freeze over the bank-fishing is good, especially for kokanee when using kokanee spawn or red or yellow bottled salmon eggs or corn. There is some ice-fishing in January with a gradual thaw in February. Access depends on snowstorms. After a snowstorm, the road to the dam is normally bladed.

In March, and once the lake is clear of ice, bank-fishing ranges from good to very good. Try the east shoreline at the state park. Live minnows are best for good catches of rainbows. Dress warmly. At the dam, brown trout angling is good with worm-tipped lures. Roads are bladed and often dry.

In April, May, and June the runoff occurs. In-flows from the Rio Chama peak in May, and so does the good spring fishing. Road conditions range from muddy in April and May to dry in June. Live minnows or salmon eggs are the best bait for shore anglers. Fishing with shallow-running lures is good, especially on the east side and from the state park south to the dam. Browns are still being caught, along with kokanee, rainbows, and a few lake trout. Fishing is good overall in May—maybe the best of the year. The easy fishing eases off in June as the spring feeding binge subsides and the fish spread out. Anglers fishing the inlet get good catches of rainbow trout on minnows and lures. By the end of June there is some good night-fishing for rainbows. The lake is full or near full.

July and August is a busy time at the state park. Water-skiers flash by, and campers and anglers are everywhere. The runoff is over, the fish are scattered, and warm sunny weather has arrived. Fishing for browns is still productive at the dam. Use lures, woolybuggers, or peacock-bodied flies fished deep. The inlet area is still hot for rainbows. Deep trolling for kokanee and rainbows is good with christmas trees, flashers, cowbells, leadcore, or downriggers in the main channel south of the Peninsula and in the south-western corner of the lake. Daytime bank-fishing is tough, but it is much better at night.

September, October, and November bank-fishing ranges from poor to good. Catches from the shore gradually improve throughout autumn and peak in November and December. The inlet area is still good with minnows and lures. Kokanee are caught trolling at twenty to twenty-five feet and

El Vado Lake

snagging starts on September 1. The first salmon runs are up the Chama River at Plaza Blanca. Check the Albuquerque newspapers and the Department of Game and Fish fishing report, for the timing and location of the kokanee run is different every year. Until winter temperatures begin to freeze the shallows, there is good bank-fishing for kokanee and rainbows (use yellow salmon eggs or fresh kokanee spawn).

The hills around El Vado Lake were once pinned to the earth with huge ponderosa pine trees. From 1900 until the end of World War I, this area was decimated by cut-and-haul logging. The topsoil is no longer held to earth by the big pines, and runoff carries tons of silt and detritus into El Vado. That's what helps make this lake such a fine carp and sucker producer. You can see remains of the logging town and the relocated cemetery of El Vado on the Peninsula in the northern part of the lake.

There is a good population of little green sunfish in El Vado, but these panfish are rarely caught by the trout anglers. To help control the suckers, coho salmon were introduced in 1972 (the state-record coho came out of El Vado in 1974). That program has not been continued. A few big (five- to ten-pound) browns are caught each year, in May near the dam or in November at the inlet. Thousands of kokanee are caught in the summer. Channel catfish may be in El Vado's future, and the Department of Game and Fish is looking at increased stocking rates of rainbow fingerling and kokanee fry. Lake trout were never stocked, but came down from Heron Reservoir, and are now growing in this lake. All in all, El Vado is a great fishery.

RIO CHAMA WILDLIFE AND FISHING AREA

For eight miles above El Vado Reservoir, the Chama River is in the state-owned Rio Chama Wildlife and Fishing Area. With a large coldwater lake below and a reasonable watershed above, it is little wonder the Department of Game and Fish calls this stretch "one of the best in the state." It's stocked with fry, fingerling, and catchable-size rainbows, brown trout fry, kokanee salmon fry, and occasionally with Snake River cutthroats. There are three ways to reach this part of the Chama: boat in, hike in, or take a dirt road and walk in. Camping (no fee) is allowed throughout the fishing area; there are no facilities.

The Chama ends its untamed run as it enters El Vado Reservoir. This inlet area is one of the few spots in New Mexico where a big trout stream

Rio Chama Wildlife and Fishing Area

enters a great coldwater lake. A dirt and gravel road, S.R. 95, runs right by the inlet bay five miles west of Heron Dam. You can also get there by boat. Launch from the public boat ramp at El Vado, head north along the eastern shoreline, and motor up the inlet channel as far as it's safe to go. With camping gear, you can enjoy some great evening fishing with no worry about boating back at night.

Four virtually unfished miles of the Rio Chama lie just upstream from the inlet. The river here flows throught a steep gorge, with canyon walls defining the Chama's course. You can hike to this area by parking at Heron Dam and following the marked trail down Willow Creek canyon. This is where Heron releases its water into the Chama. If you like low water and Indian Summer fishing, the time to hike into the gorge is in October, the month with a history of no releases from Heron. This is a great place to backpack for a few days of camping. You're fairly close to your vehicle, but once in the canyon it's just you, the river, and the fish.

The canyon walls open up in the lower four miles of the river in the Rio Chama Wildlife and Fishing Area. Cottonwoods line the banks and a dirt road leads directly to the river. About six miles west of U.S. 84 on S.R. 112, barely improved dirt roads head north to the area called Cottonwood Flats. Easy access makes this a very popular fishing spot, but your own private piece of the Chama lies just a short hike away, upstream or down. Fly fishermen like this stretch because the runs, riffles, and the easy wading are perfect for those casting a fly-line.

Rainbow trout are the normal catch in this part of the Chama River. The browns are catchable, especially in the late fall during their spawning act. Kokanee run upriver from El Vado during their early winter spawning run, snagging is legal from September to the end of December. If you're on the river when the kokanee salmon are running try drifting yellow salmon eggs through the pools. The trout will often key on the salmon spawn. Large trout move into this stretch of the Chama from El Vado Reservoir, rainbows in the spring, and browns as well as rainbows in the fall. Spring fishing is not production until the runoff starts to drop, sometime in June or July.

Fall is the classic time to be on the Rio Chama: the browns are aggressive and the rainbows are putting on fat for their winter slowdown. While the grasshoppers are still active, the fly and the bait fisherman will be doing the same thing: one will cast a feathery imitation and the other will cast the real thing; both are trying to fool a big brown before winter chases us back to a warm fireplace and the autumn memories of this great trout stream.

RIO BRAZOS

The Rio Brazos is a great brown and rainbow trout stream feeding the Chama River just south of Tierra Amarilla. This freestone river is completely on private property. The New Mexico Department of Game and Fish stocks one part of the Brazos River where land owners have signed a public-access fishing agreement. Off-limit areas are posted with no-trespassing signs.

Even with access problems, erosion from gravel pit operations, and heavy fishing pressure, many anglers think this is one of the best rivers in the state. Access is tricky. Please don't trespass on posted property.

Access is off U.S. 84 just north of Tierra Amarilla. Turn east on paved S.R. 512. Signs for the Brazos Lodge and Corkins Lodge mark the turnoff. About two miles in there is a paved right turn that does not lead to the stream, so stay on the main paved road. The first stop for the angler is the public fishing area at the Chaves Creek Bridge. This is a good spot for a family picnic and to try for some of the catchable-size rainbows stocked at the bridge. Chaves Creek is small; better fishing is found on the Brazos River.

Access to the stretch of the Brazos River upstream from Chaves Creek is on dirt roads heading toward the river from S.R. 512. Remember that this is all private property. You can also park along S.R. 512 and hike the quarter-mile cross-country to the river. If you are not familiar with the terrain, carry a compass, because it is easy to lose your way. This part of the lower Brazos (above mile-marker 5) contains good brown trout fishing. Below this section the Brazos is not much of a river: water is taken out for irrigation, and the river channel is a half-mile-wide bed of rocks with but a trickle of water.

Paved road S.R. 512 continues on toward the lodges. At mile-marker 7 the road turns to maintained gravel. Although at this point the Brazos is right next to the road, a steep cliff makes it nearly inaccessible. Continue one mile east on the gravel road (this is the Brazos Estates area) and you will see a signed public-access point with parking for about a half-dozen vehicles.

This is the only public-access point on the Brazos River. It is a short walk through a gate and down a jeep trail to the river. This is where the hatchery truck gets access to the river. You can fish upstream for a mile and a half until you get to the marked boundaries of Corkins Lodge. In the public water below this point, you can expect good fishing for the larger rainbow trout stocked by Corkins which have moved downstream. You'll also find plenty of state-stocked rainbows and, occasionally, brooks and browns. Working downstream from the public-access point, you'll find rainbows and more brown trout.

This section of the Brazos River is contained in a canyon, and about the only way in or out is at the single public-access point. There are very few pools, most of the Brazos is a free-running river made of riffles, runs, and rocks. The bait fisherman can try the one big pool just upstream from the access point. Better catches are made by fishing your bait, fly, or lure through all the fish-holding runs. The trout will be just about anyplace where you can't see the bottom. Those fishing in chest waders (hip waders won't do) should bring an extra pair of clothes, since slipping on the algae-covered rocks of the Brazos is a common occurrence.

If you drive past the public-access point, you'll reach Brazos Lodge (actually a store and four nice motel units), a restaurant, about fifty private vacation cabins, and a small stocked pond (a public fishing area). Further up the road is Corkins Lodge, which provides for its guests over a dozen rental cabins, a stocked pond, and a couple miles of the Brazos River stocked with plump rainbow trout. Corkins is the only access to the Brazos River above the Brazos Lodge. Call either of these lodges for prices and reservation information.

The Brazos Box, above Corkins, and the Brazos Meadows, in the high country, offer fantastic wild trout fishing all on private land. There are browns, brook trout, rainbows, and cutthroats in the headwater creeks. In terms of wild populations of naturally reproducing trout, the upper Brazos nurtures the best trout fishery in the state, all on private land.

The entire river is unfishable during the spring runoff. It ranges from good to very good for six- to twelve-inch rainbow trout from Memorial Day until mid-November. Lure-casters connect with small Mepps-style spinners. Fly-fishing is fantastic. There are stoneflies in early summer; caddis, mayfly, and midge hatches through the warmer months; and great streamer (and dry fly) fishing in the fall. Salmon egg and worm fishermen do best after a brief summer shower, when the water is a bit muddied. Be ready to change your fishing plans if you notice rains in the mountains to the east. It takes about three hours for a heavy rainstorm in the headwaters to come roaring down the Brazos Canyon, turning this usually clear river into a roaring torrent of brown water.

There is one other access to the Brazos River: from Tierra Amarilla a dirt and gravel road runs east, roughly parallel to the south side of the river. Don't go exploring on this road in your Mercedes, and if it's been raining don't go on it at all. It runs through private property, but it does give access

Rio Brazos

to some good brown trout fishing on the lower end of the fishable part of the Brazos River.

A tiny bit of the headwaters of the Brazos River is on the Carson National Forest. This is the Osier Fork of the East Fork of the Brazos. It is accessible through Lagunitas Campground east of San Antonio Mountain and from Osier (in Colorado). This is a good little brook trout creek located a long way from the pavement.

In autumn the lower Brazos, from the U.S. 64 bridge downstream to the confluence of the Brazos into the Chama, holds a good population of brown trout. This area is all posted private property.

HERON LAKE

If you like fishing a deep, cold, clear trout lake, check out Heron Reservoir. Located in north-central New Mexico, ten miles west of Tierra Amarilla, Heron Dam releases water into the Chama River just upstream from El Vado Lake. Most of the water in Heron comes from the high country of Colorado and is piped into New Mexico, pumped over the Continental Divide, and released into Heron Reservoir. Since these headwaters are collected before they can load up with silt, Heron is an excellent trout and salmon habitat. The result is about 5,500 acres of cold, clear water backing up behind Heron Dam. This is not a long, thin canyon lake. Heron is about three miles across.

Four types of trout as well as kokanee salmon and white suckers live in the reservoir. One- to three-pound trout, rainbows and cutthroat, are common. Brown trout are rare catches in Heron, but every year a few five- to ten-pounders are hooked. Lake trout are the prize catch in Heron. They were stocked in the late 1970s and are now in the seven- to fifteen-pound class. It is possible that the lakers are spawning successfully.

The lake and all the land surrounding the reservoir are included in Heron Lake State Park. Access is on paved State Route 95, five miles west of Tierra Amarilla. S.R. 95 follows the southern shoreline of Heron, past the paved boat ramp turnoff, and leads right to the dam. Full service camping facilities, including recreational vehicle hookups, are operated by the New Mexico State Park Division from April through October. Unimproved campgrounds are open throughout the year. Privately owned camping areas and tourist cabins (at Stone House Lodge) are located west of the dam. For privacy and quiet, boat to the north shore of Heron and choose your own campsite. The park service has regulated Heron as a no-wake lake, making it very popular with the sailboat crowd.

Heron Lake

The fishing year starts poorly at Heron. January, February, and March finds the lake frozen around the edges. In some years there is ice-fishing in the Willow Creek Arm. But the lake is usually a cold and quiet place throughout the winter chill. By late March the ice is thin or completely gone.

Iceout in April and May is the time to catch big rainbow trout, and fishing from shore or trolling in shallow water is very productive. Try the stretch along the Heron Dike, a mile west of the dam. Deep trolling at twenty-five feet is effective for lake trout, but the salmon aren't feeding yet and the trout are in shallow water. After a long winter's rest the cutthroat, rainbow trout, and a few browns can be found along the edges, in five to fifteen feet of water, on their annual spring feeding binge.

June is a crossover month at Heron. The water is starting to turn over and gamefish can be found everywhere. Trolling at depths from twenty to thirty-five feet will work for kokanee and trout. Bank-fishing is still good for rainbows, cutthroat, and an occasional laker.

July, August, and September are hard on the boatless angler. The water in Heron stratifies during the vacation months and the fish go deep. The summer sunshine is too bright, the surface temperature too high, and the oxygen content too low in the top layer of water. The bottom layer is too low in oxygen and foodstuffs. The right combination is found in the middle, or thermocline, zone. In Heron, that area is from twenty to fifty feet below the surface. That's why bait-fishing from the bank is tough during the warm summer months. You're often casting to water that's not deep enough, and the fish just aren't there. Look for drop-offs, especially around the dam, and let your bait or lure get deep. The trolling angler knows the salmon are deeper yet; you need to put your kokanee lure thirty to forty-five feet.

Around October the lake turns over, destratifying the water. Bank-fishing quickly improves because the trout are once again feeding in shallow water. October also marks the beginning of the salmon run. If you're casting from the shore in autumn or early winter, try real or imitation kokanee eggs (yellow). The rainbow trout and cutthroat key on the yellow salmon eggs dropped by the kokanee. By November the salmon snagging will have started, though it's better to wait until December for the run to peak. Bank-fishing is good until around Christmas, but when winter gets severe the fishing quickly stops. Everything stays on hold until next spring, when iceout marks the beginning of another fishing year at Heron Reservoir.

More kokanee salmon are caught in Heron Reservoir than all other species combined. Each year they're stocked as fry near the Ridge Rock campground. For the next three or four years these freshwater salmon grow in the depths of Heron's clear water. They spawn and then die, often near the location where they were stocked.

Kokanee school together by age groups, following the plankton they feed on. Limited food supply and cold water temperatures keep these salmon quiet from winter through early spring. As the water temperature warms and the sunlight reaches down, the plankton multiply and the kokanee start feeding. In June they're twenty to twenty-five feet deep, and from July through September twenty-five to forty feet deep.

Fishing these depths is easiest with a downrigger, but most still use leadcore or christmas trees. Any copper, gold, or silver lure with red accents, when fished at the right depth, will catch kokanee salmon. Favorite slow troll lures at Heron include the Z-Ray and the Kokanee Killer, and for faster trolling some use a red and white Gatorspoon. Fishermen using a downrigger and still not connecting should put their lure thirty-five to forty-five feet behind the lead weight.

If you see a group of boats trolling in one location, they're sure to be on a school of kokanee. Motor over their way (remember that this is a no-wake lake), give them plenty of room, and start trolling. Otherwise, try trolling around the island for which Island View campground is named, located a mile north of the dam. It's more important to put your lure at the right depth than to worry about a specific lure or a specific spot. If you're serious about trolling for lake trout, rainbows, or kokanee salmon, consider a downrigger and a sonar unit. Knowledge of these tools can provide consistent hookups for the deep-trolling fisherman.

The lakebed just south of the island is where Heron's two original creek beds meet. Willow Creekbed runs northeast up to the Narrows, while Horse Creek runs northwest. They meet just south of the island and head to the dam. These are the deepest areas of the lake, one hundred to two hundred feet deep.

In autumn the four-year-old kokanees start to run in tight schools. Their coloring changes, with the males gradually turning a brilliant orange-red and the females changing to a dull silver. The lower jaw on the males starts to curl up. These are signs that the salmon are getting ready for their spawning run. Trolling is still the way to fish in October. By November, and until mid-December, snagging is the key to catching a basketful of kokanee salmon. La Jara boat ramp, west of the dam, is the best place to start. Snagging from a boat, about forty yards offshore, is easier than heaving treble hooks from the bank. If you're boatless, bring plenty of replacement hooks, you'll lose a lot of tackle to the rocky bottom. The legal snagging season runs from September to the end of December, with a legal bag limit

Burns Canyon Lake

Fluorescent orange kokanee salmon electro-shocked and released by the U.S. Fish and Wildlife Service.

of twenty-four. Check the fishing reports in the Albuquerque newspapers for weekly updates on the spawning run.

The road coming into Heron, S.R. 95, is paved past Heron Dam to the Stone House Lodge. From the dam parking area you can hike down to the Chama River Canyon. Or you can drive west to Heron Dike. The road splits at the dike, heading north to unimproved campsites along the west shoreline of Heron and deadending at Horse Creek Inlet. Or head west from Heron Dike and in about two miles miles you'll be at the north end of El Vado, west of where the Chama River enters. Gravel and dirt S.R. 95 continues west and eventually gets back to pavement on Jicarilla Apache land south of Dulce.

BURNS CANYON LAKE

This little lake used to be the brood pond at the Parkview Hatchery. Its ten acres are now a public fishery named Burns Canyon Lake. No boats or floating devices are allowed here, and much of the bank is overgrown with cattails and willows. A fisherman willing to wade the shallows while casting a small lure or wooly worm will soon find a trout on the end of his line.

The riprap along the dam is fairly clear of cattails and offers a good spot for the bank fisherman. A few other clear spots require a ten-minute walk from the parking area. Because of its small size and almost hidden location, Burns Lake is overshadowed by nearby Heron and El Vado reservoirs. Burns has a good coldwater inlet and an excellent natural food supply; this makes for good growth in the six thousand catchable rainbow trout stocked here every year.

Wheelchair access is almost impossible at Burns, and no camping is allowed. The lake is open from April 1 to October 30, from one-half hour before sunrise to one-half hour after sunset. Access is off U.S. 84 at the El Vado Lake turnoff. At the U.S. 84 and S.R. 112 intersection, a paved road leads north for a half-mile to Parkview (Los Ojos). The road leads down a steep hill, past a religious shrine, and into the little village of Los Ojos. Take the marked gravel road to Parkview Hatchery. You can turn in at the hatchery for a self-guided tour of this modern facility. But if you want to go fishing, stay on the county road for another mile, and follow the road where it abruptly curves into the little parking area for Burns Canyon Lake.

CHAMA LAND AND CATTLE COMPANY

A little south of the town of Chama and east of U.S. 84, the earth gradually rises up from the Chama River Valley. Elevations climb from eight thousand to over eleven thousand feet above sea level. The groundcover changes from cottonwoods and meadows to the scrub oak, pine, and aspen of elk country. The thirty-two thousand acres of the Chama Land and Cattle Company are known as fine producers of elk and deer, but they also hold headwater streams and a dozen little high mountain lakes.

Fishing here is by reservation only, and guests stay in the headquarters lodge. Both the lakes, two to four acres, and the small streams are managed for a quality fishing experience. Bait-fishing is not promoted, and small lures and artificial flies are the rule. June to November are the prime months; and the daily rate includes lodging, meals, transportation in four-wheel-drive vehicles, and johnboats at the lakes.

The Chama Land and Cattle Company operation is biased toward the adult who needs to escape the pressures of work to enjoy some fishing or hunting. Some of the lakes are fly-fishing only, some are stocked with big rainbows, and others hold wild cutthroat. The stocked rainbows grow big and wild in these fertile mountain lakes, where twenty-inch fish are possible. The streams are loaded with small brookies, and the lakes they feed support some large brook trout. Daily rates run over one hundred dollars.

EDWARD SARGENT FISH AND WILDLIFE MANAGEMENT AREA

The Chama River and one of its little feeder streams, the Rio Chamita, meet south of downtown Chama. You can't fish either one without running into a no-trespassing sign, as both run through private property. It's a different story just north of town. The twenty thousand acres of the Edward Sargent Fish and Wildlife Management Area is public property. It was purchased by the Nature Conservancy and held until the Department of Game and Fish could obtain the money to buy it. Fishing is good on both the Chama and the Chamita, and each has a different access route.

To have a chance at the cutthroats, rainbows, and cutbows (hybrids) of the Chamita, enter the Sargent Area by vehicle. Turn west on First Street at the north end of town. Go two blocks west, past the Double Hackle Tackle Shop, and then head north on Pine Street. Pine turns into a dirt and gravel road as it enters the Sargent area. The information sign at the entrance tells you to drive only on the main road and that there's a two-fish limit. No bait-fishing is allowed.

It's a short walk from the dirt road to fish any part of the Chamita for its wild trout. Nabor Creek is a little tributary to the Chamita, which has been reclaimed with Rio Grande cutthroats. A twenty-minute hike from the marked trailhead will get you to Nabor Lake, a little four-acre reservoir on the creek.

To give the browns and rainbows of the Chama a look at your fly or lure, drive through town and head north on S.R. 17. Just outside town, S.R. 17 crosses the Chama River. Park at the bridge and you can fish upstream for about six miles, to the confluence of Wolf Creek. Highway 17 parallels the river north past the bridge, but there is no public access. Here, you must park and walk upstream from the bridge. This stretch, especially the upper portion, is almost unfished. Remember the two-fish limit and the no bait-fishing rule. The river holds mostly browns, with some rainbows from upstream stockings as well as a few cutthroats and brookies.

Tracks for the steam-powered Cumbres and Toltec Railroad parallel the river along the upper reaches of the Sargent area. Like much of the Chama watershed, this is a special place to angle for trout in the fall. Cold mornings, warm afternoons, and cool evenings are the mark of late-season, high-country fishing. To catch a wild trout, with its sparkle matching the red and gold hillside, this is the upper Chama at its best.

LOBO LODGE

When the Chama River first enters New Mexico it flows through a big piece of private property. Known to sportsmen as the Lobo Lodge, this 10,700-acre spread includes Wolf Creek, the first major tributary to the Chama River. The lodge operates housekeeping cabins, with rates running about one hundred dollars a day for a party of four.

An experienced angler can expect to hook and release a couple of dozen trout during a good day's angling. Brown trout are the wild fish in this ten-mile stretch of the Chama River. Rainbows are stocked twice a year. Wolf Creek is a strong little mountain stream full of wild cutthroats and brook trout.

Both the river and the creek are in runoff until the middle of June. But from July to September the waters are in excellent condition for both the fish and the fishermen. July and August are good for all-day fishing excursions, from sunup to dusk. By September the cold mornings and cool evenings signal the beginning of autumn. Fall fishing is better after the day starts to warm. October is the beginning of hunting season at Lobo Lodge and the facilities are normally booked full.

JICARILLA APACHE INDIAN WATERS

The Jicarilla Apache Indian Reservation encompasses 750,000 acres west of Chama. This is one of New Mexico's best-managed trout fisheries. With five good lakes there's a spot for just about anyone's style of angling. The Navajo River runs through Jicarilla lands, but is only a marginal trout fishery. Ice-fishing is popular at two of the lakes, and early summer and fall trout fishing can be very good for all styles of fishermen.

The lakes all have superb angling during the month or two after iceout. The warmth of the sun on these cool spring days turns the rainbows and cutthroats into eating machines. They feed heavily on minnows at this time of year, and fifteen- to twenty-inch fish are common to the few anglers who brave the springtime chill. Lures and the big flies that imitate baitfish or dragonfly nymphs are the tools to use in casting for these hungry trout. Boats are not absolutely necessary in the first two months after iceout;

casting from the shore produces fish. But as summer rolls in, dense aquatic vegetation along the shoreline makes a boat a good asset for the vacation-time fisherman. Canoes or johnboats with small motors are perfect for these thirty- to seventy-five-acre lakes, and a float tube is a definite advantage for the summertime fly fisherman.

The hot days of August find the Jicarilla fisheries personnel harvesting the thick growth of aquatic vegetation with a giant floating combine. All these lakes are incredibly fertile, but the plant growth in these trout lakes is a two-edged sword. It nurtures the minnows, insects, crayfish, and snails that the trout feed on, but it also dies and rots in the winter. A thick coat of ice combined with the rotting vegetation can use up all the available oxygen and the result could be a severe or total winterkill of fish in these high-country lakes. By harvesting the water weeds in summer and bubbling air, water, or propane through the ice in the winter, the managers of these Jicarilla lakes assure the angler of good ice-fishing and great spring catches of large trout.

Most of the lakes are just off paved highways with dirt or gravel access roads. The town of Dulce has gas stations, grocery stores, and motels. Camping is allowed at each lake, but no drinking water is provided. Paved roads lead to Dulce from Chama and Farmington (U.S. 64), or head north from Bernalillo on N.M. 44 and turn north on State Route 537 at the concrete tepee rest stop twenty miles north of Cuba.

Anyone wanting to fish on Jicarilla lands must first obtain a Jicarilla fishing permit, but you don't need a New Mexico fishing license. The permits are available in Dulce, at the Jicarilla Department of Game and Fish, or at the Best Western Jicarilla Inn (open all day, all year long); in Bloomfield, at Jim's Sporting Goods; or in Albuquerque, at Charlie's Sporting Goods or at Gardenswartz Sportz. Call the Jicarilla Department of Game and Fish at (505) 759-3255 for maps and current fishing information (including ice-fishing information).

Enbom Lake

Enbom is a personal-size lake that grows a lot of weeds in the summer. A canoe is a definite asset if you're fishing with flies or lures. Bait-fishing is great in the early summer and again after the first cold winds of autumn. There's not much camping room at this lake, but there are plenty of good-size cutthroats and rainbow trout. The water is very clear in Enbom, which makes fishing lures or flies a joy, you can actually watch the trout hit your lure. Enbom is located 12.8 miles south of Dulce, just off paved road J8. Handicapped access is available.

Mundo Lake

Mundo is the youngest of the Jicarilla lakes and one of the most popular. Here are plenty of well-used camping areas and a shoreline just made for bankside bait-fishing. The lake is stocked with brown trout, catfish, and with plenty of catchable-size rainbows and cutthroat; and during most every quiet evening Mundo Lake is full of rising trout. There are many crayfish in Mundo, and a small crayfish tail makes a great bait. The inlet area offers a chance at larger trout for both shore and boat anglers. This is a good-size lake of sixty acres, and it is the only Jicarilla lake that doesn't have a heavy summer growth of aquatic vegetation. Mundo is located 5.3 miles south of Dulce on paved route J8. Handicapped access is good.

Hayden Lake

Hayden is an almost hidden lake of fifty-three surface acres. Aquatic insect life is abundant here, and on summer evenings the cutthroats feed with abandon. The six miles of gravel access road make Hayden Lake a fairly private spot for the fisherman after a peaceful day of angling. Waders, a float tube, or a small boat are needed, as most of the shore is locked in with cattails. Hayden is located just northeast of the much larger Burford (or Stinking) Lake. Don't try fishing Burford; it is off-limits to fishermen, has no trout, and is managed for its great autumn duck hunting. Hayden is twenty-four miles south of Dulce on J8.

La Jara Lake

In recent years, La Jara has been the best springtime fishery on the Jicarilla lands. Rainbow trout and cutthroats big enough to challenge your tackle swim the shorelines in the first month after iceout. Lures or big flies are the best springtime tackle, as these trout feed heavily on minnows and dragonfly nymphs before the warm summer days start the great mayfly, midge, and caddis hatches. Summer at La Jara brings a quick growth of water weeds, and this is the time for boat fishing with a flyrod or casting a bubble-fly rig. Bait-fishing picks up in the fall as the large trout feed closer to shore before the winter quickly quiets everything. La Jara Lake has fifty-six acres and is fifteen miles south of Dulce at the northeast corner of J15 and S.R. 537. The easiest access is on a good gravel road off S.R. 537. Camping and shore-fishing is limited, but this is the best spot for launching a boat. Access off J15 is on a rougher dirt road leading to better bank-fishing and great campsites. Handicapped fishing is possible at these campsites. La Jara offers very good ice-fishing.

Dulce Lake

Dulce is the largest of the Jicarilla lakes and is full of small, medium, and large rainbows and cutthroat. It is just four miles south of Dulce on S.R. 17. A boat is needed if you want good access to all of this seventy-five-acre lake. Dulce follows the cycle of other high-country trout lakes. All techniques work in the spring, especially lures and flies that imitate the baitfish and dragonfly nymphs. Summer brings on the bugs and the aquatic weeds, which makes a boat and a fly-rod the best combination. The coolness of autumn makes excellent fishing for all legal styles of fooling trout. There are pull-off points right off S.R. 17 which offer good spring bank-fishing and a boat-launching area good enough for cartop boats. A dirt road goes across the dam and leads to the north shoreline and many good camping spots. This entrance fords the small outlet stream, and a high-clearance vehicle is usually not necessary.

Stone Lake

Stone Lake was once one of New Mexico's best rainbow trout lakes, but it was ruined when someone illegally used carp minnows as bait. The carp reproduced and now own this once great fishery. It is illegal to use minnows on any Jicarilla waters. Stone Lake is still managed as a trout lake, and though there are fewer trout, the stockers can grow very big. Try trolling with a three-inch orange-over-silver Rapala. You'd be imitating a small carp and attracting some very large rainbow trout.

Jemez Watershed

FISHING THE JEMEZ COUNTRY

The Jemez watershed is the closest trout fishing to the half-million people living in the greater metropolitan Albuquerque area. The area has three lakes and about seventy-five miles of fishable streams. A lot of angling pressure is put on the more accessible portions of this watershed. The Jemez River flows into the Rio Grande just north of Bernalillo, but the Jemez does not become a trout stream until you travel north of the Jemez Indian Reservation, where the Guadalupe River enters the Jemez. Each of these fine trout streams offers good fishing, all the way up to their headwaters.

The Jemez is for the paved-road angler pursuing wild browns and hatchery-raised rainbow trout. The Guadalupe is for the dirt-road fisherman angling after wild browns and seeking the quiet noise of the Santa Fe National Forest. If you are not familiar with these streams, the bridge and parking area just below their confluence is the first place to stop. The fishing usually isn't very good here, but you get to see conditions on both rivers. If the Jemez is running high and is the color of the surrounding red bedrock, it's a day for fishing on the Guadalupe side; or vice versa. Rain or runoff easily muddies these little rivers, but this spot gives you the chance to see what each watershed is doing. There is good wintertime brown trout fishing above and below the bridge. Casting for winter-stocked rainbows is good from this spot all the way up to the town of Jemez Springs. We'll look at the Jemez watershed first, and then come back and work up the Guadalupe side.

JEMEZ RIVER WATERSHED

Sheep Springs Recreation area is the first fishing spot for the angler driving up S.R. 4 north of San Ysidro. Located next to the highway on Jemez Pueblo lands, Sheep Springs is a three-acre pond stocked with rainbow trout. This is fee-fishing; you buy your permit right at the ponds. There is

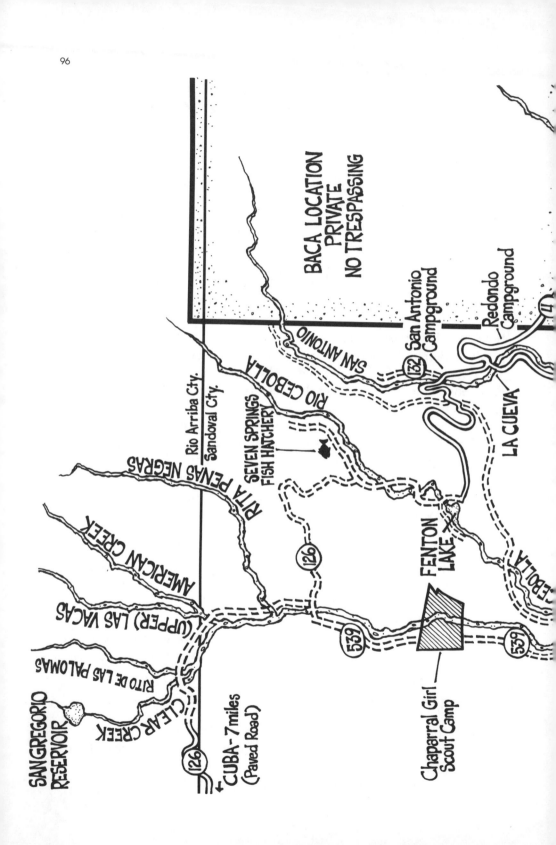

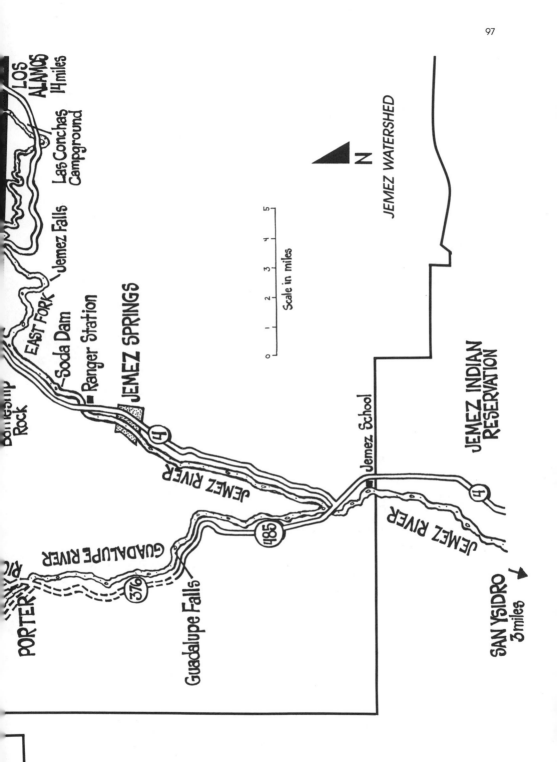

LOS ALAMOS 14 miles

Las Conchas Campground

Jemez Falls

EAST FORK

Soda Dam

Ranger Station

JEMEZ SPRINGS

Battleship Rock

4

JEMEZ RIVER

GUADALUPE RIVER

RIO

PORTER

Guadalupe Falls

376

485

Jemez School

JEMEZ RIVER

4

JEMEZ INDIAN RESERVATION

SAN YSIDRO 8 miles

JEMEZ WATERSHED

N

Scale in miles

0   1   2   3   4   5

a gravel parking lot, shade trees, and plenty of ready-to-catch trout. Sheep Springs is a great spot for a family picnic as well as for those beginning fly-rodders who are looking for an easy place to practice fly-casting. Just north of Sheep Springs Pond is the Jemez Pueblo, and north of the pueblo is the Jemez Public Schools complex. North of the schools the road (S.R. 4) drops down next to the Jemez River at the Guadalupe confluence.

The lower Jemez, from the Guadalupe confluence up to Jemez Springs, runs through a big canyon of red sandstone. Any runoff turns this portion of river into rust colored mud. Cottonwoods line the banks, and there are many good parking spots for fishing and picnics. This area is stocked nearly year round and is popular for winter as well as spring and fall stream-fishing. Low summer water levels combined with the heavy fishing pressure means a small population of trout. Summer angling is for stocked rainbows, and during the warm summer weekends the traffic is heavy. There's trout to be caught, but better hot-weather fishing is found farther upstream.

Most of the Jemez is posted "no trespassing" through the town of Jemez Springs. The Forest Service District Office on the north end of town is the place to stop for maps and camping information. Just upstream from the Ranger Station Bridge is a parking spot with good public fishing up to the Soda Dam. Above the Soda Dam the Jemez again runs through private property. About two miles upstream the river returns to National Forest land, and this is an excellent spot to wade and fish upstream toward the next landmark, Battleship Rock. This is the best of the fishing on the main Jemez, for at Battleship Rock the river splits into two tributaries, the San Antonio River and the East Fork of the Jemez.

Battleship Rock is a developed day-use area with picnic tables, a bridge over the San Antonio River, chemical toilets, and footpaths. You can fish the confluence pool for browns and rainbows or work up either of the two tributaries. Or you can fish downstream in the Jemez itself. Even if you're not planning to fish here, Battleship Rock is another good place to stop and check water conditions. If the San Antonio is high and muddy, then fish downstream with bait or work up the East Fork with a fly-rod. If they're both unfishable, maybe it's a day to try Fenton Lake.

SAN ANTONIO RIVER

Slightly smaller than the East Fork, the San Antonio tumbles and rolls alongside S.R. 4. There are three picnic areas right off the road north of Battleship, where both browns and stocked rainbows are caught. A favorite entry point is the day-use parking area at the Jemez Hot Springs pull-off. It is public fishing on the San Antonio from Battleship Rock upstream to the La Cueva Picnic Area. A mile above the village of La Cueva (with a restaurant, a gas station, a motel, and a grocery store) at the U.S. Forest Service San Antonio Campground, the stream is again on public land. The stream is stocked at the campground.

There are six miles of unstocked fishing, primarily for brown trout, upstream from the campground, with two dirt Forest Service roads giving access to the upper San Antonio. The first road (F.R. 132) heads north from S.R. 126 just past the San Antonio Campground. This rough dirt road parallels the stream and dead-ends after two miles. Above the dead-end there are two miles of rarely fished water until you reach the San Antonio Hot Springs Area. In dry weather this rough, rutted road gives access for those who want to fish this little river.

The other Forest Road is F.R. 376. It also heads north from S.R. 126, but it follows the stream high up on the slope of the river valley. Occasionally you catch a glimpse of the stream hundreds of feet below. After about four miles the road drops down to the San Antonio at the San Antonio Hot Springs (Forest Service Youth Conservation Camp). This is a heavily fished spot because the road is right next to the stream. You can fish (or drive) upstream for two miles until you get to the posted Baca Location. Downstream from the Forest Service Camp, there is about two miles of fishing before you reach the dead end of F.R. 132. The San Antonio is a small forest stream full of good trout fishing (but only if you walk away from the easily accessible spots).

EAST FORK OF THE JEMEZ RIVER

Let's travel back down to Battleship Rock, where the San Antonio meets the East Fork of the Jemez River. Making long casts while fishing up this part of the East Fork will snare nothing but trees. The way to fish here is to wade quietly upstream and flip your bait, fly, or spinner through the hundreds of little pockets where the brown trout hide out. About a mile upstream a hot spring enters the East Fork, a good spot to hike to if the water is clear but cold in early spring or late fall. This is good walk-in fishing, but few anglers fish this forest stream. There are some deep holes in this stretch, which continues up to Jemez Falls. A Forest Service dirt road leads from S.R. 4 to the campground at Jemez Falls (outhouses but with no drinking water). Rainbow trout are stocked near the falls, but

East Fork of the Jemez River

upstream it's back to brown trout fishing. Canyon walls close in on the East Fork above the falls, and it's a solitary mile and a half of quiet fishing until the East Fork crosses S.R. 4.

The canyon, just as S.R. 4 crosses the stream, opens into a nice little valley with grass meadows lining the streambank. Easy access makes this a very popular spot for family hikes. The hatchery truck stops here, and rainbow trout are caught in the pools near the road. Less than a mile upstream, the East Fork crosses briefly into the private Baca Location. A barbed-wire fence marks the boundary; if you want to fish upstream, go around this small piece of private property—don't trespass. The brown trout fishing continues in a wilderness setting for three and a half miles before the East Fork drops down once again to cross S.R. 4. It heads south and west through a few hundred yards of private property until it crosses back under S.R. 4 at Las Conchas campground, an improved Forest Service area.

From here, the little river heads north for a mile before crossing again into the no-trespassing Baca Location. This last mile of fishable water on the East Fork of the Jemez is rarely fished much past the campground. Few people will drive this far and walk past all the downed trees and wade the deep pools to get to the wild trout in the upper reaches.

LOS ALAMOS RESERVOIR

Although not actually part of the Jemez watershed, Los Alamos Reservoir is the next fishing spot east of the Baca Location. Head east on S.R. 3, past the Valle Grande, up and over the mountains, and turn north on the paved road leading to Los Alamos. This turnoff is just after the last steep switchback coming off the mountainside. Head north past the abandoned guardhouse and continue toward Los Alamos. Turn west just before the high bridge over Los Alamos Canyon. This paved road switchbacks down into the canyon. Turn west (upstream) just after you cross the little creek at the bottom of the canyon. This dirt and rocky road follows along the creek, and in about two miles it dead-ends at Los Alamos Reservoir. The little ten-acre lake is stocked with catchable-size rainbow trout in the warmer months. Fishing is best after the hatchery truck makes its first springtime stocking. Midday catching is good in June, poor in July and August, and good again in the fall. Handicapped access is reasonable.

That's the story on fishing the Jemez Country. Hatchery-raised rainbow trout are available in each of the spots accessible to the park and fish anglers.

Guadalupe River Watershed

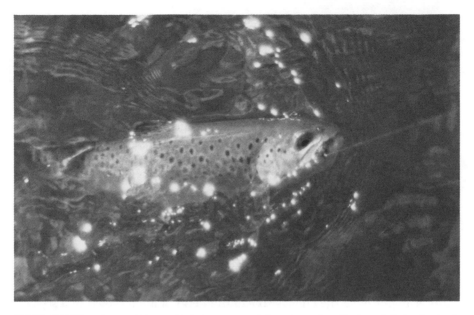

The Rio Guadalupe is a great brown trout stream, especially upstream from the tunnels, but a few trout, like this brown, live below the waterfalls.

Wild browns dominate the stream in the areas you can walk to, and a few cutthroats hide out in the headwater creeks. Bait, flies, or small lures are all productive if presented carefully to the hungry trout of the Jemez watershed.

GUADALUPE RIVER WATERSHED

Almost all the Jemez is paralleled by paved roads. Rainbows are stocked at all the likely locations, and there's good fishing for browns. Restaurants and gas stations are never more than twenty minutes away. But just a few miles west of the Jemez watershed is the Guadalupe River, its headwater streams, and two good trout lakes. The Guadalupe is almost as big as the main Jemez, but fewer people fish it. The access is on the dirt and gravel Forest Road 376. This river is managed as a brown trout stream; there's very little stocking of catchable-size rainbows. Dropping a salmon egg on a No. 10 snelled hook into a nice pool and propping your rod up on the bank won't get you much but chubs. It is the active angler, quietly casting upstream with lure, bait, or fly, who fools the wild browns in the Guadalupe.

Access to the Guadalupe is easiest from the bridge just below the con-

Guadalupe River Watershed

fluence with the Jemez River. The turnoff from S.R. 4 is just a half-mile past the Jemez School complex. The road (F.R. 485) is paved, and you drive past a little village. After the last houses, you'll see the foundation of an abandoned sawmill. Park off the pavement if you want to check out the brown trout in this lower stretch of the Guadalupe. There is about a mile of upstream fishing before you come to the base of Guadalupe Falls. Just past the falls the paved road passes through two old railroad tunnels. This is a great place for a family picnic in a New Mexico river canyon.

Fishing this area is tough because the access is easy and there are no hatchery rainbows to replace the browns caught and kept by the fisherman. It is upstream from this point that the Guadalupe becomes a quality fishing stream. The paved road turns to maintained gravel and a four-wheel-drive vehicle is normally unnecessary. The road stays in the river canyon, but it sways back and forth from the stream. Some areas require a fifteen-minute walk to reach the river; these spots might have some big brown trout just waiting to be fooled and released by an adept angler—released so that another might have the chance to feel the bend of a big brown in a stream inaccessible to the hatchery truck. Fly fishermen on the Guadalupe enjoy a strong hatch of stoneflies in June, and good caddis and mayfly hatches throughout the summer and fall.

RIO DE LAS VACAS AND HEADWATER CREEKS

At Porter, an abandoned settlement, the Rio Cebolla and the Rio de las Vacas meet to form the Guadalupe. There is a modern bridge over the river just below the confluence, and this is a popular spot for family camping vacations (no improvements). Lure- and fly-fishing can be excellent just below the campsites. The best access to this point is on dirt road F.R. 376 coming south from paved S.R. 126 west of La Queva. The Rio de las Vacas is twice as big as the Rio Cebolla and offers good small-stream angling for four miles upstream. It enters the Chaparral Girl Scout Camp, and the side road (F.R. 539) is closed to the public at the camp boundaries.

Above the Chaparral Camp there's good fishing for stocked rainbow trout and browns. This stretch is reached by F.R. 126, either from Cuba or up and over from Fenton Lake. There is some private property along this part of the Rio de las Vacas, but it is well marked and there is plenty of public fishing. Right below the Rio Arriba–Sandoval county line the headwater creeks meet to form Rio de las Vacas.

The Rito Peñas Negras is the largest of these creeks and offers cutthroats as well as browns. The other little tributaries are the Rito de las Palomas, American Creek, Rio de las Vacas, and Clear Creek. These are all very small streams that have their headwaters in the San Pedro Wilderness. The forest service provides camping at the Rio de las Vacas and Clear Creek campgrounds, and these areas are stocked with rainbow trout.

SAN GREGORIO RESERVOIR

Clear Creek was dammed in the early 1900s to form San Gregorio Reservoir, a thirty-acre irrigation impoundment. San Gregorio offers fishing for stocked rainbow trout in a high country meadow. Access is on a marked dirt road (F.R. 264) heading north from Clear Creek Campground. This road is signed and, in dry weather, is usually drivable in the family car. Two miles in on F.R. 264 you park at the marked San Gregorio parking lot.

One of the best things about San Gregorio is that you cannot drive to the lake. San Gregorio Lake is inside the San Pedro Parks Wilderness Area. The parking lot is just outside the wilderness boundary. Once at the parking lot, you load your gear on your back and take a twenty-minute hike on a good wide trail north through the tall trees of the San Pedro Parks Wilderness Area. The walk is about eight city blocks long, just long enough to discourage a lot of anglers.

Fishing at San Gregorio is for hatchery-raised rainbows and the occasional cutthroat hybrid. The access trail comes into the lake at the southeastern corner, and this is a good place to fish almost anytime. It's right between the shallows of the eastern shoreline and the depths along the dam on the southern shoreline. The feeder creek, Clear Creek, enters at the northeastern corner. This is a very small stream with little or no fishing except in the middle of spring, just after the runoff starts to clear. The west side of the lake is a combination of shallow and deep water and is best fished from an inflatable boat. Summer water-weeds make the whole southwestern part of the lake a difficult place to fish.

From June through October, fly-fishing, bait-fishing, and lure-fishing is good at San Gregorio. There are plenty of bugs to interest the fly-rod fellow; small lures are productive early or late in the day; and worm or grasshopper fishing is good all the time. Bring your own worms if you plan to fish with garden hackle. The scars left from digging for "free" worms are ugly, and such excavations cause lake shore erosion. Grasshoppers are the best local bait, and you can use your hat to catch them.

San Gregorio Reservoir

An inflatable boat or float tube is the way to actively fish at San Gregorio. A few people have taken the trouble to build a set of wheels for the back of their canoe. They then have a fairly easy way to get a boat (and fishing and picnic gear) into San Gregorio. Remember, you cannot drive to this lake, and camping is not allowed.

The best access to this region is to drive in through Cuba on F.R. 126. The road is paved for seven miles out of Cuba and then turns into a well-maintained gravel road continuing on to the Clear Creek campground.

RIO CEBOLLA

The Rio de las Vacas meets the Rio Cebolla to form the Rio Guadalupe at the long abandoned village of Porter. As the crow flies, Porter is about fifteen miles south of San Gregorio Reservoir and about five miles south of Fenton Lake.

Dropping back down to Porter, you can fish up the small Rio Cebolla. Upstream from Porter the little river runs through a grassy meadow, and a grasshopper is a natural for tempting trout in this unstocked stretch. F.R. 376 follows the Cebolla, and you can park at the bridge where it crosses the stream and fish downstream in the "Fish for Fun" area. Regulations forbid bait-fishing, and all trout caught must be released. This is a tough area to fish as most of the trout have been caught and released more than once. Angling is best in the morning or evening with dry flies, or midday with wet flies.

Upstream from the bridge you can hike and fish the two miles to Fenton Lake. Rainbow trout are stocked right below the lake where the State Parks Division has built an improved campground. Access to Fenton Lake is on paved S.R. 126 west from La Cueva.

Above the lake, the Rio Cebolla meanders through a marsh before collecting itself back into a small bushy stream with both browns and plenty of stocked rainbow trout. Springs provide the water for Seven Springs Hatchery, which in turn provides the rainbows that are stocked in all of the Jemez drainage. Above the hatchery is an unimproved campground and the Ice Pond, a small stocked trout pond at the edge of the Seven Springs Hatchery. Hatchery personnel once harvested and stored ice from the Ice Pond. In summer they used the ice to keep the water in the transport cans cold enough so that they could stock fish in distant lakes and streams. Now the pond is a favorite family fishing spot. It is regularly stocked throughout the warmer months. The best fishing in the Ice Pond is in the spring and the fall, or during long summer evenings.

As you fish upstream from the Ice Pond, it is the beaver ponds that create the best fishing in this now very small stream. The road following the Rio Cebolla is dirt, and a four-wheel-drive vehicle is the way to travel if you plan on fishing much past the campground.

The Jemez-Guadalupe watershed is an important New Mexican fishing resource. There is trout fishing for just about any style—paved roads or dirt roads; stocked rainbows, wild browns, or headwater cutthroats; lakes, streams, or creeks. Park and walk or park and fish. Most of this drainage is in the Santa Fe National Forest. The rainbows are fun to catch and good to eat. The browns are stocked only as fry. Make it a rule to pick up other people's litter and not to keep more fish than your family will eat for dinner. With good management our great-grandchildren can enjoy the wild roses, the trout, the chipmunks, and the waters we fish in the Jemez country.

FENTON LAKE

Elijah McLean Fenton was the first Anglo settler in the valley that now holds Fenton Lake. His burial site is on a hillside overlooking this popular thirty-acre trout pond. The lake was formed in 1946 by damming the little Cebolla River, and although the dam was originally built with federal waterfowl funds, duck hunting is now prohibited and trout fishing is the main sport at Fenton Lake. This spot gets crowded in the summer. It is the best fishing lake close to the most heavily populated area in New Mexico. From Memorial Day to Labor Day, the weekend traffic is heavy on the shoreline of Fenton Lake.

Seven Springs Hatchery is just up the road from the lake, and thousands of catchable-size rainbow trout are stocked throughout the warmer months. There is a good self-reproducing population of brown trout. Most of the angling at Fenton is bait-fishing with salmon eggs, but the browns are rarely fooled by this technique. It is the active angler—casting fly or lure and fishing when the sun is off the water in spring or fall—who fools the browns of Fenton Lake.

Practically speaking, the fishing year ends in December as the lake begins to ice up. It's too soft for ice-fishing, and visitors are few and far between. Around January the ice is safe, the roads are cleared between snowstorms, and a handful of warm-blooded humans make their annual winter sacrifice to the ice-fishing gods. This is a peaceful place to freeze your ears while waiting for the soft take of Fenton's winter rainbow trout.

Iceout in March or April is met by the early spring fisherman; lures and

Fenton Lake

A fine trout caught during a warm autumn day at Fenton Lake. This brown took a woolybugger cast parallel to the shoreline near the dam.

big flies are favorites as the ice clears from the southern half of the lake. Bait-fishing improves in April, getting better as Memorial Day aproaches. The lake is seldom crowded before Memorial Day, and the fly-rod fellows do well in May as the mayflies, caddis, midges, and dragonflies bring the trout to feed near the surface.

With the hot days of summer the water warms, the algae thickens, and it is vacation time for the half-million people in the Albuquerque metropolitan area. Summer fishing is tough. One hint is to try night-fishing with crayfish tails. Fenton Lake is crowded on summer weekends. Corn, cheese, worm, and salmon egg containers litter the shoreline. Stringers are stuck in the bank, with each family waiting for the strike of the stocked rainbow trout.

As fall approaches the crowds disappear, and much better fishing arrives at Fenton Lake. The surviving rainbows are big, and the brown trout begin to show in the angler's creel. As the water cools off the algae begins to disapear. The sun is lower in the sky and the trout no longer have to hide from the midday brightness. A spinning rod equipped with a clear, casting bobber will cast a gray-hackle peacock to the rising fish. This is a great technique for autumn fishing on Fenton or on any other mountain trout lake. Big grasshoppers, which are free for the catching in the meadows on the eastern shoreline, are the best natural bait at Fenton. The fly fishermen return to Fenton Lake for the daily midge hatch. Use a little nymph, No. 16 or smaller, and retrieve it with small jerks. A large No. 10 Muskrat nymph is effective if the midge rises are few. The brown trout make a fall spawning run up the little inlet. The fishing here is difficult—stay back from the bank and be quiet, and cast small lures, salmon eggs, or flies upstream. These are wild trout, easily scared by a sloppy cast or a loud footstep.

Fenton is regulated as a no-motor boating lake, and strong spring winds are the only interference to drifting in a canoe or rowboat. A nice concrete boat ramp is located near the dam. Handicapped parking and access is very good, and there are fishing piers for the handicapped angler. Fenton Lake is one of our newest state parks, and the entire western shoreline is a fee area during summer weekends. The eastern shoreline is a free-use area with no camping allowed. Improved fee-camping areas are located near and below the dam.

Fenton Lake is located on the west side of the Santa Fe National Forest. North of Albuquerque on I–25, take State Route 44 to San Ysidro. Take the State Route 4 turnoff at San Ysidro, and drive through the town of Jemez Springs to La Cueva. Turn west on State Route 126 and travel the eight miles to Fenton Lake. The road on the west of the lake is maintained gravel, passable in the family car. The road on the east side of the lake is dirt, steep, and rutted. Gas, food, lodging, and tackle are available in La Cueva.

CHAPTER FIVE

Middle and Lower Rio Grande Drainage

COCHITI LAKE

Cochiti Lake, named after Cochiti Pueblo, is an Army Corps of Engineers project on the Rio Grande between Albuquerque and Santa Fe. The project was authorized by Congress for flood and sediment control, for wildlife management, and for recreation. The important word here is *recreation.* Legally, this reservoir cannot be reduced to an area below twelve hundred surface acres. Water levels certainly rise and fall with the seasons, but this permanent pool gives a stable base for the fish populations.

Fishing at Cochiti Lake involves just about every species of sportfish found in New Mexico: rainbow trout, channel catfish and bullheads, large-mouth bass, yellow perch, white bass, spotted bass, bluegill, smallmouth bass, crappie, northern pike, walleyes, plenty of carp and suckers, and maybe even a few huge brown trout.

Cochiti Dam is one of the largest earthfill dams in the world. The dam is over 5 miles long and rises 250 feet above the old river channel. At its lowest level of 1,200 surface acres, the maximum water depths are 85 feet. At this minimum permanent-pool size, the lake is about seven miles long with twenty-one miles of shoreline. It can grow to a flood-pool stage of 9,000 acres. The upper end consists of mud flats, debris, and slow moving water in a wide river channel. The middle section is a long 1,000-foot-wide lake. There are some good side-canyons in this stretch. The lower end of Cochiti, which is about one mile wide and three miles long, comes nearest to being a "lake."

Fishing at Cochiti peaked between 1978 and 1980, about five years after the dam was completed. This is typical of reservoir fisheries. Acres of newly submerged grass and shrubs give nutrients and cover; fish populations grow and prosper; and fishermen enjoy good catches. But after the peak comes the fall. When catch rates dropped, Cochiti lost favor with central New Mexico's anglers.

For a while, Cochiti was only a wide spot on the map, but a series of

Cochiti Lake

wet years, combined with new management techniques have turned Cochiti into an excellent place to catch fish. Rainbow trout are being stocked in amounts sufficient to guarantee good catch rates. Stocked white bass are now reproducing, and crappie catches are again increasing. This reservoir is an important fishery resource because of its location in the middle of the biggest population base in New Mexico. The New Mexico Department of Game and Fish is working hard to improve the stocking program at Cochiti.

Fishing opportunities vary at the two access points to Cochiti's shoreline. Cochiti Recreation Area, located on the west side, offers paved access, a convenience store, fishing docks, good parking, a swimming area off-limits to fishermen, boat slips, an excellent boat ramp, outhouses, camping, and lots of room for shore fishermen. You can cast to shallow and medium depths, fish from a rocky point, or take a short walk to fish off the riprap of the long earthen dam.

Tetilla Peak Recreation Area is on the east side of Cochiti. Tetilla has shaded picnic shelters, bathrooms, camping spots, recreational vehicle hookups, paved roads with good parking, and not very much elbow room for bank fishermen. The Tetilla shoreline is often crowded on summer weekends. Though closed from October through March, anglers can park beside the locked gate and take the ten-minute walk down to the shoreline.

An advantage of Tetilla is its location in respect to the winds. New Mexico is known for its strong spring breezes. Those with small boats or canoes should consider using the Tetilla boat ramp and working north or south along the eastern bank. The shoreline here is dotted with little bays, and is perfect for fishing. If the wind does come up, it normally blows toward the east side, you'll be blown back toward the shoreline.

All boaters should be aware of the two wind-warning lights, one on top of the control tower in the middle of the dam, the other near the Tetilla Overlook. Park rangers note that winds and waves at Cochiti can build to dangerous proportions in a matter of minutes. No light on the wind-warning indicates winds less than 15 mph; a blinking amber light indicates 15 to 25 mph winds; and a flashing red light signals winds over 25 mph. Of course, if you're caught in a dangerous windstorm, do not try to get back to the boat ramp, but head immediately for shore and wait it out. It's better to get soaked on the shoreline than swamped in the lake.

Iceout in March is a good time to cash in on the rainbow trout at Cochiti. The lake rarely gets enough ice for ice-fishing and sometimes doesn't freeze at all, but late winter and early spring finds the trout feeding near shore. Try fishing where the wind has blown warmer surface water against a shoreline or into a protected bay. That's where the food supply is concentrated. Both bait and small lures are productive trout catchers, especially if you can troll slowly along the damface.

April, May, and June are excellent for catching panfish at Cochiti. This is spawning time for the crappie and bluegill, which will be concentrated close to shore. Since the larger predator fish key on their food supply, you'll have a chance for northern pike and walleye pike in the same shallow areas, especially early and late in the day. Good summer catches of panfish are to be had by using minnows, tiny jigs, or waxworms.

Spring is also the spawning time for largemouth bass. Once again the action is in the shallow areas, with prime spots in five to ten feet of water, next to a submerged tree or shrub. Rig plastic worms Texas-style or use a pig and jig. That's about the only way to fool the bass while hiding your hook from the snags. Historically, good areas favored by the springtime largemouth fisherman include Bland, Sanchez, and Medio canyons, all about three miles upstream from the boat ramps. Another excellent area is the eastern shoreline from Tetilla boat ramp to the dam.

White bass are another good sportfish for the presummer fisherman. White bass feed on baitfish, and baitfish feed on all that grows in Cochiti's rich soup of nutrients and water. Springtime brings on warmer weather and more and more sunshine, and this change fuels the food chain process. More plankton means more baitfish, and baitfish draw the white bass to feed. Use lead-head jigs with plastic minnow imitations, real minnows, or any diving or sinking lure that imitates a wounded minnow.

Walleye and northern pike are two of the undiscovered sportfish at Cochiti. Walleyes have been stocked at a rate of about a million fry a year since the lake first held water. Good information on places for the best walleye fishing is rare. The only noted areas are both springtime spots: the riprap along the dam and the outside of the big point across from Medio and Sanchez Canyons. Even less information is available on the northern pike population, but the northerns were in the river before the dam was built. Both the northern and the walleye populations should be in good shape. Annual Department of Game and Fish sample netting operations have turned up some big fish. These predators feed almost exclusively on three- to eight-inch panfish, a size and type prolific in this lake.

Midsummer is still prime time for white bass and trout fishing. Fishermen can score during midday by using metal jigging lures that can be fished deep. A sonar unit will certainly help in finding the whites, for they travel in large schools and if you catch one you'll have a chance at catching a bunch. Summer trout catches are best in early morning and after the sun starts to set.

The riprap along the damface is one of the best bets for spring, summer, or fall boat-fishing. But this is not the place to be when a storm comes up. Wind and waves can blow right into the damface and boats have been smashed. In good weather you can expect over a dozen hookups per rod in three hours of fishing. Minnows or small lead-head hooks with hollow plastic skirts (tube jigs) in black, white or chartreuse are deadly when the panfish are on the feed. Anglers after larger fish should cast toward deeper water with a large crank or spinner bait. To match a natural food that lives in the rocks along the shoreline, try a big eight-inch black plastic centipede.

No wake is the rule for motor boating at Cochiti Lake. Wind-powered boats are the only ones exempt from the eight-mile-an-hour speed limit. Park rangers and the New Mexico State Parks boating officer enforce the rules from their patrol boats. Cochiti is a very popular sailboard and sailboat lake. Crowded summer weekends make for some interesting contests between ten-pound test and sixty-pound sailboards. It does get crowded along the easy-access portions of the shoreline. One hint to the boatless angler is to drive to the Cochiti Area (on the west side) and park as close to the dam as possible. Then walk along the water line at the dam. This is a good place to fish on a crowded weekend.

The outlet works at the dam release water to reform the Rio Grande below Cochiti. The Department of Game and Fish stocks catchable rainbow trouts and brown trout fry in this tailwater fishery. A fair number of other fish get flushed through the outlet works and into the river. Large fish are caught. Fishermen above the S.R. 22 bridge lose plenty of tackle to the rocks in the fast current of the river channel. Fishing is allowed below the bridge for about a half-mile. The river here is spread out and has a slower current. Walleye, rainbows, channel catfish, carp, and largemouth bass are typical catches. The Mainstream Bait Shop in Peña Blanca is the best source of current fishing information on both the lake and the tailwater fishery.

Cochiti Lake is next to Cochiti Pueblo, about ten miles north of I–25 between Santa Fe and Albuquerque. All the access roads are paved. There are two marked freeway exits to Cochiti Lake. Both roads meet just north of Peña Blanca, a little village with convenience stores and a bait shop. A first-time visitor should stop in at the Visitor Center near the entrance to the Cochiti Recreation Area. Maps are available, and you get a good overall view of the dam and the main body of Cochiti Lake.

Albuquerque Area Drainage Canals

Department of Game and Fish personnel electro-shocking the Rio Grande below Cochiti Dam.

ALBUQUERQUE AREA DRAINAGE CANALS

The Rio Grande in central New Mexico is paralleled by riverside drains. These ten- to forty-foot-wide drainage canals were established to protect the low-lying areas along the river's floodplain. Sections of these ditches are stocked biweekly with catchable-size rainbow trout from November through March. Urban fishing is a rare treat in the dry Southwest, and these drains offer a unique opportunity to go angling for trout in the middle of winter.

Many of the riverside drains are fed with water channeled in from the Rio Grande. For most of the year, these ditches run strong and their water is turbid. A bright red salmon egg disappears from sight as soon as you drop it in the water. These drains, however, often clear up in late winter. The Albuquerque Riverside Drain is the best example of this type of drain.

Some of the ditches, especially those on the east side of the river, are fed by springs. These drains have a smaller flow of water and are rarely muddy; in fact, they are often cool and crystal clear, and they can offer good trout fishing throughout the year. The Corrales Drain, often called the Clear Ditch, is the prime example of this type of canal.

Rainbow trout are not normally stocked in water that rises above seventy

Albuquerque Area Drainage Canals

These volunteers are building trout motels on the Corrales Drain. Plenty of tough, stream-raised brown trout live in this mid-city spring creek.

degrees. That's why the stocking ends in March. Bullheads, catfish, brown trout, carp, bass, suckers, and sunfish are available all year long. The best fishing, however, is in the winter.

Learning to catch fish from the riverside drains can be just as much fun as working along your favorite lake or stream. Pick a drain and learn where the fish are. Each ditch has a different set of characteristics. Pick the one that's closest to your house or choose the one that fits your style of fishing.

Bernalillo Drain, on the east side of the Rio Grande, is stocked from Highway 44, in the town of Bernalillo, south to the Albuquerque city limits, but not on the Sandia Indian Reservation. A dirt road runs alongside the ditch. This is a large straight canal, lightly fished.

Corrales Riverside Drain (the Clear Ditch), on the west side of the Rio Grande, heads north of Corrales as a small spring-fed ditch. The wild brown trout in the upper three miles make for great fly-fishing. The lower four miles, which are stocked with catchable-size rainbow trout, ends at the Corrales Bridge. The Clear Ditch provides excellent fishing. This is mostly park-and-walk fishing.

Albuquerque Riverside Drain, running along the east side of Rio Grande, offers good bait-fishing and is very popular. It is stocked above and below

Albuquerque Area Drainage Canals

Sunfish are great fun for all anglers. After helping three youngsters catch their first fish on a fly-rod, this gentleman caught a panfish, and a smile, for himself.

the Corrales Bridge and the Rio Bravo Bridge. Good access is available at the Rio Grande Nature Center. This is mostly park-and-walk fishing.

Tingley Beach, on the east side of Rio Grande, provides a small lake near the zoo just off the Albuquerque Riverside Drain. Heavily fished and heavily stocked, this site offers yellow perch, channel catfish, sunfish, bullheads, walleye, largemouth bass, and in the winter, stocked with trout. Be forewarned that this is not always a quiet place.

Atrisco Riverside Drain, on the west side of the Rio Grande, is stocked below Rio Bravo Bridge, with park-and-walk fishing the rule here. This small drain is fed by springs and is usually clear, with very little fishing pressure.

Belen (west side) and Peralta (east side) Riverside Drains are heavily stocked from Los Lunas to Belen, and both are popular and have parallel running dirt roads.

Tome Drain, east of the Rio Grande, runs into Peralta Drain. This small drain is stocked above and below the Highway 47 crossing.

Belen Ponds, east and just south of Belen Bridge off Highway 47, are two small ponds maintained for children under twelve, and they provide great spots to take the kids on a nice winter day.

All the drains are stocked from November through March with nine- to twelve-inch rainbow trout from the Red River Hatchery, located north of Taos. Every two weeks the stocking truck makes its rounds, stocking fish at spots accessible to the angler. The pools just above and below the culverts are usually stocked. If you see a group of anglers fishing along a drain, you can bet you're looking at a spot that the stocking truck visits.

The best hint for catching fish in the riverside drains is to learn from the fishermen who are already there. Ask questions. Watch the style of those who've already caught some fish. Anglers fishing clear water usually work along the streambank, casting upstream with fly, bait, or lure to likely looking spots. Fishermen pursuing rainbows in the murky water of the larger drains use salmon eggs or corn, and concentrate on the pools and back eddies.

Fly fishermen have great sport casting over rising browns and rainbows in the Corrales Clear Ditch. Hatches run from No. 12 caddis and mayfly (in the spring) all the way down to No. 20 tricos (in the winter). Meadowlark Lane, Dixon Road, and the Sandoval Lateral Road are three good access points. Spin fishermen can have fun with light tackle. Equipment that can cast 1/8-ounce lures is an advantage. Heavier stuff will catch aquatic weeds on every cast.

The best tip for any style of fishing on any of the drains is to use grasshoppers. From early summer to December the streamside weeds will be loaded with grasshoppers. Besides being free for the taking, grasshoppers are a bait that these urban trout just love to take.

CABALLO LAKE

Caballo is Spanish for *horse*. The canyons of the Caballo Mountains once sheltered wild horses whose heritage traces back to the *entrada*, the entrance into New Mexico of the first Spanish explorers and their horses. These mountains rise on the sunup side of Caballo Lake, creating a fairly steep shoreline on the east side of the reservoir. In contrast, the west side has a gently sloping shoreline. Both sides of Caballo offer great warmwater fishing opportunities, especially in the springtime.

Caballo Dam is located on the Rio Grande about twenty miles below Elephant Butte Reservoir. On the map, Caballo Lake looks long and narrow;

but a visit reveals just how big this lake really is. Over a mile wide and eight to twelve miles long, this ten-thousand-acre reservoir has over seventy miles of shoreline. White bass are the premier sportfish, and walleye, largemouth, and channel catfish are all a close second. A few strippers and crappie are caught, and threadfin shad are the prevalent forage fish.

Caballo Dam was built in the late 1930s to store winter-released water coming out of Elephant Butte's hydroelectric generator for summer irrigation use. Years with little snowpack in the north country turn Caballo into a long, skinny lake. But the wet years of the 1980s have kept Caballo Lake at near-full levels. The result has been an explosion of both baitfish and sportfish. High water also inundated some of the state park campgrounds and covered up the best boat ramp. The facilities have all been moved to higher ground and there are now good boat ramps. The state park has excellent facilities including concrete boat ramps, recreational vehicle hookups, paved and all-weather gravel roads, restrooms, outhouses, improved camping spots, shaded picnic tables, grills, drinking water, and over five thousand acres of land, with most of it open to pick-your-own spot for camping.

The Department of Game and Fish has concentrated its Caballo stocking efforts on walleye. Millions of walleye fry are stocked each year. The largemouth bass population exploded through natural reproduction in the miles of shallow shoreline. White bass numbers continue strong, even with the forty-fish bag limit. Channel catfish are harvested on trotlines and on rod and reel with crayfish tails, cutbait, or shad. Catfish of three pounds are common, ten- to twenty-pound cats are taken most every month of the year. Crappie numbers are cyclical, and these panfish are usually incidental catches while casting lead-head jigs for white or black bass.

Access to Caballo Lake State Park headquarters is off I–25 at Exit No. 59, 60 miles north of Las Cruces or 160 miles south of Albuquerque. The park headquarters area is on the southwestern corner of the lake, just a half-mile north of the dam. This is the improved area of the state park, with the recreational vehicle hookups; camping, a boat ramp, and a small marina with gas, tackle, bait, and snacks. You can drive across the dam to the eastern shoreline, where there is a secondary boat ramp and, past the ramp a rough road following the eastern shoreline for about two miles north. You can also drive below Caballo Dam, where big cottonwoods line the shoreline, providing welcome relief from the summer's heat. Drinking water, camping, and restrooms are provided to supplement the decent river fishing on the Rio Grande.

Highway 85 (U.S. 85) follows the western shoreline from the dam and park headquarters area north to the upper end of the lake. There are rough gravel roads leading in from U.S. 85 to the shoreline. Most of these access points lead to very shallow water, and a hundred-foot cast might put your hook into a tumbleweed in three feet of water. You can launch a canoe or a small cartop boat in these areas, but not a trailered boat. The easy access and decent shoreline at the state park headquarters area make it best for the boatless fisherman.

Anglers fishing from a boat have ten thousand surface acres to choose from. After noting wind conditions (for winds can build dangerous three-foot waves in no time at all), launch your boat at the headquarters boat ramp and work south, fishing the shallow and medium deep water along the bays and points as you head toward the dam. Switch to deep-water techniques as you work along the riprap of the damface. Then head north on the eastern shoreline, using medium-depth fishing techniques along all the points and coves. If the wind is still reasonable, you can deep-water troll as you head back across the lake to the state park headquarters area, the place you started from. After lunch, fish up the lake, from the boat ramp north three miles to KOA Point. These three areas—the eastern side north of the dam, the damface, and the western side from the dam north to a mile north of KOA Point—are the most productive fishing areas on the lake.

Landmarks on Caballo include the dam; the state park headquarters area; Apache Creek (on the eastern side just north of the dam and the secondary boat ramp); KOA Point (named after the full-service KOA campground on U.S. 85, which is four miles north of the dam and near, but not on, the lake), Animas Creek inlet (just north of KOA Point); the Narrows (north of Animas, where the lake is squeezed down to a width of a half-mile); the Upper Lake (the lake opens up above the Narrows); and Palomas Creek (where Palomas Arroyo enters the upper end of the Upper Lake). Above Palomas is the North End and the inlet of the Rio Grande, an area that contains almost a thousand acres of mudflats. The North End is unfishable at low water levels.

The fishing year at Caballo starts in March. The whites are schooling at the North End; there's good catfishing in shallow water, and excellent walleye fishing in the Rio Grande below Caballo Dam and below Percha Dam, three miles below Caballo.

April and May are the best fishing months of the year, but you must watch wind conditions. Strong spring windstorms can come blasting down the Rio Grande Valley, turning Caballo into a whitecap nightmare. On calm or slightly breezy days the afternoon temperatures will settle in the comfortable seventies, and the black bass will be doing their spawning maneuvers in fairly shallow water. Anglers can score on a dozen nice large-mouth by casting loud surface lures or by using the silent techniques of flipping plastic worms, pig and jigs, or plastic lizards. Because the white bass are medium to fairly deep, crankbaits or lead-head jigs will entice these prolific fish to the creel. Walleye, which will be moving from deep to shallow waters, are best fished along the dam and up the eastern side.

June still offers great angling opportunities, but the fish are more dispersed. The sportfish are on the feed, and if you find them and cast a shad imitation you will connect. Troll deep-running crankbaits to find the white bass; catch one and you've found a whole school. Or do some night-fishing with minnows in the shallow bay by the marina; shore anglers catch many whites with this technique. Walleye fishing is still good, it is best when slow trolling the bottom in medium-depth water along the eastern side. Flipping plastic worms or jigs produces for the largemouth angler.

July and August bring afternoon thundershowers, hot weather, and tougher fishing. Walleye are deep during the day, but they feed heavily at dawn and dusk; try the rocky points on the eastern side for Caballo's walleye. The North End and the western shoreline, from the dam north to KOA Point, are the best spots for whites. Black bass are harder to pin down, but plastic worms still seem a good bet for midday fishing; and topwater buzz baits bring exciting strikes early and late. The campgrounds are full on weekends, yet the fishing is uncrowded (except on busy Memorial Day) on this ten-thousand-acre lake.

September and October bring the gold color of autumn to the cotton-woods along Caballo's eastern shoreline. Walleye fishing is very good throughout the lower five miles of Caballo Lake. Daytime temperatures are in the seventies. Both white and black bass are caught on crankbaits north of the dam, on the eastern side. Big catfish, weighing up to thirty pounds, show up on trotlines. This is the most pleasant time to fish Caballo: nice weather; light winds; and good hookups with walleye, white bass, and largemouth.

November and December see little fishing pressure at Caballo. The white bass, which are deep but catchable, are at their best south of KOA Point and from there to the dam. The catfish are in fairly shallow water, best in the shallows of the North End and in the coves near the dam. The black bass and walleye are still active, but not enough fishermen use Caballo to establish good fishing spots.

January and February bring cold weather to Caballo. Few anglers fish Caballo in the winter. Daytime temperatures are in the fifties, but the shallow coves are iced over. Some walleye are caught toward the end of February.

Model A Bombers are the most popular fishing lures at Caballo. These crankbaits imitate the prevalent forage fish, threadfin shad. Longtime Caballo anglers watch the seagulls to help locate schools of shad. When the gulls see the commotion of white bass corralling shad, they flock to feed on these baitfish. Anglers can work the edges of this feeding binge with crankbaits or Mr. Twister–type lures, catching ten- to fourteen-inch white bass. Or they use pearl white slab-spoons, letting the heavy spoons go down twenty feet or more before jigging the lure. Sixteen- to twenty-inch white bass will be the catch as the larger whites tend to stay deep, feeding on the shad scattered by the smaller whites.

Check with the state park personnel for that day's best fishing spots and techniques. These state park employees are proud of their knowledge of fishing at Caballo Lake. The marina and the boat-ramp parking lot at sundown are good spots for current fishing information. Caballo is a big lake with an amazing variety of shoreline, and it only takes minutes for boat fishermen to change from shallow- to medium- to deep-water fishing techniques. Whether you are trying for largemouth, white bass, walleye, or big channel cats, keep changing techniques. Caballo is often slow to give up its secrets. And if you get hot on some springtime largemouth— remember the special black bass regulations—daily limit is eight, but only four may be less than fourteen inches. Consider catching and releasing all the largemouth bass you connect with—and keeping all the white bass you can eat. The whites breed like rabbits in an irrigated potato field, while the existence of trophy-size bigmouth bass depends on you and me carefully releasing the large ones.

CHAPTER SIX

Upper Pecos River Watershed

THE UPPER PECOS RIVER WATERSHED

The Sangre de Cristo Mountains reach up and send their last peaks skyward in the Pecos Wilderness. Storms caught by these mighty peaks blanket the high country with winter snows. The spring melt then feeds Pecos fishing expeditions with the cold, clean water New Mexico's trout demand. Dr. Elliott Barker, the grandfather of wildlife management in New Mexico, wrote a timeless description of this watershed: "The wilderness area is characterized by alpine forests, mountain meadows, bunch-grass parks, the finest aspen woods in the world, timberline ridges, and peaks of 12,000 to 13,500 feet."

The fisherman's joy in this high country are the alpine lakes, each one covering from two to ten acres. In modern times these lakes are stocked by helicopter, but the angler walks or rides on horseback to cast for cutthroats or rainbows and to camp in the 223,000-acre Pecos Wilderness Area.

Some of these mountains feed the Rio Grande to the north and west through the Rio Santa Barbara, the Rio Nambe, the Santa Fe River, and the Rio Peñasco. Other creeks head east to feed the Mora or the Gallinas. But the bulk of these mountains form the Pecos Watershed, providing trout fishing from right under the highest peaks all the way south to the town of Pecos, thirty miles downstream. From small cutthroats in the headwaters to the browns and stocked rainbows living in the larger feeder streams, this whole area is an excellent place to cast for trout. Expect crowds during the summer, and be prepared to walk a bit if you need to cast your line in privacy.

PECOS RIVER AT THE TOWN OF PECOS

The twenty miles of the Pecos River from the town of Pecos downstream to I–25 offers good trout fishing with very little public access. There is good

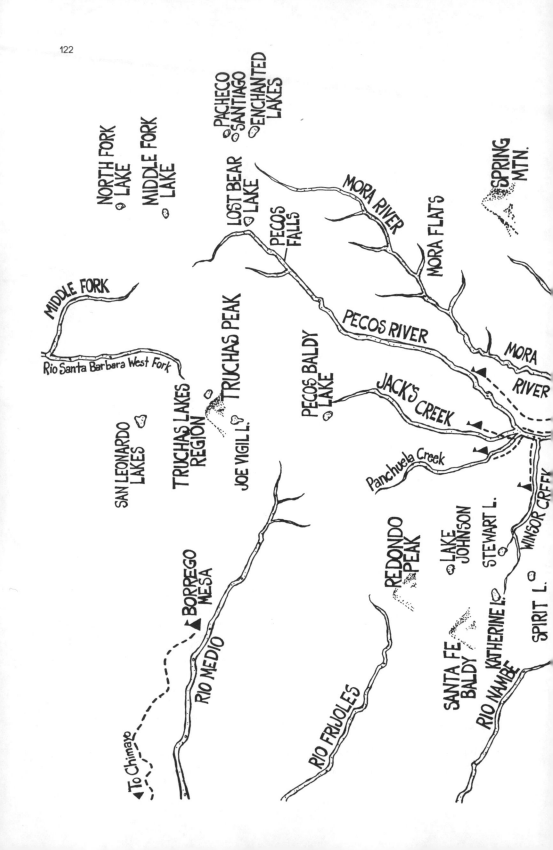

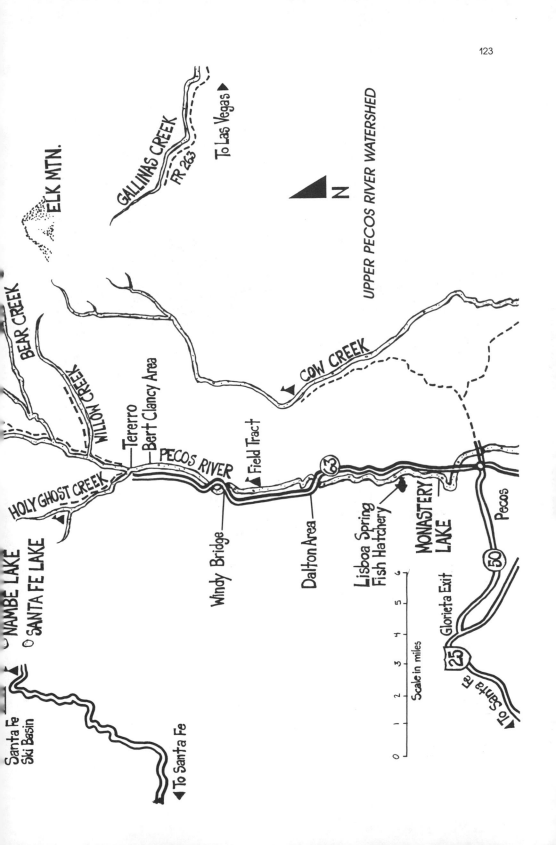

UPPER PECOS RIVER WATERSHED

N

GALLINAS CREEK

FR 263

To Las Vegas ▶

ELK MTN.

BEAR CREEK

WILLOW CREEK

COW CREEK

Tererro

Bert Clancy Area

PECOS RIVER

Field Tract

HOLY GHOST CREEK

○ NAMBE LAKE

⊙ SANTA FE LAKE

Santa Fe
Ski Basin

▲ To Santa Fe

Windy Bridge

Dalton Area

Lisboa Spring
Fish Hatchery

63

MONASTERY
LAKE

Pecos

50

Glorieta Exit

25

To Santa Fe ▶

Scale in miles

0 1 2 3 4 5 6

Pecos River at the Town of Pecos

A fast-moving stream in the Sangre de Cristo Mountains.

wild-trout fishing here *if* you can get permission to enter private property. Don't do it without permission!

With gas stations, restaurants, motels, tackle shops, and grocery stores, the town of Pecos is the base for fishing the Pecos River Watershed. Access is from I–25 south of Santa Fe or Las Vegas—take the Glorieta or Rowe exit. Fishing is good both upstream and downstream from either of the two bridges in the town of Pecos. Most of the fishing here is done by active anglers, moving along the bank while casting short distances with salmon eggs or by casting across stream with lures. The fly fisherman definitely needs chest waders to reach all the runs and fish-holding pockets.

COW CREEK

A good little stream, Cow Creek, parallels the river across the mountains east of the town of Pecos. Access is via Forest Road 86 or 83 just east of Pecos. This is a favorite creek to fish with worms just after the runoff starts to drop. The roads are gravel and dirt; ask for conditions at the ranger station in Pecos before you head out. The stream is heavily stocked near Cow Creek Campground (a fee area), a good spot to set up a tent for a few days.

MONASTERY LAKE

The first stop for fishing north of Pecos is just past the Benedictine Monastery. Take a left turn at the marked, Monastery Lake entrance. Monastery Lake is a six-acre, heavily stocked trout pond and a favorite for family fishing trips. This is a day-use area with a good parking lot located a short walk from the lake. No boats or floating devices are allowed here, and the bait fisherman usually catches the most fish. Switch to a casting bubble in the evening. That's the way to present a fly to the trout rising in the middle of Monastery Lake. Handicapped access is good. Help keep the litter picked up at Monastery Lake; this family fishing spot is leased from the Benedictine Monastery by the New Mexico Department of Game and Fish, and they need our help in keeping the shoreline clean. Just west of the lake is the Pecos River. This stretch, owned by the monastery, is closed to public access.

Just north of Monastery Lake, signs mark the entrance to Lisboa Springs Hatchery, a good place to see how the stocked rainbows are raised. There are shade trees and clean toilets, and you can buy a handful of trout food and let the kids feed the fish. A self-guided tour is great fun for the young people. Just downstream, right next to the road, is a popular bait-fishing pool, which is a good spot to harvest a few hatchery-raised rainbows. The river is also stocked right behind the hatchery, but private property takes over just upstream.

The next public fishing spot is upstream at the first Bert Clancy Fishing Area (also called the Dalton Picnic Area). This day-use area covers both sides of a bridge three miles upstream from the hatchery. Fishing the section below the bridge is great fun for the angler with waders; walk the trail down to the end of this public section and then wade back upstream, fishing as you go. The area above the bridge is a better spot for the bait fisherman. Pick any of the pools and cast to the head, and use just enough splitshot so that your worm drifts slowly down the pool. Some anglers use lures as weight, putting worms on the treble hooks and letting this rig drag slowly along the bottom.

Public access continues upstream to the old mill section where tiny Dalton Creek comes in. On the Pecos there is good public fishing with difficult

Monastery Lake

access, even though the road is only a stone's throw away. Heavy brush and deep, swift flows make this a good stretch for the angler who likes a challenge.

Private property takes over again for a mile and a half through Camp Lasalle until you get to the Field Tract Campground. This is a developed, fee-camping area run by the forest service, and offering access to a short stretch of the Pecos. Passing by another half-mile of posted property takes you to the Windy Bridge, where there's a short piece of downstream fishing and a good run of cliffside trout water upstream. It's private property again as you pass by the stocked ponds at the Broken Drum (Tres Lagunas) Guest Ranch and drive on to the second Bert Clancy Fishing Area. This is the last popular fishing area on the paved road. There is a pool or two for the bankside fisherman and upstream fishing for a quarter-mile to the next bridge over the Pecos River.

HOLY GHOST CREEK

Holy Ghost Creek meets the Pecos at this bridge just before the road turns to gravel. This small but fishable little creek is stocked near the Holy Ghost Campground (fee camping), located about two and a half miles of dirt and gravel road (Forest Road 122) upstream from its confluence with the Pecos. Unless you've scouted it first, don't try this road in a recreational vehicle or while pulling a trailer.

PECOS NEAR TERRERO

Some of the best fishing on the Pecos is upstream from the Holy Ghost confluence. Just before Terrero, turn off the main road and cross the Pecos bridge; then turn north and cross the Holy Ghost bridge. The gravel road is now on the west side of the Pecos and it follows the Pecos upstream for a couple hundred yards before ending at a parking area. Walk and wade upstream, casting as you go. Expect browns and rainbows from the pools, runs, and riffles in this rocky canyon. Bring a sack lunch so you don't have to quit at dinner time.

PECOS ABOVE TERRERO

The road following the Pecos River turns to gravel and dirt above Terrero, and the mud will definitely slow you down during the spring runoff or later

The Willow Creek Shelter beside the Pecos River.

with the summer rains. Check road conditions with the people at the ranger station in the town of Pecos or at the convenience store in Terrero. Forest Road 63 climbs above the river canyon running past Terrero, and it's a steep walk down to the quiet fishing below.

The first easy access is at the Willow Creek Day Use Area. This tiny creek is fairly good for little cutthroats and a few rainbow trout; and Forest Road 645, a dirt route, follows Willow Creek toward its headwaters at Elk Mountain. The best part of the Willow Creek Day Use Area, however, is its location on the banks of the Pecos River. Upstream access is limited, but it's public fishing downstream for as long as you care to hike; and the farther you go downstream, the more you'll have this river to yourself. Willow Creek is the only area on the Pecos where large groups can reserve a big shelter. Call the Department of Game and Fish for reservation information *one year in advance.*

MORA-PECOS RIVER

If you drive a mile and a half upstream the next good spot, Mora Campground, is easy to find. It's also right on good fishing water. Fee camping is either on the Mora-Pecos River or on the Pecos itself. The Mora-Pecos, which is *the* main tributary to the Pecos River, has good fishing for stocked rainbows in the campground area as well as excellent brown and rainbow fishing just a short upstream walk away. Downstream fishing on the Pecos finds plenty of stocked rainbows, plus a good population of stream-bred trout. A twenty-minute walk down the main Pecos will put you in an area the hatchery trucks can't reach. There are very few pools for the bankside bait fisherman, but anyone who learns to read a stream will find enjoyable angling.

Upstream from the Mora Campground is a mile and a half of stocked water on the Pecos River. This stretch is regulated as a catch-and-release area, with no bait-fishing allowed. If you walk upstream a short distance, you will find some good small-water fishing. Most of these trout have been caught and released more than once. It is fun to fish here if you enjoy using a fly-rod or lightweight spinning tackle.

The road to the Iron Gate Campground takes off a mile above Mora Campground. This is the best access to fishing the upper Mora (Mora Flats) in the Pecos Wilderness Area. It offers excellent small-stream fishing for wild brown trout. Since Forest Road 223 is often rough, be sure to check conditions in advance.

The Pecos has now turned into a small stream. The road leads up to its dead end at the summer-home area of Cowles. Here, the high-country creeks come together to form the main Pecos River. Winsor, Panchuela, and Jack's creeks all have fee campgrounds, and fishing for stocked rainbows is good. The little stream that is still called the Pecos winds north to its headwaters. A walk away from any of the campgrounds will take you into the territory of some wild trout—cutthroats, rainbows, and browns. Each of these campgrounds supports trail heads to the high country, the alpine lakes, and the "finest aspen woods in the world."

MAIN TRIBUTARIES OF THE PECOS RIVER
(ABOVE THE TOWN OF PECOS)

Cow Creek—a heavily stocked, good small mountain and meadow stream, with a campground. Access is east of the town of Pecos on Forest Roads 86 and 83.

Holy Ghost Creek—a heavily stocked, fast-moving mountain stream, located on Forest Road 122 just south of Terrero campground.

Willow Creek—a little cutthroat creek stocked with rainbows, located on Forest Road 645 one and a half miles north of Terrero, with good access to the Pecos River.

Mora-Pecos River—a heavily stocked, main tributary of the Pecos River, located three miles north of Terrero, with a big campground and many brown trout upsteam.

Winsor Creek—a very good but small brushy creek stocked with rainbows and holding cutthroats, located west of Cowles on Forest Road 121; campground.

Panchuela Creek—a large, good creek, stocked but brushy, with beaver-dam fishing near the campground; take Forest Road 121 to Forest Road 305 north of Cowles.

Jack's Creek—a small, swift, unstocked creek; go north past Cowles to the end of the road, brook trout are found upstream, cutthroats, browns, and rainbows near the campground.

Upper Pecos River—an excellent mountain and meadow canyon stream with wild trout: browns, rainbows, cutthroats; trails lead-in from Jack's Creek or from Iron Gate Campground.

PECOS WILDERNESS AREA LAKES

Stewart (5 acres), Spirit (7 acres), and Johnson (6 acres) lakes are all stocked with rainbows and cutthroats. Katherine (12 acres) Lake is stocked with cutthroat. No camping allowed on lake shores. Trails lead in from Santa Fe Ski Basin or from Winsor Creek and Holy Ghost campgrounds.

Pecos Baldy (8 acres) and the Truchas lakes—Ruth, Hazel, and Alice (each 4 acres)—are stocked with rainbows and cutthroat. San Leonardo (5 acres) lake is stocked with cutthroats. There is no camping on lake shores. Jose Vigil Lake has no fish. These little lakes are just north of Truchas Peak, on a six-mile trail from Jack's Creek, or an eight-mile trail south from Santa Barbara Campground.

Middle Fork (5 acres) and North Fork (2 acres) lakes are both stocked with rainbows and cutthroats. From State Route 3, just north of Mora, take Forest Road 113 west for eight miles of four-wheel-drive road, then walk the four-mile trail. Camping allowed at both lakes.

Enchanted or Encantada (3 acres), Santiago (3 acres), and Pacheco (5 acres) lakes are all stocked with rainbows and cutthroats. From Ledoux, the road leads past Morphy Lake State Park and continues west to Trail 274 and a three-mile hike. No camping at Santiago Lake.

Lost Bear (2 acres) Lake is stocked with cutthroats, and is located upstream from Pecos Falls.

Fishing the Pecos River Watershed

Holy Ghost Creek, just upstream from the Pecos River, is a perfect stream for a small rod.

Nambe (2 acres) Lake, at the head of Rio Nambe, has only a few fish.
Santa Fe (3 acres) Lake, at the head of Santa Fe River, has very few fish.

FISHING THE PECOS RIVER WATERSHED

The Pecos River, where large fish are caught every year, is one of New Mexico's best public trout streams. March and April offer a chance at fishing before the high snows start to melt. With the water clear and cold, bait-fishing will be your best bet. From May to mid-June, when the runoff peaks, flows are heavy and the Pecos can become a roaring river. Consider fishing the edges of the feeder streams with worms.

In late June the runoff has subsided and the stoneflies will be hatching in full force. The water will be high and very clear, with great lure fishing. Bait-fishing picks up as the water level drops and the hatchery rainbows are stocked. July brings great fly-fishing as the insects start hatching in earnest. Afternoon showers occur almost daily, and the high country trails are finally clear of snow. August brings the hot days of summer to the Pecos; try the Mora-Pecos or any of the headwater creeks for a good summer day's outing. September cools the waters of the main Pecos, and lure, fly, and bait all produce trout. In October the first serious high-country snows hit the peaks. By late fall the high-country fishing has cooled off, but the main Pecos is full of hungry trout, with the browns especially active because this is their spawning time.

FISHING THE HIGH-COUNTRY WILDERNESS AREA

Fishing the high-country lakes and streams is serious business in the Pecos Wilderness Area. Because snowstorms are not uncommon in the middle of summer, the hiker must be prepared for all weather conditions. Permits are no longer required for overnight trips into the wilderness area. Obtain the *Pecos Wilderness Map* from the Forest Service ranger station; it outlines regulations and the terrain you will encounter while backpacking the Pecos high country. Camping is not allowed on the shores of the high-country lakes, but you are welcome to camp away from the fragile lake basins. Because vandalism of vehicles at trailheads is common, you are urged to leave nothing of value in your car. A safe trip into this rugged territory depends on good planning and the right response to the joys and risks of the wilderness. The Forest Service puts it clearly:

> Survival depends on the ability to meet natural challenges and to overcome emergencies. Chances of finding help on short notice are remote. Notify someone of your planned itinerary, so they can try to locate you if your schedule is not met. Helicopters are extremely expensive and you may be liable for costs if you need one in an emergency. Remind everyone in your party of the logistics problems of accidents that would be only a minor inconvenience at home. Count on no one but yourself.

Consider fishing the high-country lakes by taking a guided horseback or llama-pack trip. Check with the Forest Service ranger station in Pecos and at the general store in Terrero for leads on commercial outfitters.

CHAPTER SEVEN

Lower Pecos River Watershed

PECOS RIVER NEAR I–25

Interstate 25 crosses over the Pecos River at San José, about thirty-five miles south and east of Santa Fe. The freeway is an important breakpoint on the Pecos. Upstream from I–25 lies some of the best trout fishing in New Mexico. Downstream from the four-lane highway the Pecos slows and loses the cold sparkle that makes for good natural trout water. The Pecos River Valley widens, and the river begins its long journey down the eastern side of New Mexico.

There are very few wild brown trout south of the freeway. It is the hatchery truck that provides good wintertime trout fishing. Paved road S.R. 3 parallels the river, and the hatchery truck stops at each of the little diversion dams. Access can also be found in the villages of San Miguel and Ribera. Winter and spring is best, from October to the beginning of the runoff.

VILLANUEVA STATE PARK

Villanueva State Park, twelve miles south of I–25 on S.R. 3, offers excellent access to the river and is where plenty of rainbow trout are stocked. With camping facilities clean and well kept, this is one of the prettiest state parks in New Mexico, and a great place for a family fishing outing, especially before the spring runoff muddies the river. Autumn at Villanueva is gorgeous, with the cottonwood trees displaying their fall colors; the fishing for stocked rainbow trout can be very good during this season. In mid-summer, higher water temperatures and too much silt make this part of the Pecos poor trout water. Handicapped access is reasonable with the help of a friend. Villanueva State Park is also accessible from I–40 on paved S.R. 3, seventy miles east of Albuquerque.

South of Villanueva there is little or no access to the Pecos River, and few if any sportfish. The river has lost its appeal to trout. Catfish, chubs, and minnows populate the water, but few people fish this quiet stretch.

However, northwest of this part of the Pecos River lie two trout lakes that get their water from the mountains west of Las Vegas. Storrie Lake is the first of these and McAllister Lake, the second. Water from these two lakes eventually drains into the Pecos River.

STORRIE LAKE

Storrie Lake is a fine fishing lake located three miles north of Las Vegas on the road (S.R. 3) leading to Mora. Water levels can change drastically on this thousand-acre (when full) irrigation reservoir. Normally, the lake is full enough for good rainbow trout fishing; and an added attraction is provided by spring catches of crappie. Brown trout are a rarity, but a few browns enter by the diversion channel from Gallinas Creek. There are bullheads in Storrie, and the Department of Game and Fish has stocked channel catfish. Dace and chubs, as well as crappie, catfish, sucker, and bullhead fry are the forage fish.

Public access to Storrie is limited to the southern and eastern shorelines. These are the lands of Storrie Lake State Park. Fee camping, recreational vehicle hookups, a playground, bathrooms, showers, paved and gravel roads, and sheltered picnic tables all make this a modern, fully improved facility.

Catching fish at Storrie is directly keyed to the shallow and sloping shoreline. When the trout are cruising the shallows, as in the spring or fall, bank fishermen make their catches by using salmon eggs, corn, worms, or cheese. But midday summer fishing is often tough because the rainbows are in deeper water, hiding out from the brightness of the summer sun. This is the time to fish bait, lure, or fly in the deeper water near the dam; or fish early in the morning, or better yet, at night.

From iceout until November, thousands of rainbow trout are stocked by the Department of Game and Fish. Thirty thousand or more catchables, as well as fifty to seventy thousand fingerlings, are delivered annually. Though three-pound trout are rare in Storrie Lake, creel checks show good catches of ten- to fifteen-inch rainbows.

Boat fishermen have the advantage at Storrie. Drifting with the breeze constantly moves your position, and by fishing at different depths you're sure to discover the place where the rainbow trout are holding. A good boat ramp is located on the south end of the dam. Consider fishing north from the ramp, along the damface, and then following the shoreline on the north end of Storrie; this will put you first in the deep water and good rocky structure along the dam, and then in medium and shallow depths

Wind surfing is becoming a popular pastime on Storrie Lake.

along the northern shoreline. Spring winds and summer thunderstorms are normal occurrences at Storrie. The wide-open skyline usually gives boaters a visual warning of incoming storms.

Although the lake is fed by a diversion channel out of Gallinas Creek, the foothills to the west also drain into Storrie. In most years, a strong growth of bullrushes is found on the northwestern shoreline, where these intermittent feeder creeks enter the lake. This is a great spot for early summer boat-fishing with small lures or flies that imitate dragonfly or damselfly nymphs. Because this is private property, there is no access here for the shoreline angler.

Another spot accessible only to anglers with a boat is the main water inlet. Located on the west side, the Gallinas Creek division dumps fresh cold water into Storrie. The oxygenated water attracts both trout and trout food. The inlet works are not always releasing water, but this area is worth checking out if you are boat-fishing along the western shoreline.

Crappie, which were not stocked in Storrie by the Department of Game and Fish, were most likely a "bait bucket" introduction by a careless and illegal fisherman. (Minnows are illegal bait here and in most trout lakes.) Crappie catches peak in June. Try the area around the boat ramp for these panfish. Use lead-head jigs in yellow or black.

Channel catfish were stocked in Storrie to fill the niche taken over by

the bullheads. While a school of little bullheads will provide almost continuous action, anglers after the larger trout, crappie, and catfish are sometimes bothered by the nature of bullheads to strike incessantly at bait being
fished for the larger sportfish. Perhaps the channel cats will take over the
ecological position held by the bullheads.

Fly fishermen find an excellent midge hatch on summer evenings and on
calm days in the spring and fall. Caddis, mayflies, scuds, damselflies and
dragonflies round out the aquatic insect list. Float tubes are a rare sight on
Storrie because, most fly fishermen bring a canoe or a johnboat. Streamers,
both bright (zonkers) and dark (spruce flies), produce strikes, especially
along the damface.

In the spring and in autumn, anglers connect with rainbow trout by
casting lures from the shore. The best lure technique in the summer is to
troll along the northern shoreline or to cast lures from the dam. Medium
and small spinners and lures, whether dark or bright, work fine; and small
lead-head jigs with little plastic curly tails also produce. Cast these jigs and
let them sink, retrieve with a twitch, a pause, and then another crank on
the reel.

If your style of fishing isn't producing strikes, move your casts to deeper
(or shallower) water. Listen for that unmistakable sound of other anglers
catching fish; note their fishing style and copy it. The damface is often
productive when the shallow waters are not producing. If the fish are rising,
switch to a fly-rod or cast a bobber and a small wooly worm with spinning
gear.

Though much of the shallow shoreline works against the summer lakeshore fisherman, fish can still be caught; but you have to experiment to
find a particular day's location (depth) and technique. Ice-fishing is hap-
hazard at Storrie Lake because the ice is not always safe. The best fishing
starts a month after iceout, usually in late March or April and continues
through June. Summer daytime fishing can be tough, and July and August
catches are better when the sun is off the water. Good angling returns in
September and continues until the middle of December.

McALLISTER LAKE

One-hundred-acre McAllister Lake is the only fishable lake inside Las
Vegas National Wildlife Refuge. The refuge is an 8,750-acre birdwatchers'
paradise, where the eagles, falcons, and long-billed curlews keep the Au-

dubon crowd smiling, and the rainbow trout keep the fishermen coming back. McAllister is a lake rich in the natural food and good trout habitat needed to grow big fish. It is stocked with fingerlings and catchable-size rainbow trout. Bank-fishing is good in the spring and continues until the watergrass and cattails crowd the fishermen to the few remaining open spots. Good summer catches are made by fishing the deeper water from a boat, or by wading the edges of the bullrushes.

The inlet water at McAllister comes by ditch from Storrie Lake. In wet years, when the water levels are up, the fish and the fishermen prosper. Occasional years of limited snowpack, little rainfall, and hot summer days can produce a fishkill, but during most years McAllister is one of New Mexico's best growth-rate lakes. It is located on the verge of the "trout line"—any farther south or east and water temperatures rise too high to support a good trout lake.

Because the lake is managed for both waterfowl and trout, it is closed to winter fishing. The lakes, ponds, marshes, and prairies in the refuge are in the Central Flyway, an important spot for migrating waterfowl. The old-timers have the most consistent fishing from September to the winter closing date, October 31. The lake reopens at noon on March 1. A good September trip can combine dove hunting in the refuge with fall fishing on the McAllister; check at the refuge office for details.

A boat is a definite asset on this lake, and a good concrete boat ramp makes for easy launching. An outboard is a necessity for fishing on windy spring days. Boats are limited to trolling speeds, and on calm days a rowboat or a canoe is adequate.

Natural baits are best for many local fishermen. They sweep the weedy shallows with quarter-inch mesh handnets and catch "hellgrammites" (actually dragonfly larvae), which are a great bait for this lake. Wooly worms and small spinners are especially productive along the weedbeds. Fly fishermen should bring their waders (and a float tube) and work the edges with nymphs, streamers, and woolybuggers.

The Las Vegas National Wildlife Refuge is reached by driving east from Las Vegas on State Highway 104 for two miles, and then south on State Highway 281 for four miles. Stop at the refuge office for information on the September dove hunt, as well as to see the natural history exhibits. McAllister Lake is about two miles south of the office. No camping is allowed. Road access is paved or improved gravel. Wheelchair access is decent at the boat ramp.

SANTA ROSA LAKE

The next good spot for public fishing on the Pecos River is at the first irrigation reservoir, Santa Rosa Lake, located about 120 miles east of Albuquerque and 7 miles north of the town of Santa Rosa. This is a warmwater fishery. Walleye, catfish, bluegill, largemouth bass, and crappie make Santa Rosa a popular fishing lake. Water, however, is the limiting factor at Santa Rosa: there is no permanent pool, and water levels can fluctuate from full to empty in less than a year. But a series of wet years can produce great crappie, bass, and walleye fishing.

Santa Rosa Dam is an Army Corps of Engineer project completed in 1981. The dam was originally named Los Esteros, after an intermittent feeder creek located four miles north of the dam. New Mexico State Parks Division operates a full-service facility at Santa Rosa Lake, with paved roads, bathrooms, showers, electric hookups, fee camping, a picnic area, a primitive camping area, an excellent boat ramp, an information center, and a handicapped-access nature trail.

Fishing at Santa Rosa is for walleye, largemouth and smallmouth bass, crappie, and bluegill. As long as this lake holds water the fishing can be rated as good to very good. A series of average to above-average years of rainfall means excellent crappie fishing and good bass and walleye catches. One dry year drops the lake severely, but excellent catches are possible in the remaining waters. Back-to-back years of below-average snowpack in the high country can reduce Santa Rosa Lake to nothing more than twelve thousand acres of dry mud flats, with the remainder of the Pecos River flowing down the western edge. It's important to watch the weekly newspaper fishing reports or call the Department of Game and Fish tape recorded fishing report for up-to-date information on Santa Rosa. The lake peaks at fifteen thousand surface acres. It can drop to zero.

Rock cliffs form the entire western shoreline of Santa Rosa Lake. The Pecos River once flowed along these cliffs; and this submerged river channel is now the deepest part of the lake, running from the dam at the southwestern corner of the lake north along the western shoreline. Medium to fairly shallow depths are typical in the body of the lake. The eastern and southern shorelines consist of thousands of acres of shallows, perfect habitat for little fish. Half-submerged juniper and piñon trees mark the gradual slope of the bank, and large inlets and bays make for a very irregular shoreline.

The northern part of Santa Rosa offers the most diverse structure in the lake. Thousands of years ago the Pecos River carved the mile and a half

Horseshoe Bend in what is now the northern end of Santa Rosa Lake. The old river channel defines a strip of deep water all the way around the bend. Los Esteros Creek enters on the northern side of Horseshoe Bend. The creek is intermittent, but its inlet channel is a good place to fish. There are shallows in Horseshoe Bend, as well as tall vertical cliffs, islands, points, submerged brush and underwater cottonwood trees; this is a good place to fish for bass, walleye, crappie, and catfish.

Extensive shallows help make this a productive lake. The submerged brush provides good cover for the baitfish; and the larger sportfish frequent the shallows to feed. Big walleye, catfish, and largemouth bass work along the southern and eastern shorelines in the evening, at night, and in the early morning hours. After the sun hits the water the sportfish head for the security of structure and the deeper water.

Though oversimplified, this pattern offers the boat angler a good plan for fishing Santa Rosa. Casting shallow-running lures while quietly drifting along the southern and eastern lakeshore is effective from the predawn hours until the morning sun breaks full. These shorelines are an easy run from the boat ramp, and a quick ride returns you to the campground for breakfast, coffee, and the morning constitutional. Good midmorning to midafternoon fishing is found at the northern part of Santa Rosa Lake. Fish the medium to deep structure around the islands, points, and dead-end canyons of the Horseshoe Bend area. Don't miss the Los Esteros Creek inlet. Long summer days give you time to head back for a big midafternoon meal and a much-needed nap. Late afternoon and evening fishing could be concentrated in the main body of the lake. Jigging or slow trolling a deep running lure is effective in this medium to deep water.

Wind is a safety concern for boaters on New Mexico's reservoirs, and Santa Rosa Lake is no exception. Spring winds are often fierce, and summer thunderstorms can churn up whitecaps in a matter of minutes. Anglers using small johnboats or canoes should consider fishing along the southern shoreline. In this way, you can fish over a mile of shallow to medium deep water and if the wind comes up you can head back to the boat ramp. If a storm grows dangerous, you're close to shore and can put in until it blows over.

Shore-fishing is limited at Santa Rosa Lake. Boatless anglers catch fish, especially in the springtime; but the only easy access point is at the boat ramp. You can cast to fairly deep water right off the ramp, or scramble along the rocks and fish the deep water toward the dam. A short walk east of the launching ramp puts you next to shallow water, but much of this area is too shallow for good shore-fishing. Driving across the dam and parking at the Rocky Point Campground puts you close to deep water near the old

Santa Rosa Lake

Sumner Lake and State Park is a large warmwater fishing area ideal for anglers with or without a boat.

Pecos River Channel. There is no vehicle access to the rest of the shoreline and handicapped access is possible only at the boat ramp.

Some very large walleye and bass have been caught in Santa Rosa Lake. In the spring and early summer, bass are often full of bullhead fingerlings, baitfish that are dark in color with a bit of sparkle to their skin. Bass caught from middle to late summer have stomachs full of crappie young, a yellow and brown forage fish. Keep these colors in mind when you reach into the tackle box. Bait fishermen using waterdogs take some of the biggest walleye out of this lake. Crappie fishing is good at night if you use a lantern and minnows. Yellow or black jigs are good choices for daytime crappie fishing.

Shade trees are nonexistent at Santa Rosa Lake. If you're planning a summer visit, don't forget a hat and sunglasses. The town of Santa Rosa town is full of motels, restaurants, and grocery stores. The Los Esteros Bait and Tackle Shop, the only spot to pick up waterdogs or minnows, has been on the east side of town since the dam was built, and the people there keep track of productive techniques and hotspots on the reservoir. The shop is part of a Texaco station across from the Holiday Motel. Make sure to check the fishing reports before you go to Santa Rosa Lake, for there may not be any water left.

THE TOWN OF SANTA ROSA

Santa Rosa is right on I–40, about a hundred miles east of Albuquerque. The town, located in the middle of the Pecos River Valley, is loaded with natural springs. Creeks, ponds, marshes, little lakes, and sinkholes abound here, and there is some fishing available. The Power Dam Lake, just south of town, is a small misnamed pond stocked with rainbow trout. The Blue Hole, a famous, clearwater sinkhole very popular with scuba divers, is not stocked and contains only a few carp. When irrigation water is released, sportfish are flushed out of Santa Rosa Reservoir and into the Pecos River. Since the Pecos River runs through the middle of town, there is a chance for decent sportfishing. However, when the Pecos is devoid of water, angling is limited to the few deeper holes and pools.

SUMNER LAKE

Lake Sumner is an irrigation reservoir operated by the Bureau of Reclamation on the Pecos River in east-central New Mexico. The dam was built in 1937, one mile south of the junction of Alamogordo Creek and the Pecos River. The lake was originally called Alamogordo Lake, but the name was changed to Sumner Lake in 1974. The town of Fort Sumner is ten miles south of the lake.

This is a big warmwater lake, 4,650 acres when it's full but often only half that size. Yet water levels are stable enough to afford good fishing for white bass, crappie, walleye, catfish, northern pike, largemouth bass, carp, and bluegill. The land area around the southern end of the lake is in Sumner Lake State Park. Though only a few of the park roads are paved, a good gravel road-base makes the improved areas of the state park accessible year round. Improvements at the park include a fee-camping area; one paved boat ramp and a number of unimproved boat-launching sites, recreational vehicle hookups; drinking water; picnic tables under shelters; a group shelter; acres of shoreline with no-fee camping, and a park office with a good topographical map of the entire lake.

Access to Lake Sumner is off U.S. 84, thirty-five miles south of I–40 at Santa Rosa or ten miles north of Fort Sumner. A sign (Lake Sumner State Park) marks the paved turnoff (S.R. 203) to the lake. Gently rolling hills are typical of the landscape in this part of eastern New Mexico, and the same topography is found underwater at the reservoir. This type of submerged landscape provides an excellent structure for deep-trolling crank-baits, a good technique for Sumner's walleye and white bass.

Sumner Lake is shaped like a big capital-letter Y. The lower end and deepest waters are at the dam. This southern end is the main body of the lake, and it includes the state park campgrounds; three nice side-canyons; the boat ramp; and great access for the shore fisherman to fish shallow, medium, or deep waters. The upper end of Sumner splits into two long arms: the Alamogordo arm runs northwest, while the Pecos Arm runs northeast.

Lake Sumner Bait Shop, which is located on State Route 203 just before you reach the lake, has a good supply of minnows, lures, and catfish bait. This is *the* spot for up-to-date information on where and how Sumner's sportfish are being caught. Most fishermen stop at the Bait Shop after a day's fishing to report their success, the best locations, as well as the techniques that worked for them.

The first marked turnoff from S.R. 203, just before you reach the lake, is a gravel road leading north to the campgrounds, side bays, and to the shore-fishing on the east side of the lake. State Route 203 continues toward the south end of the lake; a gravel turnoff leads to the fishing below the dam, while the paved road climbs and crosses over the dam and then curls around to the westside state park entrance. You will find a cafe, a convenience store, and a bar just before reaching the park headquarters. The paved boat ramp is located here, as well as fee camping with bathrooms and hot showers in the improved campground area. North of the park headquarters is the lease area, state land divided into lots and leased to people who desire a permanent or vacation home located next to Lake Sumner.

Lake Sumner is a great lake for the boatless fisherman. You have your choice of casting to shallow, medium, or deep water, with good access to miles of shoreline. You can fish with the wind at your back or with the breeze blowing in your face. There are protected bays, wide-open shorelines, and river-fishing in the canyon below the dam.

Just west of the dam is West Canyon, a protected little bay with steep rock sides. Shore access is good, with parking on a gravel road just west of the dam. Rock cliffs form the shoreline and lead down to five to twenty-five feet of water. This is a favorite spot for crappie fishing in the springtime. You could also park east of the dam and fish the shallow water of East Bay, a good spot to cast a big shallow running crankbait before sunup on a warm summer morning. You can also walk along the earthen part of the dam and cast a lead-head crappie jig to deep water. This is a good springtime spot for walleye.

The turnoff to the eastside campgrounds leads to Violation Bay. There are picnic tables with shelters, outhouses, electric hookups, and drinking water available in this fee-camping area. Violation Bay is protected from the wind and is a good crappie and bass fishing spot. Float tubes are a favorite way to fish the bay for largemouth bass. There are many turnoffs from the gravel road leading up this east side. Each side road leads to shore-fishing in shallow to medium deep water. The rocky points are good after-noon white bass and early morning catfishing spots. Except for the protected Violation Bay, the wind, when it's up, usually blows in your face if you're fishing the east side of Sumner Lake.

The shoreline around the paved boat ramp on the west side is a favorite for the shore fisherman. You're close to the amenities, and the wind is usually at your back. At high-water levels, there is an island two hundred yards off the boat ramp. When the reservoir is in low-water conditions, you can walk out and fish from this "island." Up and down the shoreline from the boat ramp the water varies from one- to three-foot shallows to five- to twenty-foot depths. This is another good spring crappie spot, es-pecially when casting to submerged trees or brush in three to six feet of water. Summer catfishing, at night or at dawn, is also good from the boat-ramp area.

Anglers fishing from a boat have a pair of warnings coming from expe-rienced Sumner fishermen. First, the wind: watch out for summer thun-derstorms and our annual spring windstorms. Whitecaps appear quickly on Lake Sumner. There is a wind-warning light at the main boat ramp. A flashing white light means gusts over 15 mph; a flashing red light means winds over 25 mph and that you should get off the lake. The second warning concerns the many submerged hazards—rocks and trees—that show when the water levels drop in late summer.

Walleye, white bass, northern pike, and largemouth bass are four of the best reasons to bring a boat to Lake Sumner. Although walleye and white bass certainly don't spend all their time in deep water, the best daytime catches are made by slow-trolling jigs or crankbaits in fifteen to twenty-five feet of water. The largest point on the lake is where the Alamogordo arm and the Pecos arm meet to form the main body of the lake. This is prime structure for walleye fishing. Both arms north of the junction point have cliffs with steep dropoffs. These bluffs are good white bass and walleye water. The area just out from the dam is a consistently good spot for fishing walleye. Trolling or casting orange-bellied or fluorescent-colored crankbaits is one of the proven walleye techniques. Don't be afraid to use deep-running cranks. Some even use downriggers or an ounce of lead to get their lures down in the twenty- to thirty-foot range.

Largemouth bass usually keep closer to shore than the walleye, and the bass often key around an obvious piece of structure. Sumner's submerged trees, brush, and rocky points all attract largemouth. Bass fishermen in boats drift along the shoreline casting lures or working a pig and jig or plastic worm in shallow to medium depths. Lake Sumner offers miles of shoreline and over a dozen good bass bays in each of the two upper arms.

The angling year at Lake Sumner starts in March. A few crappie and catfish are caught, but it is the walleye (at twenty- to thirty-foot depths) that start the fishing year. March water temperatures are around 45°F. By mid-April the best fishing of the year has begun. The white bass are finally active and crappie catches are excellent. Some of the best catches come from the Alamogordo and Pecos arms. May is the top month for sportfish catches at Sumner, when water temperatures run from 55°F to 65°F and fishing is good on the entire lake. The first half of June is still excellent, but water temperatures are rising and readings are well over 70°F by July. Except for catfish, the easy fishing disappears in this hot summer month. August is a transition month. The fishing gets better as water temperatures drop to 65°F. By September the angling success is way up. Autumn fishing peaks in October and is good to the end of November. Trout are stocked every two weeks below the dam from November to March. December and January finds the lake almost empty of anglers, yet a warm week or two makes for excellent wintertime catches of white bass and walleye. February is too cold for sportfish or for fishermen.

Sumner Lake is one of the most underused of New Mexico's warmwater fisheries. The lake is about the same distance from Albuquerque as Elephant Butte or Conchas (about 150 miles), yet it receives just a fraction of the fishing pressure. There's good spring crappie and walleye catches; good summer white bass, catfish, and largemouth fishing; and fall fishing for all species is often very good. Crowds, even on the Fourth of July, are usually pleasant and mild mannered. This is an excellent family lake with a safe and a gently sloping shoreline and good camping facilities. Handicapped access is good at the main westside boat ramp, the eastside campground (Violation Bay), and many spots on both sides of the lake. Like all of New Mexico's warmwater reservoirs, Lake Sumner is windy in the spring, hot in the summer, and beautiful in the fall.

BOSQUE REDONDO

Bosque Redondo is a bit of historic New Mexico located just off the Pecos River south of Fort Sumner. The fishable water, which encompasses only fifteen acres, is stocked in the winter with rainbow trout. Actually a series of long narrow ponds, the area has been turned into a park by the city of Fort Sumner. There are cottonwood trees for summer shade, and the grassy meadows around the lake are mowed. These simple amenities make Bosque Redondo a nice place for a quiet picnic and an afternoon of relaxed angling; and handicapped access is good. To get to these little trout ponds, head east from Fort Sumner on U.S. 60/84. Turn south on the paved road across from the carwash at the east edge of town. Stay on the paved road as it goes due south, and in about two miles you will reach the ponds, where largemouth bass, bluegill, ducks, and catfish live year round.

SOUTHEASTERN NEW MEXICO TROUT PONDS

East of Fort Sumner, on the eastern edge of New Mexico, the Department of Game and Fish stocks a number of small fishing lakes. Though small, these ponds provide local anglers with their only chance to go trout fishing without driving a couple hundred miles. Two of these ponds are located near the town of Clovis. Green Acres, eight acres, is stocked in the winter with rainbows and holds a few bass and catfish. Oasis State Park contains a four-acre lake which holds catfish and yellow perch and is stocked in the winter with rainbow trout. Ned Houk Pond—in Running Water Draw State Park, just north of Clovis—contains yellow perch and catfish.

Lovington, Hobbs, and Jal all have winter-stocked trout ponds. Chapparal Lake, near Lovington, has catfish as well as winter-stocked rainbows. Maddox Lake and Green Meadow are both located near Hobbs. Maddox—which is not stocked with trout but has good catfish, sunfish, and largemouth bass fishing—is a power-plant cooling pond offering good bass fishing in the winter. Because shoreline access is not very good, a canoe or a lightweight cartop boat is the key to good catches. Green Meadow is stocked in winter with rainbow trout. Eunice and Jal lakes, south of Hobbs, are bass and catfish ponds, and both are stocked with rainbow trout in the winter.

Roswell is the next downstream fishing stop in the lower Pecos Watershed. Spring River Park Lake, another children's pond, is located in the middle of town. Ten miles west of Roswell is Bottomless Lakes State Park, a series

Southeastern New Mexico Trout Ponds

of sinkholes set next to rock cliffs that mark the edge of the Pecos River Valley. Fishing is for winter-stocked rainbows and only Mirror, Inkwell, and Cottonwood lakes are stocked. These are all small, deep ponds, where corn, salmon eggs, and shrimp are the favorite baits for catching trout.

LAKE VAN

As U.S. 285 heads south out of Roswell, Lake Van and the Dexter National Hatchery are the next points of interest. Located just east of the town of Dexter, Lake Van is a twelve-acre pond in a nice community park. Modest fees for fishing or picnicking are collected at the park office. Fishing is for bass, catfish, and bluegill, but mostly for winter-stocked trout. The lake is surrounded by shade trees, and a cafe is found right at lakeside. Water-skiers use the lake from April through September (yes, water-skiers in a twelve-acre lake—park rules require all boats to go in a counterclockwise direction!). Fishing is best after the hatchery truck makes its first visit, usually in the first week of November. Small boats are allowed and handicapped access is good. Lake Van Community Park is one of the nicest family fishing spots in southeastern New Mexico.

DEXTER NATIONAL FISH HATCHERY

The Dexter National Fish Hatchery is a few hundred yards east of Lake Van. This was once a federal U.S. Fish and Wildlife Service warmwater hatchery, raising bass and catfish for waters throughout the Southwest. The mission of the hatchery changed in 1978, and it is now a refuge and study center for the rare and endangered fish species of the Southwest. The ultimate mission of the hatchery is to restock endangered or threatened fish species in their historic habitats. To that end, the fisheries professionals at Dexter rear, maintain, and study these original New Mexico fish.

Over the last one hundred years, man has radically changed the watersheds of the Southwest. Timber, grazing, roadwork, irrigation reservoirs, and the introduction of sportfish like brown trout and bass have wiped out most of New Mexico's original fish. It is the job of the U.S. Fish and Wildlife Service employees at Dexter National Fish Hatchery to find specific locations where these native fish can survive and reproduce. A typical example of this restoration process is the work in progress with squawfish on the San Juan River.

Squawfish were once the major predator fish in the San Juan River. The

Dexter National Fish Hatchery

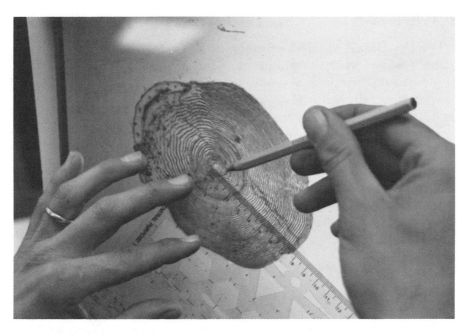

New Mexico Department of Game and Fish biologist Jack Kelly examines a fish scale to determine its age. This enlarged scale is from a smallmouth bass.

original Indian inhabitants, and later the Spanish and Anglo settlers, caught thousands of these big fish by using nets and spears. Squawfish were so abundant that they were collected by the wagonful and used as fertilizer in cornfields. But dams changed the San Juan River from wild, warm, and silty into cold, clear, and tamed. Massive changes in habitat and overharvesting transformed the squawfish into a rare species threatened with extinction. The San Juan River just below Navajo Dam is now a world-class trout fishery. Miles below the trout fishing area, the river seems able to support the reintroduction of squawfish; and the employees at Dexter are working to reintroduce these mighty fish into their home waters. Someday we may even be able to go fishing for trophy-size squawfish.

There is a visitors center at Dexter, and from April through October the public is invited to tour the facilities to see Colorado squawfish, gambusia, pupfish, razorback suckers, and a dozen other rare southwestern fish. The folks at Dexter National Fish Hatchery have also done extensive work with Apache trout, Gila trout, and Rio Grande cutthroats. Check out the work these people are doing to save our endangered fish species. It's worth a visit.

BRANTLEY DAM

Brantley Dam is the next irrigation reservoir on the Pecos. Brantley is brand new, and its waters will overtake and include Lake McMillan. The New Mexico Department of Game and Fish has an extensive management plan for sportfish in this huge, new irrigation reservoir. With recreation facilities in the plans, only the passage of time will reveal how the fishing turns out in the shallow waters behind Brantley Dam.

Avalon Lake, just downstream from Brantley, is the last big irrigation reservoir on the Pecos River. Avalon is four miles north of Carlsbad. Although the lake holds nearly one thousand surface acres when full, it is very shallow. Water drawdowns are typical, and Avalon offers little to the fisherman. It contains channel catfish, largemouth, walleye, and white bass.

PECOS RIVER IN CARLSBAD

In the middle of Carlsbad there are two lowhead diversion dams on the Pecos River. These dams create a long wide spot on the Pecos, and angling here is for white bass, catfish, and winter-stocked trout. White bass fishing is often good from February through April; try black and silver lures or minnows. A city park runs along the river through town, and there is a boat ramp, playground, and swimming area. The Pecos, both above and below Carlsbad, is good catfish and white bass water.

BLACK RIVER AND RED BLUFF RESERVOIR

South of Carlsbad the Black River enters the Pecos. Though the Black River flows through what is almost entirely private property, the lower end is stocked in the winter with rainbow trout at Higby Hole. A four-pound, nine-ounce crappie—the state record—was caught in the Black River using a minnow for bait. Twenty-five miles south of Carlsbad, the Pecos flows out of New Mexico (when it has any water in it) and into a Texas lake called Red Bluff Reservoir. At high water levels, Red Bluff backs into one thousand acres of New Mexico. This reservoir has excellent hybrid striper, bullhead, catfish, and white bass fishing and there's a boat ramp very near the state line.

Canadian River Drainage

VERMEJO PARK RANCH

Vermejo Park is both a working cattle ranch and a sportsmen's resort facility. Located inside the old Maxwell Land Grant forty miles west of Raton, the park's almost 400,000 acres hold the best high-country fishing in New Mexico. The developed lakes hold trophy-size browns and rainbows, while the streams support wild populations of Rio Grande cutthroat, cutthroat hybrids, and eastern brook trout. Fishing these waters is by reservation only, with rates running from one hundred to two hundred dollars per person per day, including lodging and meals. Camping is not allowed.

Vermejo Park is full of elk, turkey, cattle, coyotes, cowboys, and trout. The lakes and streams are reached by traveling on improved gravel roads. While a good car is adequate, a four-wheel-drive vehicle is a safer bet to handle the mud and ruts from the summer showers. The terrain runs from 7,000 to 12,900 feet above sea level, and the park operates three separate lodges. One of the few problems for the angler at Vermejo is deciding where to fish. With two exceptions, fishing at Vermejo is with fly or lure only. A state license is required on some of the lakes and all of the streams, but is not required on the class-A (stocked) lakes. Because you never know where you'll be fishing until you actually get to the ranch, be safe and buy a fishing license before you go to Vermejo. Wheelchair access ranges from good to very good at most of the lakes, but it is difficult at the lodges.

Merrick Lake, twenty-five acres, is the only stocked lake where bait-fishing is allowed and is the site of a weekly outdoor barbecue. Merrick, the closest lake to the headquarters lodge, is stocked with rainbow trout.

Munn Lake is the most productive of Vermejo's lakes in terms of the growth rate of big trout. Its forty acres hold an abundance of one- to five-pound rainbows. These large trout feed heavily on snails, a weighted peacock-bodied wet fly seems to imitate the snails and definitely catches fish. An afternoon mayfly hatch is a common summer occurrence.

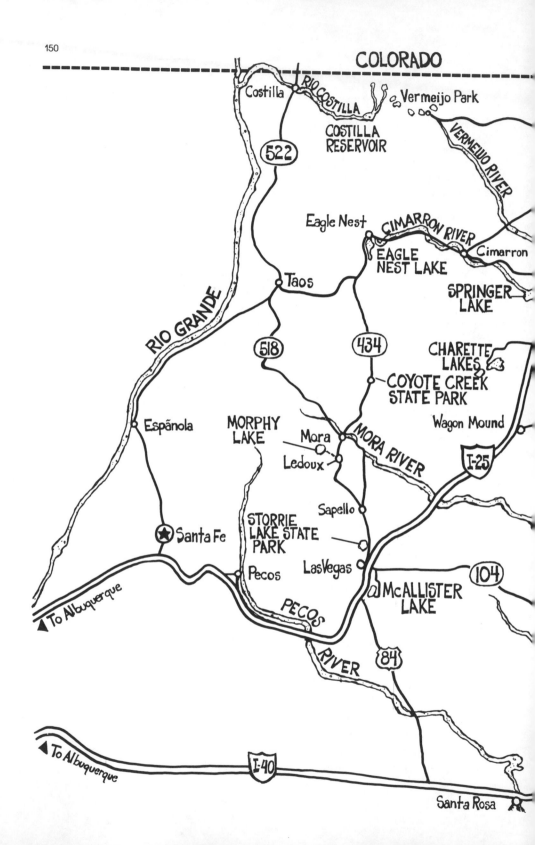

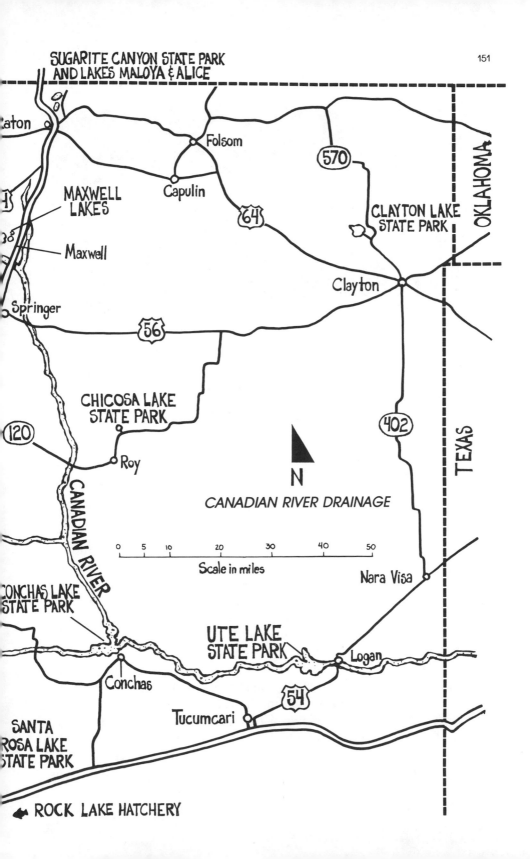

SUGARITE CANYON STATE PARK
AND LAKES MALOYA & ALICE

Raton

Folsom

570

OKLAHOMA

MAXWELL
LAKES

Capulin

64

CLAYTON LAKE
STATE PARK

Maxwell

Clayton

Springer

56

CHICOSA LAKE
STATE PARK

120

Roy

402

TEXAS

N

CANADIAN RIVER DRAINAGE

CANADIAN RIVER

0   5   10   20   30   40   50

Scale in miles

CONCHAS LAKE
STATE PARK

Nara Visa

UTE LAKE
STATE PARK

Logan

Conchas

54

SANTA
ROSA LAKE
STATE PARK

Tucumcari

ROCK LAKE HATCHERY

Vermejo Park Ranch

Large rainbow trout are common catches at Vermejo lakes. Fishing here is always excellent and also expensive. The largest trout in this catch (18 inches) was full of snails and was brought in on a #12 gold ribbed hare's ear fly fished deep.

Bernal Lake, a ten-acre brown trout lake with an eighteen-inch minimum size for keepers, is restricted to fly-fishing only. This lake is fun but demanding, for there is an almost continuous hatch of tiny midges.

Bartlett and Adams Lakes are seventy-acre sister lakes with good populations of browns and rainbows. Both lakes provide great evening action on woolybuggers cast with a spinning rod and casting bubble rig.

The two Underwood Lakes rest in a high mountain meadow, with each covering about ten acres. They support a good selection of rainbow trout. The lakes, set in a hillside depression next to one of the main ranch roads, produce fine catches of fifteen-inch rainbows.

Costilla Reservoir, which holds back the waters of the two Costilla creeks, is big (one hundred to five hundred acres) and holds browns, brookies, cutthroat, and rainbows. These are all wild fish; Costilla Reservoir is not stocked. Don't let that keep you away, however; this big mountain lake is full of trout. Bait-fishing is allowed.

Mary's Lake, named after Mary Pickford, is an up-and-coming twenty-acre brown and rainbow trout fishery with great insect hatches. Mary's Lake offers great fly-fishing. This is a shallow lake, full of ducks in the autumn.

Glacier Lakes, which straddle the Colorado border, are small trout ponds at an 11,500-foot elevation. A four-wheel-drive, high-clearance vehicle is necessary to reach the lake's cutthroats and big brook trout. The state record brook trout came from these lakes.

Beaver Lake and Seven Lakes are small and unstocked trout waters with wild populations of rainbows, cutthroats, and brook trout. Both are a short distance from Costilla Lodge and feed Costilla Creek No. 2.

The Vermejo River, which runs past the headquarters lodge, is loaded with wild five- to twelve-inch Rio Grande cutthroats, one of our state's original trout. The fishing on this little river gets better as you move upstream, especially when you reach the left fork (Recardo Creek) above the old stagecoach station.

Costilla Creek No. 1 and No. 2 offer great small-stream fishing for cutthroats on No. 1 and for brook trout on No. 2. Creek No. 1 is regulated for fly-fishing only. Both have excellent fishing just above their confluence with Costilla Reservoir.

Lake No. 1 and No. 2 are named after the two Costilla creeks that they feed. Lake No. 1 (fifteen acres), located next to a fairly good access road, offers an incredible view, and this is a favorite spot during nice weather. Expect one- to three-pound rainbows and a good chance to see some elk. Lake No. 2 (five acres) is a three-mile hike to an 11,600-foot-elevation mountain lake full of wild cutthroats.

Successful fishing at Vermejo means finding out what the trout are feeding on and then imitating that natural food with your tackle. Johnboats with oars are stocked at most of the lakes, and electric trolling motors are available at the lodges. Handicapped access is good. Fathead minnows are the main trout food in the spring, and a good selection of lures or streamers will put you into some big fish. Summer brings on the insect population, and the fly-rod is very effective. Most of the trout lakes in Vermejo support large populations of snails, and the larger fish feed heavily on these little mollusks. Try a weighted-peacock nymph fished slow and deep. Trolling on midsummer days with a lure or wooly worm is a standard technique, but better midday catches are made by just drifting and letting your lure or fly bump the bottom in five to ten feet of water.

Vermejo Park is managed for a quality outdoor experience in the high meadows of the Sangre de Cristo Mountains. The fishing is superb.

CLAYTON LAKE

Clayton Lake is a one-hundred-acre recreation lake in the northeastern corner of New Mexico, about fifteen miles north of the town of Clayton. Anglers, mostly from out of state, spend most of their time going after stocked rainbow trout. Walleye, bass, bluegills, bullheads, and catfish round out the sportfish population. Walleye are the overlooked sportfish at Clayton. The old state record of thirteen pounds and over thirty inches long was caught in the fall of 1981. Clayton Lake is a complete state park, with good roads, a group shelter, camping spots, a playground, bathrooms with showers, and a good boat-launching ramp.

Officially called the Clayton Lake Fish and Waterfowl Area, these four hundred acres of grassland and lake were purchased by the Department of Game and Fish in 1954. The lake was formed by damming the very intermittent Cieneguilla Creek. Though the lake's maximum surface area is listed as 170 acres, it rarely goes over 100 acres. The inlet creek runs only after a rainfall, which, on a yearly basis, is barely enough to overcome the evaporation rate.

As its name indicates, Clayton Lake is managed for both waterfowl and fishermen. The fishing season opens at noon on March 1 and closes October 31. Boats are limited to trolling speeds and are allowed on Clayton only during the fishing season. After the fishing season the lake acts as a waterfowl refuge. The state park is open throughout the year (though the facilities are closed in the winter), and it is used as a base camp for hunters after the fishing season closes. No hunting is allowed on the lake or on the surrounding state park land.

Clayton Lake is an important fishing hole for the trout fishermen of Texas and Oklahoma. Thousands of out-of-state anglers drive to New Mexico each year to try their luck. Many stop at the town of Clayton, spending valuable tourist dollars on provisions, tackle, and nonresident fishing licenses. The Department of Game and Fish responds with a generous stocking program. Twenty to thirty thousand catchable-size rainbow trout are stocked each year in Clayton Lake. Channel catfish, both fry and catchables, are stocked by the thousands. The bluegills and bullheads naturally reproduce while the Department of Game and Fish stocks walleye and bass fry.

A quiet nighttime walk to the boat dock with flashlight in hand will show the visiting angler why Clayton Lake is capable of supporting such a mixed bag of sportfish. The flashlight's beam will reveal hundreds of minnows, dozens of crayfish, and thousands of little water creatures. Minnows are legal bait in Clayton Lake, a minnow trap is a convenient way to collect the next day's bait. Crayfish, which can be caught at night with a hand net, make great natural bait for anglers pursuing larger fish.

Trolling lures around the shoreline is a typical and productive technique for trout during the spring and fall. Working bait or lures closer to the bottom is a good technique during hot summer days. On summer evenings, the rainbows will be rising for bugs in the surface film. Fly fishermen can enjoy fishing from a boat in the inlet area. Anglers with spinning rods can use a little wooly worm and a casting bubble.

Night-fishing with cutbait is the way to connect with the larger catfish. The bluegills and smaller bass may always be found around the shoreline, and worms, grasshoppers, flies, or small lures will produce catches all day long. But the walleyes at Clayton Lake are not easy to catch.

Most of the action at Clayton is for rainbow trout, and the pressure is concentrated from Memorial Day to Labor Day. Most of these anglers will never see a walleye taken from Clayton Lake; but they are here, hiding out during the summer-vacation season. The old state record walleye was caught here. A sixteen-pounder was caught and released during a Department of Game and Fish netting operation. The local conservation officer has scuba-dived in Clayton Lake, and he reports a good population of big catfish and walleye, concentrated in the deep water around the riprap of the dam.

Just after the February opening of the Clayton fishing season, while the spring winds are blowing, the walleye are spawning. Try fishing the south-eastern shoreline near the dam. Use big crankbaits. Later, in May, try deep diving lures along the damface. The same technique works in September and October. Bait fishermen should fish in deep water using crayfish and a lead sinker. A lead-head spinner worm rig is productive when backtrolled along the old creekbed. The depths around the dam are an important location to anglers after walleye. This reservoir submerged some big trees along the old creekbed, and that is where the walleye and big bass hide out.

Clayton Lake is located off S.R. 370, about fifteen miles north of Clayton. Clayton is about eighty miles east of I–25, from Springer. The access road is paved and the route from town is marked with Clayton Lake signs. Handicapped access, with help from a friend, is good.

EAGLE NEST LAKE

Eagle Nest offers just about everything needed to make a good trout lake: good fishing for cutthroat trout, rainbows, and kokanee salmon; a healthy watershed to collect the spring runoff; acres of shallows to grow the bugs, minnows, and creatures the trout need to feed on; and plenty of deep water to protect the fish from a winterkill. All told, Eagle Nest is one of New Mexico's best trout lakes.

Eagle Nest Lake is normally listed at fifteen hundred surface acres, but an above-average runoff can boost the lake to more than three thousand acres. The lake has been near full for most of the 1980s. This increase in size coincides with the new public fishing lease purchased by the Department of Game and Fish. CS Ranch owns and operates the lake for ranch and downstream water needs, but the public owns the fishing recreation rights (at least until the year 2000). There's a boat ramp and a marina with boat rentals. Fishing success from either the shore or from a boat is better than average. Besides trout and kokanee, most bait fishermen will eventually catch a few of the white suckers that also live in Eagle Nest Lake.

This excellent trout lake is located off U.S. 64 near the town of Eagle Nest, between Taos, Red River, and Cimarron. Camping is prohibited, for this is a day-use lake, with no overnight stays allowed. Rain or melting snow can really make a mess of the access roads, which are dirt and gravel. Though Eagle Nest Lake is heavily used, there are miles of public shoreline, and you can easily take a short hike to your own private fishing space.

Eagle Nest Lake is heavily stocked with undersized rainbow trout, es-pecially since the new lease took effect. More important are the millions of rainbow, cutthroat, coho, and kokanee fingerlings released in the last few years. Eagle Nest, which has everything needed to grow big fish from little fish, is known as a put, grow, and take lake.

The easiest bankside angling is on the western shoreline. Parking is close to the fishing and the wind is usually at your back. Bait-fishing from the bank is popular, and salmon eggs, corn, cheese, marshmallows, and worms have all produced fine catches. A good local bait can be obtained by cap-turing and using a small crayfish tail. Handicapped access is difficult but possible on the western shoreline.

Boaters typically troll with downriggers or lead core for kokanee, with cowbells or heavy lures for deep summer trout, or with big flies or lures for surface action. The best way to catch trout on midsummer days is to troll, deep and slow, with cowbells and worms. This is a deadly technique if you bounce the rig right along the bottom. Eagle Nest is a high, mountain valley lake, the winds can get fierce. Spring windstorms are common, boaters should stay aware of wind speed.

Large rainbow and cutthroat trout (weighing four to seven pounds) have been caught at Eagle Nest. One clue for a chance at these big trout is to be on the water just as the sun goes down on a calm autumn evening. Fish until after dark, working quietly along the shoreline in three to six feet of water. If you're after big trout, fishing the first month after iceout can also be productive. The lake's southern end, where the main inlet stream enters, is a favorite trolling spot anytime. Be aware of snags when trolling the shallow water in the southern end, this area has broken quit a few props.

Fly-fishing with nymphs, big wet flies, or streamers can be excellent on semicalm days. The north end of the lake, normally the downwind side, often has good fly-fishing when the wind dies off at sundown. The evening rise can be fabulous in mid-June. If you have difficulty matching the hatch, then try a woolybugger. Big wooly worms, either cast or trolled, account for many trout in Eagle Nest Lake.

A sonar chart recorder will show large populations of fish in this lake, but many of those will be suckers. Estimates of Eagle Nest fish populations show that more than a third of a million adult white suckers live in Eagle Nest. The Department of Game and Fish has netted this unwanted species in huge quantities (from 50,000 to 150,000 pounds per year), and it poses a continuing problem. New solutions, such as the trial stocking of coho salmon, are being investigated by the department's fisheries research team.

The public campgrounds closest to the lake are below Eagle Nest Dam on the Cimarron River. One tent area and three large and improved fee campgrounds are operated by the state parks division. Expect crowded camping conditions during the summer-vacation season, for these are the only public campgrounds near the lake. The towns of Eagle Nest, Cimarron, and Angel Fire have recreational vehicle parks and other overnight accommodations. There are two off-limit areas around the lake: a half-mile section of the northeastern shore, next to a large private residence; and the shoreline and water within one hundred yards of the dam. These areas are posted.

Eagle Nest Lake has sprawled across the wide Moreno Valley for more than seventy years. Public access to this privately owned lake is now assured. The Department of Game and Fish has worked with the New Mexico legislature to obtain money for the lease at least through the year 2000. Many vacationing families enjoy the good morning and evening fishing at the lake, while they spend the midday wetting a line in the Cimarron River below the dam. Eagle Nest is also one of New Mexico's most popular ice-fishing spots. You may catch a few suckers if you're using bait, but that's okay because the fine trout fishing more than makes up for it.

CIMARRON RIVER

Starting just below the dam at Eagle Nest Lake, beautiful Cimarron Canyon contains this solid little river. Angling is very good for wild brown trout, and these waters are heavily stocked with catchable-size rainbow trout. U.S. Highway 64 runs beside the Cimarron River for its entire fishable length. This nine miles of public fishing runs through the Colin Neblett State Wildlife Area, the largest piece of New Mexico owned by the Department of Game and Fish.

There are three improved campgrounds and one tent-site area in the canyon, all run by the state parks division. Fishing is good in these heavily used spots. The two big day-use areas are often vacant and offer access to good fishing.

The biggest reason for the good fishing in the Cimarron is the consistent flow of water out of Eagle Nest Dam. Downstream irrigation users require a strong stream of water, assuring a cool flow in the summer. Street signs announce parking and no-parking areas in this tight little canyon, and the critical streamside vegetation (the riparian area) stays in good shape. Good riparian management makes for good trout habitat, which, in turn, makes for good fishing. The self-reproducing browns maintain a good fishery for the lure and fly fisherman, while the heavily stocked rainbows provide good sport for anglers preferring salmon eggs or corn.

The Cimarron River flows in a steep canyon, its banks overgrown with trees and shrubs. An elevation drop of eighty feet per mile provides only a few quiet pools for the bankside fisherman. One good tactic is to sneak along the edges, casting upstream with bait, fly, or lure. Another productive technique is to wade upstream with a little closed-face spinning outfit. The fly-fisher will be making short casts with weighted nymphs or with a hard-to-sink, low-floating dry fly.

Stonefly nymphs are a major source of food for Cimarron trout. These underwater creatures hatch into big mothlike creatures in the spring. Browns and rainbows see the nymphs all year long. Bait fishermen can find the naturals under rocks. Imitations in brown or black, such as No. 10 wooly worms or stonefly nymphs work just as well. Fish these flies with splitshot, and try to bounce them just off the bottom. An ultra-light spinning rod is the perfect gear for this technique. Stoneflies will catch trout almost any day of the year. The trick is to wade quietly upstream, casting your fly just above every spot that looks like it might hold a fish.

The campgrounds are very accessible, with paved roads, water, and outhouses provided. There is now a camping fee in the Colin Neblett Wildlife

Area. The Gravel Pit Lakes Campground offers good fishing for stocked rainbows in some old riverside ponds. Access here is good for handicapped anglers.

Tolby and Clear Creek are the two fishable tributaries to the Cimarron in the wildlife area. Tolby comes in just upstream from the U.S. 64 bridge below Eagle Nest Dam. Clear Creek, which is smaller, enters about three miles downstream. Both have populations of wild cutthroats.

The downstream end of the Colin Neblett Wildlife Area is found at the village of Ute Park. The valley floor has widened, and the Cimarron slows and meanders through this private property. This is wild brown trout water, and no rainbow trout are stocked. Further downstream, the river is on Philmont Scout Ranch property. Public access is allowed on Philmont property only where the stream is not fenced off from U.S. 64. If you cross a fence to fish the Cimarron you are trespassing on private property. There is no public fishing below the Boy Scout ranch.

For a quarter-mile above the Ute Park area, at the eastern or downstream end of the Colin Neblett Wildlife Area, the Cimarron River is managed as a fish-for-fun area. This stretch offers excellent fishing for browns and rainbows, but it is catch-and-release only and no bait-fishing is allowed.

For its size, the Cimarron is one of the most heavily used (and heavily stocked) rivers in New Mexico. The campgrounds are often filled with recreational vehicles and campers from Texas, New Mexico, and Oklahoma. The river is crowded only in the camping areas; the nine miles of fishable river offer plenty of room for all. Eagle Nest Lake is only fifteen minutes away, and many anglers fish the Cimarron during the day while catching the evening feeding spree on the lake. The Cimarron also offers a good chance at catching fish during runoff. The dam tempers the cold and murky water from the lake's feeder creeks, giving the springtime angler a chance to fool the Cimarron's wild browns and holdover rainbows. The Colin Neblett Wildlife Area is on U.S. 64, between Taos and Raton, just east of Eagle Nest.

SPRINGER LAKE

Springer Lake has always been a fairly good trout lake, and that fact has been especially appreciated by the local anglers because it's nice to have a rainbow fishery just four miles off the highway. A problem developed in 1963 when suckers began to take over the lake. The Department of Game and Fish decided to solve the problem by stocking northern pike. These toothy feeders quickly grew very large while eating up the white sucker problem. When fishermen discovered these five- to fifteen-pound pike, the quest was on to catch the larger fish. The state record from Springer stands at thirty-six pounds and that northern pike was four and one-half feet long!

Springer Lake is more than 400 acres, and a boat is the key for consistent catches of pike. You can cover more water searching for the depth, lure, and speed that will attract these voracious feeders. A long earthen dam runs along the eastern side of the lake, and many pike addicts troll back and forth along the rocky riprap looking for that day's feeding zone. Early morning or late evening finds the pike fisherman casting or trolling along the opposite shoreline. This shallower western bank is lined with reeds, perfect hunting ground for a hungry northern. Casting lures from the bank along the northwestern shoreline occasionally produces pike for the boatless angler.

The Department of Game and Fish has also stocked Springer Lake with thousands of channel catfish and bullheads. Bottom-fishing with cutbait is the method of choice for most anglers; use a big hook to keep from catching a dozen four-inch fish. Bait-fishing with live minnows is popular, so bring a minnow trap if you want to catch your own bait. Still-fishing with big minnows is also one of the best ways to connect with big northern pike. Perch, which are beginning to take hold in Springer, congregate near the riprap along the earth dam. Any lightweight lure, fly, or bait (especially small worms) works well when these panfish are on the feed.

Trout fishing is kept alive in Springer with large stockings of catchable-size rainbow trout. Fingerlings don't do well here because there are too many predators anxious to feed on the little trout. Bait-fishing on the bottom, with worms or salmon eggs, is difficult because the small catfish keep hooking themselves on your trout bait. Move to a different spot or use a bobber to keep your bait off the bottom. The rainbow trout will hit lures cast from the riprap when they're in the mood, and the casting bubble and wooly worm is hot when the dragonflies are hatching (in midspring), especially when worked from a boat along the western shore.

Springer is open throughout the year, but ice-fishing is prohibited. Camping (with no fee) is available on the northern and southern ends of the lake; the dam takes up the eastern side and the western bank is private property. Drinking water is not provided, but there are a few outhouses. Springer Lake is located just west of the town of Springer (seventy miles north of Las Vegas). Take the I–25 exit at Springer and follow the signs to the Springer Boys' Ranch, just west of town on S.R. 468. This paved road turns to maintained gravel and ends two miles later at Springer Lake.

Springer Lake is home to seventeen-pound northerns, seven-pound channel cats, plus perch, trout, and bullheads.

Launching your boat is easiest at the primitive ramp on the southern end, remember that you are limited to trolling speeds. Wheelchair fishing is good from both the northern and southern shorelines. A good gravel road on the dam connects both ends of the lake. Trout, perch, catfish, and big northern pike—Springer Lake is home to them all.

MAXWELL LAKES

Over a dozen potholes, sinks, marshes, and lakes are found in and around the Maxwell National Wildlife Refuge. Primarily managed for wildfowl, Maxwell also contains some good fishing lakes. The refuge is located off I–25, just north of the town of Maxwell, which is about twenty-five miles south of Raton. Stubblefield Lake, located just outside the refuge, is the largest, and bigger than all the rest combined; it is full of channel catfish, largemouth bass, walleye, and perch. Laguna Madre, connected by a canal to Stubblefield, is not separately stocked. Maxwell 13, which is inside the refuge, holds catfish and bass and is stocked with catchable and fingerling rainbow trout. Maxwell 14, also in the refuge, contains bass, catfish, and sunfish.

Fluctuating water levels keep these lakes from being consistent and long-term producers of limit catches. But any given year can produce fine angling (or it may not). A call to the refuge office (375-2331) will get you up-to-date reports on water levels.

Because of their size, shoreline, and warmwater species, Stubblefield and Maxwell 13 are best fished from a johnboat, although bank fishermen do just fine. The refuge fishing season opens March 1 and closes October 31, and fishing is not allowed at night. Stubblefield is open year round. Fishing worms or stinkbait for catfish is good anytime. Trout fishing in Maxwell 13 is best before and after July and August. Walleye catches are best in March and April. Largemouth are caught throughout the season by active anglers fishing safety-pin spinnerbaits or plastic worms along the weedy shorelines.

Remember that water levels can really fluctuate. In wet years the fishing is good from March through October. In dry years the fishing can be lousy. But big fish are caught in these lakes. While the normal catches are pan-size, sixteen- to twenty-inch fish (walleye, bass, catfish, and trout) are creeled each year. Enjoy the grasslands, the wildlife, and the good angling at Maxwell Wildlife Refuge.

CHARETTE LAKES

Charette Lakes are a surprise, sitting high atop a dry plateau, east of the Sangre de Cristo Mountains. When these two natural depressions were filled with water diverted from Ocate Creek, the fishermen gained Charette Lakes, a great place to catch both trout and yellow (ring) perch. The upper lake has pretty much silted in and has been turned over to the ducks. Except for years of above-average snowpack, the silt captured by the upper lake protects the lower lake from getting murky during the runoff. The stony meadows and rocky cliffs bordering the lower lake keep it from silting up under heavy rainstorms, and this all makes for good early spring fishing.

Because of their status as waterfowl resting areas, the lakes are closed to fishing during the winter (from October 31 to March 1). In early March it's still a bit chilly, but come April the rainbow trout and perch fishing is good. Charette produces so many perch that these panfish have begun to compete with the rainbows for habitat. For years, the district fisheries

Charette Lakes

Northwest Area Fisheries manager Bob Akroyd (looking up) directs his crew as they net Charette Lake perch for transport to Springer Lake.

professionals have netted the perch during their spring spawning swarm; thousands have been transplanted to other area lakes, solving the crowding problem at Charette while providing good panfish angling elsewhere.

The springtime dragonflies signal the start of good trout catches in shallow water. Try a small black spinner, a black wooly worm, or a dragonfly nymph. The perch, which spend the spring along the steep rocky cliffs, grow just large enough to make a great meal. Try small lead-head jigs cast in deep water, along the rocks. Worms and grasshoppers are the consistent favorites for the bait fisherman.

Lower Charette normally covers four hundred acres, and even though you're limited to trolling speeds a boat is a good asset. The boat ramp is in good shape, but at low water-levels you may have launching difficulties with a large powerboat.

The rocky points are the first place to check if you are new to Charette. These points, located along the southern and northern shorelines, allow you to try many different depths while either trolling from a boat or casting from the bank. The lake is sixty to ninety feet deep (depending on water levels) near the dam. The fly-rod angler should bring a float tube and head for the shallow cove just south of the boat-ramp parking area. Cast big nymphs and let them sink, then retrieve slowly through the deeper pockets.

Spring winds will cut down the pleasures of fishing on a warm May day, but it won't bother the fish—they'll be just as catchable. Summer thunderstorms can be fierce, so get your craft off the lake if you see one approaching. Summer slows the trout fishing a bit as the water temperature warms. As in most trout lakes, the fish will be suspended during midday at the level providing the right amount of oxygen. Find that medium level and the trout can be caught. In July and August, fish from dawn to midmorning—just after sunup is best. Because yellow perch are not bothered as much by the warmer water, a drive to the steep rocky cliffs along the north bank can produce some fine perch fishing. There is no limit on perch, and their sweet filets freeze well.

Fall is the best time to limit out on fifteen-inch rainbows. Don't forget to bring your wooly worms or gray-hackle peacock flies and a casting bubble. That's the key for the spinning rod to match the fly-rod during the evening rise.

Sterile grass carp have been introduced into Charette in an attempt to control the weed problem. Because they are sterile, these big goldfish cannot reproduce and take over the lake. These carp eat aquatic vegetation, one thing with which Charette is occasionally overblessed. Carefully release the carp you catch at Charette, for these carp are helping to make the lake better for both the fish and the fishermen.

A dirt and gravel road goes completely around the lake, but rain turns the low spots into mud. A four-wheel-drive vehicle is recommended if you plan to camp away from the main parking area. Drinking water is provided near the boat ramp, and there is camping (with no fee) all around the lake, with picnic tables and outhouses provided. Bring your own shade if you plan to visit during the hot summer months; the nearest trees are a long way off.

Access is gained by traveling about sixty miles north of Las Vegas on I-25 to the marked S.R. 569 Charette Lakes turnoff. Head west toward the mountains on this maintained gravel road. At the eight-mile point the road narrows a bit and continues on, winding up a steep cliff to the top of the plateau. This short switchback section has been improved, and a stout pickup driven in low gear should have no problem in pulling a trailer or boat. The lake is about thirteen miles from the freeway. Bring everything you'll need because the nearest supplies are twenty-five lonely miles away (in Springer).

Rainbow trout and perch are the sportfish at Charette Lake. Hidden on a high, treeless plateau east of the Sangre de Cristo Mountains, Charette offers good boat- and shore-fishing.

CHICOSA LAKE

Chicosa Lake is the only place in New Mexico where an errant cast might find you hooked to a thousand-pound longhorn steer. This state park holds both a herd of longhorns and a good population of rainbow trout. When water levels are normal the growth rate is fantastic, but the problem of low water levels in late summer can hurt the trout population. It all depends on the August thundershowers. Chicosa Lake State Park is in the Kiowa National Grasslands, just north of Roy, in the northeastern high plains of New Mexico. During the middle to late 1800s, these rolling hills were the grass highways of the mighty cattle drives. One hundred years later the highways are paved, the grasslands fenced, and the modern family enjoys camping and fishing at Chicosa Lake State Park.

The facilities are fantastic for such a small lake: three-sided shelters for picnics and camping, restrooms with hot showers, water spigots for each shelter, swings for the kids, and plenty of stocked trout for the angler. As at all our state parks, there is a day-use and camping fee. Spring and fall, which are best for the fisherman, are also when the waterfowl stop for a rest on their yearly migration. It is common to see a dozen different kinds of ducks on an April afternoon. This is a popular layover spot for Texans on their way to Eagle Nest and Red River.

Fishing is best from April through early July. Hot summer days and the lack of summer rains bring on a thick growth of algae and water weeds (sterile grass carp have been put in Chicosa to help eat up this aquatic vegetation problem). These summertime low water conditions hurt the trout fishing, so watch the weekly fishing reports. Early autumn rainfall refreshes the lake, and fall fishing is good. A bubble and fly rig cast on a spinning rod is the best way to catch early morning trout, but this type of fishing isn't effective much past 8:00 A.M. on hot summer days. Lures work on cloudy days, and bait-fishing is good if you move your casts around and find the level where the fish are feeding.

The lake has a minimum size of forty acres, but rainfall and runoff can triple that figure. Access is off I–25 about forty-five miles north of Las Vegas. Take the Wagon Mound exit and turn east on S.R. 120 toward Roy. It is thirty-four miles to Roy. State Route 120 winds through Roy and then heads north to Chicosa. Don't turn north on S.R. 39 in Roy; stay on S.R. 120. State park regulations stipulate that no boats or floating devices are allowed in Chicosa Lake.

MORA RIVER

The Mora River has its headwaters in the Sangre de Cristo Mountains, north of Las Vegas, New Mexico. Except for a few tiny headwater creeks, the Mora flows entirely on private land. Running twenty to forty feet wide, this river is a good brown and rainbow trout stream. There is some public fishing below the town of Mora. Follow S.R. 3 north from Las Vegas, past Storrie Lake. S.R. 3 turns west and heads toward the town of Mora, right where the Mora River goes under the highway. From this point upstream, for three miles, the river is on the south side of the road. This is where the hatchery truck unloads catchable-size rainbows in the Mora River, and it is the only public use area. The rest of the Mora is on private land, most of it posted. Get landowner permission before fishing any other part of the Mora.

COYOTE CREEK

Coyote Creek is a small, brown trout stream with its headwaters on private land in the mountains south of the Angel Fire resort complex. The river flows south and eventually feeds the Mora River. Action for anglers is found in the midsection of Coyote Creek, on public land at Coyote Creek State Park. The park is typified by large grass meadows in the stream's floodplain, surrounded by deciduous and conifer shade trees. Wildflowers are lush, the campgrounds are clean, and access is on a paved road (S.R. 38) out of Mora.

Catchable-size rainbow trout are stocked in the warmer months, beginning in May. A few of these trout will survive through the winter, and an occasional fifteen-inch rainbow will be caught. There are plenty of wild reproducing browns, mostly in the six- to ten-inch size.

Coyote Creek is a small stream, ten to fifteen feet wide and one to two feet deep. Plenty of beaver dams create some nice ponds for drowning worms, grasshoppers, or salmon eggs. The most consistent fishing is not in the beaver-engineered pools and side flows, but in the two-foot-deep runs where the creek is contained in its natural channel. With willow trees and shrubs lining the banks, the creek is best fished by wading upstream, casting fly, lure, or bait through all the fish-holding runs.

In early spring the runoff and cold weather keep most fishermen away. But those who visit on a nice April or May afternoon can score with worms and small lures. Fly fishermen might choose to visit this creek in late June, when Coyote Creek explodes with caddis and mayfly hatches. Spin fishermen do just as well with four-pound test line in an ultralight spinning rod by casting wet flies with just enough splitshot added to get their cast off. This easy fishing ends in mid-July when water levels drop.

August and September fishing is more challenging because of lower water levels. Summer rain showers are common, and in years of average precipitation this spring, seep, and creek-fed stream still offers plenty of cool water and hiding places for brown and rainbow trout.

Grasshoppers are the preferred summer bait at Coyote Creek. The fly fisherman can get by with a gold-ribbed hare's ear or pheasant-tail nymph and two dry flies, an Adams and an elk hair caddis, all tied on No. 12 hooks. Lure fishermen should use the tiniest Mepps, Panther Martins, and Z-Ray type lures that their spinning rod can cast. Try those weighing one-eighth of an ounce or less.

Facilities at the state park are clean and well kept. Roads, which are gravel and dirt, are usually drivable even after a rainstorm. As in most state parks, there is a day-use fee and a camping fee. Drinking water, sheltered picnic tables, designated camping spots, clean outhouses, and plenty of shade trees make this a delightful area to visit. A large grassy meadow, complete with playground equipment, is perfect for the kids. Fishing access for the handicapped is reasonable, for the park roads often run right next to the creek.

Coyote Creek State Park is in north-central New Mexico between Eagle Nest and Las Vegas. From I–25 at Las Vegas, head north on S.R. 3 to Mora. In Mora, turn north on S.R. 38, the turnoff is marked with signs pointing toward Guadalupita. It is about seventeen miles to the village of Guadalupita, and a few miles past the village you reach the marked entrance to the state park. If you stay on S.R. 38, one mile past the state park you find a grocery store and gas station with rental cabins and a private, fee campground, all located right on Coyote Creek. Continuing north, the road turns to gravel and leads to Black Lake, where the road is again paved to Angel Fire.

Coyote Creek is famous for its wildflower display. Spring explodes with purple iris; summer is full of wild roses and flowering shrubs. Though this is a very small stream, it flows with a gentle gradient, perfect for fish and fishermen. If the stream seems to be more full of anglers than trout, pack a snack and hike downstream (or upstream). When you get to what is obviously private property, then turn around and fish your way back to the campground. One mile of the creek upstream from the state park boundary is open to public fishing. You don't have to bother with waders; it is cool and refreshing to wade in jeans and tennis shoes, catching wild browns and stocked rainbows from the waters of Coyote Creek. And take some time to enjoy the wildflowers, their summer colors are as pretty as the trout.

MORPHY LAKE

The dirt road to Morphy Lake State Park is only three miles long. If the roadgrader has made one of its rare appearances, the trip to fish Morphy Lake will be a pleasant one. More often than not, however, the snow, rain, mud, deep ruts, and the runoff make a pickup or a high-clearance-vehicle necessary, though many anglers take the chance with the family car. Each summer thousands of visitors fish this alpine lake for trout. Every year it is heavily stocked with catchable-size rainbows.

Midwinter storms shut off road access to all but a few hearty snowmobilers. Around March, four-wheel-drive vehicles carry in the early spring anglers.

By mid-May, when the roadgrader will have flattened the ruts, the best spring fishing begins. Morphy is an irrigation-storage lake with a fluctuating size from twenty-five to fifty acres. When the pond is full in the spring, bank-fishing is good. Shallows near the parking area offer good angling for the fisherman wearing waders.

The lake is drawn down in the summer for irrigation needs in the farmland below the dam. The shallows shrink back and fill with algae and minnows. The surface-water temperature rises and summer midday fishing means getting your hook into deeper water. A small raft or canoe is great for fishing the depths off the southern shoreline; try worms held right off the bottom. Watch for midday summer rainstorms, for they can bring the trout up to the surface on an afternoon feeding spree. A good spot for early-morning or late-evening angling is the big rocks that meet the northeastern shore just past the end of the camping area. Much of the bank-fishing is done along the steep southern shoreline, from the parking area to the dam. The lake is loaded with minnows, and the lure angler who makes his first cast before the sun hits the water can score with the few large rainbow trout that cruise the edges for breakfast.

Autumn brings the end of the fishing year to Morphy Lake. The water cools and the level rises as irrigation needs diminish. The western foothills carry the yellow flag of fall while the rainbows put on their autumn-feeding binge. Catch a grasshopper and fish it on a clear casting bubble. The fly fisherman does well on the northern and eastern banks, where there is room for a backcast. A small cartop boat is fun on this lake and gives any fisherman a better chance to cast to a good spot. Don't try to bring a camper or a boat on a trailer unless you have already experienced the access road.

Morphy Lake sits in a natural basin, eight thousand feet above sea level. Looking due west, your eyes travel up the hills to the top of Cebolla Mountain. All around are giant pines and little chipmunks. During quiet evenings the trout rise, forming disappearing circles on the lake. This is a good place to bring a nonfishing friend for a few days of midweek rest. It is quiet and good to sit next to a peaceful lake with mountains in the distance, watching the evening stars appear as daylight fades.

Morphy Lake is a 238–acre state park with picnic tables, clean outhouses, and fee camping, but with no drinking water. Boating is limited to electric trolling motors or oars. Wheelchair access is reasonable for bank-fishing the shallows near the parking area, but impossible for most of the rest of the shoreline. Parts of the three-mile dirt access road are often muddy and lined with deep ruts. From the town of Mora, turn south on paved State Route 94 and travel five miles to the little village of Ledoux. The Morphy

Lake turnoff (Forest Road 635) is marked with a warning about bad road conditions. Once on Forest Road 635, bear right at two unmarked turnoffs. Two and one-half miles from Ledoux, the road comes to a bridge crossing the Rito Morphy. Once you cross the bridge, the lake is three-quarters of a mile farther.

CONCHAS LAKE

A quick report on Conchas Reservoir would read like this: an excellent walleye and largemouth lake with over fifty miles of shoreline; about ten thousand acres, with the irrigation and flood control reservoir completed in 1939; a state park with two marinas and eight boat ramps; a favored spring crappie lake with some smallmouth fishing, good channel catfish, and plenty of bluegills hogging the shoreline; many submerged stumps, logs, timber, and brush; acres of shallows and miles of rock ledges and points with quick drop-offs and dozens of creek channels; water usually clear; high winds in spring; lousy winter fishing, but great in the spring and fall, and good in the summer. This impoundment of the Canadian River is just north of I–40, thirty-two miles northwest of Tucumcari.

Conchas is one of New Mexico's best walleye fisheries. Slow trolling with Lindy rigs or deep running plugs is the most consistent technique. Jigging lead-head jigs with twister tails might be more productive, but you must concentrate because walleye rarely smash, grab, and run with your lure. The take is more a tap than a strike, and it requires concentration to detect and react to these big perch.

Better walleye spots include Little Green Island, Rattlesnake Island, Brush Point, Cedar Point, and along the riprap of dam. These are popular areas because they are landmarks, not because they're secret fishing spots. Look for walleye at certain depths, in shallow water early and late in the day and deeper during midday. A good chop on the water will move walleye out of the depths to feed in five to ten feet of water. The wave action breaks up the bright New Mexico sunshine and allows these big eyed (walleyed) fish to hunt in shallower water. Walleye are caught in different situations at different times of the year. The best walleye fishing at Conchas is from mid-April to the end of May. But good catches are made anytime the water temperature is over 50°F. Keep trying different locations, depths, and presentations, and you *will* catch fish.

Fishing at night from the shore is an overlooked but productive summer walleye technique. Use large floating or shallow running crankbaits (Rapala-type lures) and long-casting spinning gear. Walleyes feed almost exclusively on panfish, and they do it when the sun is off the water. This approach to walleye fishing can produce big fish. Bring patience and a big net.

Crappie fishing starts as early as February, but it isn't really worth the effort until March. Catches peak in April or May, which is spawning time. The crappie will be in two to eight feet of brushy water, and can be caught with inexpensive lead-head jigs with plastic twister tails. Shore-fishing off the rocks at the North Recreation Area is good at night with minnows and Coleman lanterns.

Largemouth bass are easiest to catch in April, May, and October. In the spring the bass are often on the rock shelves around the islands and along the walls of the Canadian arm. Fall fishing is best in the submerged salt cedar trees. These generalities, however, should be taken with a dose of salt. Bass at Conchas are exactly where you find them. Pig and jig combinations are arguably the best rig when weather, water, or fishing is cold. Plastic worms can always score, and topwater buzzbaits are great fun early in the day in the summertime. Crankbaits and spinners are good midday lures. Trementina Creek is a consistent favorite for catching bass in the Conchas arm, and the backside of Big Island near Campers Island is a favored spot on the Canadian arm.

You can't talk largemouth at Conchas without talking tournaments, for this reservoir is often loaded with a fleet of high-powered, metal-flake bass boats. These men and women are working against the clock, and don't have much time for mid-lake conversations. Ask your questions at the marina after the contest. Tournament fishers, both men and women, will be glad to talk you into some good bass fishing just as soon as the contest is over.

Smallmouth bass, which have been stocked here, produce plenty of action, especially along the rocky structure of the Canadian arm, but in fact, all over the lake. Smallmouth populations at Conchas have exploded, just like the crappie and walleye, and casting a Roostertail-type spinner along the rocks just up from the North Area Marina is a great way to start a day of bass fishing.

Catfish are the nighttime equalizers at Conchas Reservoir. Many people arrive late, set up camp, and simply run out of daylight fishing time. But instead of leaving the fishing until tomorrow, they rig up for channel catfish. Usually, it is bait on a No. 8 treble hook that will catch a catfish, use just enough lead (a slip sinker) to get the cast out. Summer night-fishing for channel catfish at Conchas is very good.

Bluegill are the backup fish at Conchas. Catches are good almost anytime, but especially in summer when the grasshopper populations have peaked. Children can catch the hoppers and then catch the bluegills. These little panfish are in and around almost every bit of submerged brush near the shoreline of Conchas Reservoir. Bluegill are also the prime forage fish for this lake's walleye and largemouth population.

The Fishing Year at Conchas

December: water temperature below 50°F; slow.

January: cold; nobody is fishing.

February: slow; no pressure, the water is still too cold for sportfishing.

March: improving all over for all species as water temperatures rise near 50°F, good crappie fishing at night, good walleye fishing in main channel, fish for black bass by deep-jigging close to shore in water ten to fifteen feet deep in midafternoon and deep (twenty to thirty feet) early and late; fishing grows better as the month progresses; some bad winds.

April: with water temperatures just over 50°F, this is the beginning of the best hundred days of the fishing year, good smallmouth fishing along rocky shorelines; and largemouth fishing all over on spinners, plastic worms, and pig and jigs; some bass fishing on topwater lures midday, walleye fishing good when jigging twenty to forty feet deep and also with crankbaits in eight to ten feet of water, good crappie fishing at night or jigging in submerged brush in ten feet of water; bad winds likely.

May: walleye fishing in shallow water, two to twelve feet deep; super fishing with midlake water temperatures at 55°F; good daytime crappie catches; midday topwater for bass, early and late with spinners for bass and walleye.

June: walleye fishing still good from early to midmonth trolling in five to ten feet of water, crappie catches best in the evening, topwater bass fishing still good, fishing slows near the end of month as water temperatures climb toward 70°F.

July: bass and crappie fishing more difficult, but walleye good when back-trolling in fifteen to thirty feet of water; water temperatures over 70°F; good catfish angling; summer thundershowers.

August: good catfish angling; water at 75°F; good black bass fishing on topwater early in the day; hot; thunderstorms, some good late-night walleye fishing.

September: good walleye fishing by trolling shallow water early and deeper water at midday; good bluegill fishing on grasshoppers from the shore; good black bass fishing early and late on topwater lures; water cooling; light pressure but some good fishing.

October: good bass and walleye fishing, but not easy; light pressure; good catfish angling.

November: still good fishing on warm days; very light pressure; walleye and bass fishing by jigging fifteen to thirty feet deep; catfish catching very good; water is getting too cold for good sportfishing.

The dam and dike which form Conchas Reservoir are at the confluence of the Conchas and Canadian Rivers. The lake, typical of New Mexico's eastern plains reservoirs, is long and somewhat narrow. Since the dam is at the confluence of two rivers, a "lake" runs up two arms, with one meandering north and the other heading west. Both arms total about ten thousand surface acres.

Conchas Reservoir, north of the dam, runs up what was once the Canadian River. This arm of the lake is contained by steep rock walls, with small side-canyons leading to box end arroyos. The lake here is about a half-mile wide. This channel heads generally in a northerly direction, but it takes two, three-mile-long S-curves before opening up into a giant mudflat where the Canadian River enters. José María Canyon, Spring Canyon, Big Island, Campers Island, Perro Arm, and Cedar Point are the important landmarks on the Canadian arm of Conchas Reservoir. It's about eleven miles from the dam to the upper end of the Canadian arm.

West of the dam, Conchas Reservoir runs up the old Conchas riverbed. The reservoir here is about a mile wide, twice that of the Canadian arm, and much of the shoreline is made of gently sloping banks leading down to acres of shallow water. Rattlesnake and Green Island, Cuervo Creek inlet, Conchas River inlet, and Trementina Creek inlet are the important landmarks. This Conchas arm is about six miles long from the dam to the Conchas River inlet.

An excellent boater's map is published by the U.S. Army Corps of Engineers and is available at the project office located at the north end of the dam. Get one of these maps and study it. This lake has more rock and tree hazards than a desert golf course. Both marinas have fishing maps available.

The eastern plains of New Mexico are home to some dangerous springtime windstorms and gigantic summer thunderstorms. Small craft warnings are normal spring happenings at Conchas. Stay aware of changes in wind direction. New Mexico state parks personnel have installed two towers with wind-warning systems. These little wind generators flash an amber light in winds from 15 to 25 mph, and they flash a red light in winds over 25 mph; one is located at the dam, and the other near the cafe at the North Recreation Area. Small-craft owners are advised to know the limitations of both their equipment and their experience.

Boaters should check in at either the marina or the tackle shops for the latest fishing information. General information can be gleaned from the weekly fishing reports in the Albuquerque newspapers as well as from the recorded fishing reports prepared by the Department of Game and Fish. State park personnel often have up-to-the-minute fishing information. Check these sources before launching your boat and you'll have a good start on a fine day's fishing.

There are two improved recreation areas at Conchas, one on each side of the long dam. A third unimproved area is located on the lake side of the dam. These areas comprise Conchas Lake State Park. The Army Corps of Engineers operates a little oasis and overlook area at the northern end of the dam. All the rest of the land around Conchas Lake is private property, with no access and no trespassing unless you have prior permission.

The North Recreation Area is located north of the dam and includes picnic and fee-camping areas, a mobile-home park, restrooms, cafe, a convenience and tackle store, a marina with gas and boat slips, a bait shop, drinking water, and boat ramps. The Central Recreation Area is on a shelf of land on the lake side of the dam, and except for outhouses, this is an unimproved area for camping or day use. The South Recreation Area is complete with motel, marina, paved airstrip, restaurant, golf course, bait-and-tackle shop, boat ramps, fee-camping and picnic areas, recreational vehicle dump station, and drinking water.

Shore-fishing at the Central Area is in shallow water with much submerged brush and a gently sloping shoreline. The North Area shoreline is comprised of rocky cliffs rising from five to twenty feet above the water. The South Area has a shallow sloping shoreline. One can also hike along the riprap of the dam and enjoy some excellent fishing, especially in May.

Conchas Lake State Park is located in east-central New Mexico, twenty-five miles north of I–40 from the Newkirk exit on S.R. 129 or thirty-one miles northeast of Tucumcari on S.R. 104. From Las Vegas and I–25, take S.R. 104 and S.R. 65 west for seventy-five miles to Conchas Reservoir.

UTE LAKE

Ute Lake is an exceptional recreation reservoir near the Texas border, twenty miles northeast of Tucumcari, New Mexico. An eleven-pound largemouth, the old state record, was caught at Ute. A six-pound, nine-ounce smallmouth bass, also a state record, came out of Ute Lake. This reservoir is also one of New Mexico's best walleye lakes. Add the white bass (the locals often call them "sand bass"), the crappie and bluegill, and the big channel cats—and Ute Lake amounts to one of our best warmwater fisheries.

Stable water levels make this a unique reservoir. Most reservoirs in the dry Southwest are built solely for downstream irrigation needs, but Ute Dam was built primarily for recreational uses; and steady water levels give Ute a solid, dependable fishery. The original dam, completed in 1963, created about four thousand surface acres of reservoir; but in 1985 the spillway was raised an additional twenty-seven feet, and runoff from Ute's tributaries, Ute Creek and the Canadian River, built Ute's surface acreage to the eight thousand mark.

Ute Lake is the center for a full-service recreation community. There are five boat ramps, a full-service marina, tackle-and-bait shops, restaurants, recreational vehicle parks, swimming areas, vacation homes, boat-storage lots, motels, grocery stores, vacation homes, and a big state park with both improved and unimproved camping areas. Most of the roads are paved, and even the gravel roads are safe for passenger cars.

Winter fishing at Ute Lake is a quiet affair. The vacation crowd is long gone and the sportfish are hiding out, waiting for warmer weather. Although the lake rarely freezes, January anglers are few and far between, but hunters are attracted by the waterfowl, hundreds of duck and geese flying twice each day between the local grainfields and Ute Lake. The fishermen, however, wait for spring.

April and May are the top months to fish for crappie and big bass at Ute Lake. There are some good walleye catches in March, but the warmth of April really turns on the bass fishing. June is a changeover month: the vacation season has started and boats now pepper the lake, white bass angling is good, and fishing from shore with minnows is decent, even at midday.

Summer's high temperatures and hot sun end the easy fishing at Ute Lake. July and August are identified by the white plumes of the water skiers. Dozens of Texas and Oklahoma license plates prove the popularity of this recreation reservoir. The place does get crowded, especially around the developed boat ramps.

There is still plenty of good fishing on those hot summer afternoons. In quiet canyons, bass anglers will be flipping plastic worms on the shady side of submerged brush. Fishermen after walleye will be watching their rod tips as Lindy rigs tipped with nightcrawlers bounce across the bottom, and white bass fanatics will be jigging flashy lures off rocky points in fifteen to twenty-five feet of water. The shorebound angler can use grasshoppers and go after bluegills close to the bank.

The walleye, white, and black bass all move closer to the surface after the summer sun starts to set. Spinners, like the Mepps or Panther Martin, are a good bet for walleye. Spinner baits or crankbaits work well for bass, especially in chartreuse. And if you find a bunch of white bass smashing a school of minnows, cast out a noisy topwater lure.

The boatless summer angler should fish Ute early and late, when the sun is off the water. Mornings, starting before the sun is up, is best. The dawn fisherman has a chance to catch walleye, white or black bass, or crappie—all before the water-skiers have had breakfast. Nightcrawlers or minnows are favorite baits. Buy your minnows the night before and keep them fresh in a ventilated bait bucket kept in the lake near the shore.

In autumn the sportfish cruise in shallower water, and fishing is excellent from September until mid-November. The white bass and walleye will be nearer the surface and easier to catch during midday; the black bass hit topwater buzzbaits. The spring winds are only a memory and the summer crowd is long gone. Try the submerged riprap along the dam for fall fishing, whether from a boat or from shore. Use plastic worms or lead-head hooks with plastic minnow imitations.

Ute Lake offers complete facilities for the visiting angler. Coming up S.R. 54 from Tucumcari, past mile marker 317, you can turn west on a paved road leading to the undeveloped Mine Canyon Area. There's a gravel boat ramp at the end of the pavement. This is a no-fee camping area. Shore-fishing is possible if you don't mind a short walk down the steep hillsides.

If you drive past the Mine Canyon turnoff and take the next paved road west, S.R. 552, you end up at the south end of the dam at the the South Area of Ute Lake State Park. The gravel road is okay even in a heavy rain, and leads to a concrete boat ramp and an unimproved, no-fee camping area. There's good access for shore-fishing, and this is the place to go for fishing off the dam face. You can also park and walk down to fish in the Canadian River below the dam. The river is rarely fished, but it offers an occasional surprise to the angler willing to cast where few bother to go.

If you pass up the unimproved areas on the south side of Ute Lake and stay on S.R. 54 you go over the Canadian River and into the town of Logan, New Mexico. Gas stations, convenience stores, motels, and liquor stores beg for your presence. A sign in the middle of town points the way west to Ute Lake. The road leads through town and then on to the North Area entrance, headquarters for Ute Lake State Park. Bathrooms, showers, an excellent boat ramp, boat-trailer parking, and improved fee-camping areas highlight the North Area facilities. The headquarters office is the information center for Ute Lake State Park. Pierce's Boatel and the Original Minnow Bait and Tackle Shop are right across the street. This is a busy place during vacation season.

If you continue past the headquarters' turnoff, the paved road leads along the north shore of Ute Lake. Side-roads lead past vacation homes and down to the shore. The paved road continues west and then makes a sharp turn north. There's an improved fee-area campground just past the turn. Bank-fishing here is difficult, for the lake is down a sheer cliff. A motel and a recreational vehicle park are located just north of the state park campground. Farther up the paved road is the Logan Park Marina, a private, full-service facility and a good place to get boating and fishing information about all of Ute Lake.

Just north of the marina is another state park fee-area with an excellent boat ramp, paved parking, swimming, bank-fishing, and camping facilities. This is another busy place during the vacation season, with good bank-fishing access.

The road then turns to gravel and leads to the unimproved fee-camping in the Rogers Park Area, the northernmost state park facility on Ute Lake. There is no boat ramp, but the Rogers Area offers good access for the bankside angler.

Fishing Ute Lake

Fishing for catfish is almost always good at Ute Lake. Early mornings are best, with the cats cruising shallow water and looking for breakfast before the noisy boat activity starts. Cast to deeper water after 9:00 A.M., then switch to shallow water once the sun goes down. Springtime is excellent for catfishing, but catches are good throughout the year. Chicken livers are definitely the favored daytime bait. Small bluegills are a good natural bait for night-fishing. Catfish go on a strong feed whenever water is entering Ute Lake, but you must get past Horseshoe Bend or go up the Ute Creek arm to take advantage of the concentrated feeding.

Each spring, during the last of March and the beginning of April, the New Mexico Department of Game and Fish is out in force at Ute Lake. Near the dam, they launch a netting operation to collect spawning walleye. Eggs and milt are mixed on the spot, then rushed to Rock Lake Hatchery, where the fertilized eggs soon hatch into millions of walleye fry. The fry are kept until they've grown out of their yolk sack; then they are stocked in waters throughout the state. Extra walleye fry are traded for other species from neighboring states. Ute Lake's first white bass fingerlings came from such a trade. Each summer, Ute Lake gets back millions of healthy little walleye fry. Good water conditions and good management are the reasons why Ute Lake is such a good walleye fishery.

Walleye can be caught during the spring spawning run. They are in shallow and fairly clear water; on a gravel bar, along a rocky point, or along the shoreline. Fish where the wind blows into the shore. The wind forms the wave action that keys the walleyes' spawning instinct, and the rolling water mixes their milt and eggs.

The best overall walleye catches are made in April and May. Cloudy days are best for shallow-water plugging, use crankbaits or spinners that imitate three-inch bluegills. Summer walleye catches are made in deeper water, specifically off rocky points. Use rigs like the Lindy, which get a worm-tipped hook right down on the bottom. The riprap along the dam is a good place to fish for walleye anytime during the year, and the damface is accessible to the shoreline angler by driving the paved road to the South Area. Fishing for trophy-size walleye is best on a quiet summer night, after 9:00 P.M. Fish very silently with a seven-inch Rapala-type lure. Make sure your spinning reel is loaded with new line, tie your knots carefully, and cast where shallow water meets deep.

Tournament fishing at Ute Lake has proven the strength, size, and population of this lake's largemouth bass. A state record largemouth came from this lake, and the experienced bass caster can figure on a half-dozen two- to three-pound fish in a good day's fishing.

Stable water levels have promoted the growth of reeds in Ute lake, and flipping plastic bass baits is a very productive technique. You may hook into a walleye or two, but that just proves the effectiveness of fishing in the bullrushes. Casting noisy topwater lures, like buzzbaits, is another good technique for bass fishing in the reeds. In the middle of a hot summer day, however, you need to move off the reeds and fish the shady side of submerged brush; or try a plastic worm next to the floating muck found in the back of a canyon. Bass, just like people, can be found in shaded areas during hot sunny days. If the bullrushes aren't producing, then find some deep, shaded structure.

Panther Martin or Roostertail-type spinnerbaits are very effective for school bass. These yearling largemouth are great fun to hook on light spinning tackle. Concentrate your effort along the shorelines, casting to water not over eight feet deep. Early summer and midfall is the most productive time for this type of percentage fishing. Choose a spinner with bucktail over the rear treble hooks; the seductive wobble of the squirrel hair seems to attract solid strikes.

Largemouth bass hooked by tournament fishers are released to grow and to be caught again. Catch-and-release fishing assures all anglers of a chance at a trophy bigmouth. The recreation angler should feel no guilt in keeping a dinner's worth of fat largemouth; but release the big ones, an act that will help bring a smile to next week's Ute Lake fishermen. In 1987 special largemouth bass regulations were imposed on Ute Lake to improve management of the bass and the fishermen. Bass less than fourteen inches long must be returned to the water. Check the current fishing proclamation for the latest regulations.

Bluegills are the saving grace for the shorebound angler. These little sunfish are a valuable part of the food chain at Ute Lake, and their habit of living near the shore makes them great sport for anglers without boats. Worms are the favored bait, but grasshoppers produce better catches. A fly-rod will present hopper flies effectively, and the rod's light action puts a bit of sport in the landing of these hand-size creatures. Bluegills will be found next to submerged vegetation and close to shore.

Smallmouth bass in Ute Lake are usually incidental catches. Bronzebacks were last stocked in 1982. Ute can produce big smallmouth bass; the state record of six pounds, nine ounces was caught here in 1972 on a crankbait. If you are after smallmouth, look for big rocks in five to ten feet of clear water. Bait fishermen should try waterdogs fished early in the morning. Spin fishermen should try lures that imitate shad or baby bluegill. Big fish eat little fish; that is the key to catching any trophy fish, including smallmouth bass.

The white bass in Ute Lake go through a cycle. Good, bad, and average years depend on spawning success and food supply. Whites travel in schools; catch one and you can usually hook into a half-dozen. During midday the whites are in fifteen to twenty-five feet of water. Jigging is the way to catch their attention; use a silver lure that flutters as it drops, or try a lead-head jig with a plastic shad hiding the hook. When you see a number of fish busting the surface of Ute Lake, they are usually whites feeding on shad. Cast a noisy black-over-white surface lure through the middle of the action. An old plug with a propeller on its nose is another great lure when the white bass are hitting on top. Some people crimp down the barbs on the treble hooks. Surface action doesn't last very long, and with the help of a pair of needle-nose pliers, they can quickly remove the barbless hooks from the bass and get out another cast. White bass make great eating, and keeping them does not hurt the population. Great, average, or poor white bass fishing depends on both spawning success and their food supply, not on fishing pressure.

The Logan Park Marina, the bait-and-tackle shops, and Pierce's Boatel are the places to stop for a free map of Ute Lake and an earful of the latest fishing information. Consistent locations for good fishing include the bay between the North Area State Park and the dam, the deep water between the North Area boat ramp and Cedar Point, and the shoreline east from Brushy Cove.

The new and higher water levels have turned Ute Lake's expert fishermen into novices. Familiar and productive shallow areas are now under thirty feet of water, and thousands of dry shoreline acres are now productive shallows; but the experienced anglers are excited about the potential of this warmwater fishery. The new higher water levels have doubled the surface acreage, which should turn an already great Ute Lake into one of New Mexico's best walleye, bass, and catfish lakes.

CHAPTER NINE

Sacramento Mountains

SACRAMENTO MOUNTAIN OVERVIEW

Centered around the Sacramento Mountain resort town of Ruidoso, the Lincoln National Forest and the Mescalero Apache lands offer good fishing for the vacation-time angler. There are high-country trout lakes, little brook trout creeks, and two good rainbow and brown trout streams. Use a Lincoln National Forest map, available from most U.S. Forest Service offices, to plan a fishing trip in this south-central part of New Mexico. A wildlife habitat improvement stamp is required for all fishermen, trappers, and hunters in the Lincoln National Forest. The fees collected from this stamp are used for habitat improvement in this national forest. Get your stamp at a Departmet of Game and Fish office, or find out if your favorite tackle shop sells the stamps.

BONITO LAKE AND CREEK

Bonito Lake, actually a reservoir, offers the best public fishing in the Ruidoso area. Bonito Creek was dammed to form a municipal water supply reservoir for the desert city of Alamogordo. New Mexico's Department of Game and Fish annually stocks Bonito with thousands of catchable-size and fingerling rainbow trout. This sixty-acre lake also holds a good population of wild brook trout as well as a few bass and carp. Bonito is open for fishing from April 1 to the end of November, from 6:00 A.M. to 10:00 P.M. Don't bring a boat to this lake, for no boats or floating devices are allowed.

Spring is one of the best times to catch rainbow and brook trout in Bonito. In April, right after the lake is open for fishing, both the brook trout and the rainbows will be cruising the edges. Lures, bait, and flies are all effective during April and May, especially in the main arm where Bonito Creek enters the lake. On these cold and quiet springtime afternoons, the only other fishers on the lake will be a pair of osprey and an eagle or two.

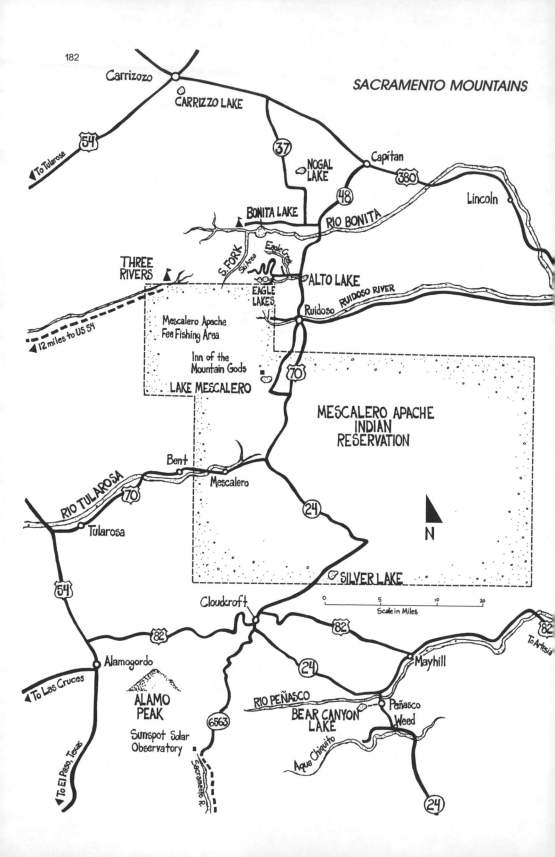

SACRAMENTO MOUNTAINS

Carrizozo
CARRIZZO LAKE
To Tularosa
54
37
NOGAL LAKE
Capitan
380
48
Lincoln
BONITA LAKE
RIO BONITA
S. FORK
Eagle C.
THREE RIVERS
ALTO LAKE
EAGLE LAKES
Ruidoso
RUIDOSO RIVER
12 miles to US 54
Mescalero Apache Fee Fishing Area
Inn of the Mountain Gods
70
LAKE MESCALERO
MESCALERO APACHE INDIAN RESERVATION
Bent
RIO TULAROSA
70
Mescalero
24
N
Tularosa
54
SILVER LAKE
Cloudcroft
Scale in Miles
0   5   10   20
82
82
82
To Artesia
Alamogordo
24
Mayhill
To Las Cruces
ALAMO PEAK
RIO PEÑASCO
BEAR CANYON LAKE
Peñasco
Weed
6563
Sunspot Solar Observatory
To El Paso, Texas
Sacramento R.
Agua Chiquito
24

Bonito Lake and Creek

Bonito is a beautiful mountain valley lake near Ruidoso. No boats are allowed.

Each year, they hunt Bonito's trout until warmer weather and crowds force them north.

Summer shuts down the easy fishing at Bonito, and it becomes difficult to find the depth and location where the trout are holding. The two shallow inlet bays are always popular, but summer catches are better in the water just off the shallows. Most of the lake has a steep shoreline, with the water dropping quickly to its fifty-foot maximum depth. Because boats are not allowed, you must work along the shoreline if you want to cover as much of the lake as possible. The trout rise to a midge hatch each morning and evening in the two inlet arms, offering good fishing for those casting a fly.

Be prepared to join the crowd if you're headed to Bonito Lake in the summer. During the vacation season, the campgrounds are crowded on Thursday night and often completely full by early Friday evening. The city of Alamogordo operates campgrounds (for a fee) on the two small inlet creeks at the northern end of the lake. The city and the U.S. Forest Service each operate separate and improved (fee) campgrounds one mile west of the Bonito Creek inlet. All campgrounds are reached on paved roads, but only the forest service area has paved roads inside its campground.

September, October, and November bring colder weather and better fishing to Bonito. Lures and big flies are very effective as the brook trout and rainbow trout go on a fall feeding spree. The main inlet arm is the favorite spot to cast for these autumn trout.

The North and South forks of Bonito Creek meet a mile west of the lake near the two improved campgrounds. Both offer late-spring fishing for stocked rainbows and a chance at fooling the wild brook trout. A special place to bring the kids is the Blue Hole, a spring-fed sinkhole that feeds the South Fork near the campgrounds; this thirty-by-sixty-foot pool is a good spot for watching wild trout. These clear waters hold many little brookies, and a small baited hook or small flies will fool these clearwater trout.

A dirt road parallels the North Fork above the fee campgrounds, and no-fee camping is allowed along its shoreline. Recent floods wiped out the character of this little creek, and it will take many years for the stream to recover from these hundred-year flood events. Summer conditions produce a dry and rocky creek bed, with water flowing under the rocks. Farther up in the high country, both creeks offer wilderness fishing for small wild trout. Bonito Creek below the dam is stocked with rainbows during the spring runoff, but it often dries up by late June. In above-average-water years, the creek holds a sizable population of brook trout.

While fishing the Bonito Creek inlet arm of Bonito Lake, you may see a number of good-size fish rolling and boiling on the surface. Nearby anglers will close in, casting bait, lures, or flies. Eventually someone will snag one of these carp, thus dispersing the anglers back to their quest for trout.

Bonito Lake is located about fourteen miles north of Ruidoso, off N.M. 37. Take the well-marked S.R. 107 turnoff; the lake is less than five miles from the turnoff. Handicapped access is almost impossible at Bonito Lake.

MESCALERO APACHE INDIAN RESERVATION

On reservation land in the Ruidoso area, the Mescalero Apache have developed four lakes and the upper Ruidoso River into good trout fisheries. These waters are stocked with trout from the Mescalero Federal Trout Hatchery. Since this is fee-fishing on reservation lands, a New Mexico fishing license is not required. The use of minnows as bait is illegal on all Mescalero waters.

Mescalero Apache Indian Reservation

Looking toward the dam from the north end of Bonito Lake. During the peak summer months, Bonito is frequently crowded.

Upper Ruidoso River

By driving up the Upper Canyon Road from the middle of Ruidoso, you can follow the Ruidoso River upstream for three miles to Mescalero Reservation lands. Purchase a permit at the reservation boundary and you can fish this small stream for catchable rainbows. No camping is allowed. This is a productive area for upstream casting with light spinning tackle tipped with salmon eggs, small spinners, or a weighted fly. The river splits into three forks, and if you want to walk a bit, the North Fork is the one to follow.

Eagle Lakes

Camping and good trout fishing in a wilderness setting are found at Eagle lakes. This area is on Mescalero Apache land and access is from a paved road (S.R. 532) a mile off the Ski Apache highway. Buy your fishing and

Mescalero Apache Indian Reservation

A little-known set of trout ponds, Eagle Lakes are on the Mescalero Indian lands near Ruidoso on the road to Ski Apache. Tribal fishing and camping permits are available on site. Eagle Lakes offer great fly-fishing for stocked rainbow trout.

camping permits at the guardhouse by Upper Eagle Lake. The lower lake is a ten-minute walk from the guardhouse and is a bit smaller than the Upper Eagle. Summer fishing is excellent with a fly-rod, and small lures are effective. These are small, one- to two-acre lakes fed by a tiny coldwater creek. Recreational vehicle hookups are available, and handicapped access is good. No boats or floating devices are allowed.

Silver Lake

Located on the highway between Cloudcroft and Ruidoso, Silver Lake is an exceptionally clear six-acre lake stocked with rainbow trout. Purchase a fishing and camping permit at the guardhouse and try your luck in this crystalline lake. Summer daytime fishing is best with a fly-rod, but lures and bait are effective during mornings and evenings when the bright sunshine is off the water. Aquatic vegetation is lush in this crystal-colored lake, and bait fishermen will do best with a bobber. The dam offers a chance to cast to deeper water or to try bait-fishing on the bottom. Silver Lake is a well-known trout pond right off the highway (N.M. 24), and both lake and campground get crowded on summer weekends. No boats or floating devices are allowed, and access is good for the handicapped fisherman.

Mescalero Lake

Mescalero Lake is the large reservoir at the Inn of the Mountain Gods. One need not be a guest at the inn to fish this hundred-acre lake. Just drive in and find your way to the boat dock, purchase a fishing permit, and start fishing. You cannot bring your own boat, but rentals are available. Consider bringing your own electric trolling motor. The lake is stocked with about twenty-five thousand cutthroat and rainbow trout each year, and there is a small population of wild brown trout. The food supply is excellent, and this lake supports a good population of minnows and insects. Fly fishermen do well anytime on Mescalero Lake. Lures are effective in the morning and the evening, while the bait fisherman has good luck in catching smaller trout from the shore. The golf course, which borders part of the lake, is an area off-limits to the fisherman. There are some very big trout in this lake, and evening fishing—casting lures from a boat (not trolling)—is the way to connect. Handicapped access is available. Mescalero Lake rarely freezes and is open year round.

RUIDOSO RIVER

The Ruidoso River, downstream from the Mescalero Apache Reservation boundary, is open for public fishing. Access is off Upper Canyon Road, which follows the river downstream to downtown Ruidoso. In the upper reaches the little river flows through a residential area, and in the city proper it runs behind the main street (Sudderth Drive). The Ruidoso is stocked with catchable-size rainbow trout and brown trout fry from about a quarter-mile below the Mescalero boundary downstream to the Ruidoso Middle School. The rainbows are stocked at four or five places where there is road access for the stocking truck.

Ruidoso means "noisy," and the stream is a roaring river in April and May. By early June the river is very fishable. There are very few quiet pools for the sit-down bait fisherman, but if you work your way upstream and cast

Ruidoso River

A small brook trout from Nogal Lake.

a small lure, weighted nymph, or a salmon egg you will catch trout. Grass-hoppers are the favored summertime bait. The Ruidoso River downstream from the Middle School is on private property and is not stocked.

ALTO LAKE

Alto Lake is located right off the highway (S.R. 37), two and a half miles north of Ruidoso in the little village of Alto. This is a municipal water-supply reservoir stocked every summer with thousands of catchable-size rainbow trout. Parking is available just off the highway. Eagle Creek feeds Alto Lake, and if you follow the highway (S.R. 532) toward Ski Apache you are following Eagle Creek. Forest Road 127 follows the main fork of Eagle Creek, a tiny creek with some brook trout fishing. The South Fork of Eagle Creek comes off Eagle lakes (see the section on the Mescalero Apache Indian Reservation).

NOGAL LAKE

Nogal Lake is located off S.R. 37, twelve miles north of Ruidoso. The turnoff (F.R. 105) is marked; you drive north on this gravel road for a mile. Nogal has an undependable water supply, and although it is no longer stocked with catchable-size rainbow trout, it is stocked with brook trout. In years of average to above-average rainfall, the lake has good fishing for small brookies.

CARRIZOZO LAKE

The town of Carrizozo, on the dry plains north of the Sacramento Mountains, has a small municipal trout pond located just north of town. Carrizozo Lake is stocked in the winter with rainbow trout.

THREE RIVERS

On the western side of the Sacramentos, at the edge of the White Mountain Wilderness, is a Lincoln National Forest campground called Three Rivers. Access is on a gravel road (F.R. 579) east from U.S. 54 between Alamogordo and Carrizozo. You drive past the Three Rivers Petroglyph National Recreation Site and continue twelve miles northeast to the campground. There is some fishing for small wild trout if you walk up this tiny stream.

TULAROSA RIVER

The Tularosa River is a fairly large stream draining the western side of the Sacramento Mountains. Because it is on Mescalero lands, there is no public fishing on the headwaters. But once west of the reservation boundary, the Tularosa is stocked with brown trout fry and catchable-size rainbow trout. The best fishing is from the reservation southwest to Round Mountain—about five miles of good cold water. Access is from the U.S. 70 bridge over the Tularosa and from gravel roads in the quiet town of Bent. The Tularosa is rarely fished, but there are some good-size brown trout in the deeper runs.

SACRAMENTO RIVER

About a dozen miles south of Cloudcroft on S.R. 64 you will find the marked turnoff to the Sacramento River. The access road is F.R. 537 and the turnoff is just before the Sacramento Peak (Sunspot) Solar Observatory. A few miles downstream the forest service built a small dam across the Sacramento River, and the resulting two-acre reservoir (it is only a few feet

Sacramento River

deep) was stocked with brook trout. This is a beautiful little stream and pond for those who don't mind fishing where an eleven-inch trout is considered a trophy.

RIO PEÑASCO, AGUA CHIQUITO, AND BEAR CANYON LAKE

Southeast of Cloudcroft on S.R. 24 is the Rio Peñasco, the small Agua Chiquito Creek, and Bear Canyon Lake. The Rio Peñasco and the Agua Chiquito both run mainly through private property, but the Peñasco is stocked with catchable-size rainbows (and brown trout fry) throughout the summer, and is open to public fishing at a number of spots upstream and downstream from Mayhill. The public area on the downstream end is the quarter-mile up and down from the county line between Otero and Chaves counties. Another good spot is from Mayhill upstream to the recreational vehicle camp. The Agua Chiquito is a small brook trout creek with public fishing on forest service land southwest of Weed and Sacramento on F.R. 64. Bear Canyon is a small winter-stocked trout pond five miles southwest of Mayhill near the village of Peñasco. Access is on two miles of decent gravel road (F.R. 621). Bear Canyon is also loaded with bluegills—great fun for the kids.

The Gila Watershed

GILA COUNTRY OVERVIEW

In Gila country, you can take a summer fishing trip along a trout stream littered with bear scat instead of trash. On a warm day in January, you can lake fish for rainbow trout fresh out of Glenwood Hatchery. On a midnight summer fishing expedition you can hunt big flathead catfish in the pools of a moonlit desert river. Or consider an autumn hike up a wilderness stream, with a smallmouth bass on almost every cast. It all happens in the Gila country of southwestern New Mexico.

The headwaters of the Gila River get their start under the snow and Englemann spruce of the high country. Tiny creeks loaded with little trout form the three forks of the Gila River, mountain streams that are home to beaver and marked with footprints of elk and wild turkey. Some of the headwater creeks hold naturally reproducing populations of the rare Gila trout. These little waters form the East, Middle, and West forks of the Gila River.

Sixty miles southwest and five thousand feet lower, the Gila River leaves New Mexico and enters Arizona. The river canyon is a green meander through the dry desert of southwestern New Mexico. Roadrunners and lizards ply the shoreline. Cottonwoods shade the big pools. Hiding in the deep runs are flathead catfish large enough to eat T-bone steaks.

Between these two extremes, in and around the Gila National Forest, the fisherman finds catfish, bass, trout, and the Gila Wilderness Area. In 1924, Aldo Leopold, one of the prime movers of our nation's conservation ethic, convinced Congress to designate 750,000 acres of the Gila National Forest as our nation's first Wilderness Area. That meant no roads, no timber sales, no improved recreation areas, limited cattle grazing, no dams, and some great fishing. The Gila River is the last undammed wild fishing river in New Mexico; and it starts in our nation's first official Wilderness Area.

The three main tributaries of the Gila—the East, Middle, and West

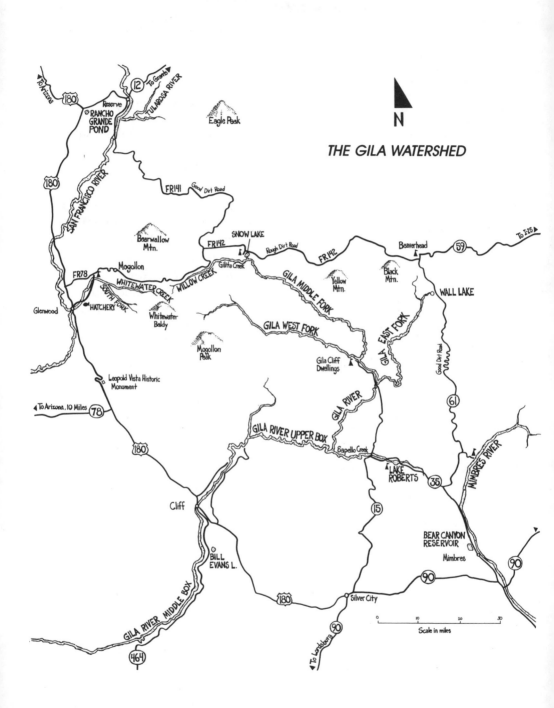

N

THE GILA WATERSHED

To Arizona
180
12 To Grants
TULAROSA RIVER
Reserve
RANCHO GRANDE POND
Eagle Peak
180
SAN FRANCISCO RIVER
FR141
Good Dirt Road
Bearwallow Mtn.
SNOW LAKE
FR142
Rough Dirt Road
FR142
Beaverhead
59
To I-25
Mogollon
Gilita Creek
GILA MIDDLE FORK
Yellow Mtn.
Black Mtn.
FR78
WHITEWATER CREEK
WILLOW CREEK
SOUTH FORK
WALL LAKE
Glenwood
HATCHERY
Whitewater Baldy
GILA WEST FORK
GILA EAST FORK
Good Dirt Road
Mogollon Peak
Gila Cliff Dwellings
61
Leopold Vista Historic Monument
GILA RIVER
To Arizona, 10 Miles
78
GILA RIVER UPPER BOX
Sapello Creek
MIMBRES RIVER
180
LAKE ROBERTS
35
Cliff
15
BEAR CANYON RESERVOIR
BILL EVANS L.
Mimbres
90
90
GILA RIVER MIDDLE BOX
180
Silver City
0   10   20   30
Scale in miles
464
90
To Lordsburg

Gila Country

The Gila Wilderness encompasses 1,000 square miles and protects the headwaters of the three forks of the Gila River.

forks—all begin inside the Wilderness Area. Though these are mostly trout waters, smallmouth bass have taken a strong hold in the Gila Watershed. The East Fork, especially, has some very good smallmouth fishing. To form the Gila River, these mountain streams meet at the village of Gila Hot Springs, near the Gila Cliff Dwellings National Monument. Rainbow trout are stocked near the many campgrounds. As the Gila leaves the Monument Area, it turns west and picks up the characteristics of a desert river.

Downstream from Gila Hot Springs the Gila River has carved the Upper Box. This thousand-foot canyon contains miles and miles of horseshoe bends. The river runs through a rough, rocky, and dry desert countryside, but sportfish are plentiful. Brown trout, a few rainbows, many smallmouth bass, and plenty of channel catfish live in these rarely fished waters.

As you move downstream the warmer water loses its appeal to trout, though rainbows are stocked where the Gila goes under U.S. 180. Even further downstream the smallmouth bass disappear. West of U.S. 180 the Gila flows into the Middle Box, which is untamed desert country. Near

Red Rock it enters the Lower Box and exits into Arizona. The flathead catfish keep getting bigger as you get closer to Arizona.

SAN FRANCISCO RIVER WATERSHED

The San Francisco River heads in Arizona, flows east into New Mexico along U.S. 180 and then goes through Reserve. The river heads south for fifty miles, turns west, and travels back into Arizona to join the Gila River. The only easy sportfishing on the San Francisco River is in the state of Arizona at Luna Lake, just over the border and twenty-five miles west of Reserve. Although a few Arizona rainbow trout do escape downstream to live in the wild canyon of the San Francisco, the San Francisco is not a river to plan your vacation around.

Access is off U.S. 180, either from the town of Luna or upstream from Reserve. Look up Trout Creek (north and east of Luna) on the Gila National Forest map for directions to a tiny creek with some good rainbow trout fishing. Downstream from Reserve the San Francisco offers good angling for catfish. Access is easiest just south of Glenwood at the San Francisco Hot Springs.

NEGRITO CREEK AND RANCHO GRANDE POND

Negrito Creek is a little spring-fed tributary to the San Francisco just east of Reserve. Negrito holds some of the best small-stream trout fishing in the entire Gila Watershed, especially in its midsection. This is walk-in fishing for wild trout; use the Gila National Forest map for road and trail information.

Rancho Grande Pond is a little two-acre public fishing spot near the intersection of U.S. 180 and S.R. 12. The little ponds are on private land, hidden behind a motel and restaurant, six miles west of Reserve. The ponds are open to public fishing; please help keep it that way by picking up the litter. This is a good spot for a cup of coffee while the kids drown some worms. Trout are stocked in winter, and there is a good resident population of sunfish.

WHITEWATER CREEK, GLENWOOD HATCHERY, AND THE CATWALK

The small town of Glenwood is a busy place in the summer. Glenwood is an oasis for the traveler on U.S. 180. Whitewater Creek runs through the middle of town and after a drive through the dry countryside, the flowers, running water, and restaurants do stop the traffic. Glenwood Hatchery is about two hundred yards west of main street (U.S. 180), right on Whitewater Creek. Catchable-size rainbow trout are stocked in a fishing pond at Glenwood Hatchery, but aquatic vegetation and the hot summer sun make the water chemistry unfit for good daytime fishing. A different kind of angling starts five miles upstream, at the Catwalk.

In the narrows of Whitewater Canyon, a steel catwalk, originally part of a mining operation, has been rebuilt and is maintained by the forest service. This is an enjoyable place to visit and the starting point for some good fishing for small trout. The road, which goes past the hatchery (F.R. 95), deadends at this National Forest Recreation Area, known as the Catwalk. Forest Road 95, which changes to maintained gravel and crosses the creek twice before ending at the Catwalk, is normally driveable in the family car.

Whitewater Creek enters a steep-sided canyon at the end of F.R. 95, five miles east of Glenwood Hatchery. The U.S. Forest Service maintains a trail and a day-use area (no camping allowed) with drinking water, picnic tables, and outhouses all under big shade trees. Watch out for the beehive in the hollow tree near the last outhouse.

Whitewater Creek is not stocked and the fishing is mostly for wild rainbows and a few brookies. A ten-inch brook would be a trophy catch. The angling starts as you hike and wade upstream from the developed day-use area. Pools and shaded runs make good trout habitat in this canyon oasis. It's about a two-mile hike (or wade) up to the Gila Wilderness Boundary. A little tributary, the South Fork, comes in just before the boundary. Few fishermen will hike or fish this far from a parking lot. Since this is a little stream with wild brook trout, use light tackle and a quiet approach.

Whitewater Creek heads in the Mogollon Mountains, to the east of U.S. 180. There are other smaller creeks that come down from these hills, and some of them, like Big Dry Creek, contain Gila trout. Big Dry is closed to fishing at its headwaters to protect the Gila trout. Like most of the little creeks in the Gila Wilderness Area, the only way you can get there is by driving on a rough road and then riding on horseback or traveling on your own two feet. Except during heavy rain or runoff, water from Big Dry Creek rarely gets down the rocky arroyo to U.S. 180. A rare endangered trout in its headwaters; fair to good fishing for rainbows and browns in the middle section, and little water at all in its downstream canyon—that's what you can expect at Big Dry Creek.

THE MIDDLE BOX OF THE GILA RIVER

Head for the deep quiet pools that punctuate the Middle Box of the Gila and you'll find some big flathead catfish. Except for the spring runoff, the fishing in this tough desert river is good anytime you can get there. Access is easiest off U.S. 180 just south of Cliff. Take the turnoff toward Bill Evans Lake (F.R. 809) and stay on F.R. 809, but don't climb the hill to the lake. The paved road follows the river past a few ranch houses, and in a few miles you are on a gravel road in the Burro Mountain Section of the Gila National Forest. The road parallels the river, and at St. Peters Rock (use a Gila National Forest map) the canyon walls close in and mark your entrance into the Middle Box.

You can also get there by driving up from Lordsburg on lonely S.R. 464, which ends at the village of Redrock. This is the lower end of the Middle Box. Cross the river at Redrock and go upstream, through the Department of Game and Fish Redrock Wildlife Area.

Use stout fishing tackle if you intend to land a big catfish; the channel cats run to seven pounds, but the flatheads get big enough to require huge (3/0) hooks and seventeen-pound test line. Tie your rod to a tree if you intend to take a nap.

Except to the canoe adventurist and the desert rat, the Lower Gila River from Redrock downstream to Arizona is inaccessible. This incredible country demands something approaching an expedition mentality. The catfish are plentiful, but you may see a gila monster or scare a rattlesnake. Although the scenery is incredible, the rough terrain keeps most anglers away.

BILL EVANS LAKE

Bill Evans Lake is a clearwater fishery near Cliff that is three hundred feet higher than the river feeding it. Its water is pumped up a steep hill from the Gila River and then drawn off and piped to the Phelps Dodge Tyrone Mining plant. Such a continuous exchange of water means good fishing for largemouth, crappie, bluegill, catfish, and winter-stocked trout. The lake has a surface of sixty acres, and the gravel access road goes around two-thirds of the shoreline. The Department of Game and Fish obtained a perpetual fishing easement to the lake from Phelps Dodge, and free-use camping is allowed. Other than outhouses, there are no campground improvements.

Bring some shade and be ready for a midday nap if you head to Evans in July or August. Summer fishing from the shoreline is good only if the sun is off the water. Cloudy days with a slight breeze or nighttime are the good times for summer fishing. Daytime catches are decent if you have the patience to find the depth where the fish are holding. A boat can certainly make that search easier. Jig a fluttering spoon or put down a nightcrawler with splitshot. The important thing is to get deep and cover a lot of water. Summer catfishing is good with stinkbaits. Some anglers favor using small panfish for bait. Catch the little bluegills with tiny hooks and little pieces of worm. Cast out deep for daytime catfishing; night-fishing is more productive in shallower water.

Spring and fall are easier times for day-fishing at Bill Evans. Trout and bass are fooled by casting lures along the riprap of the dam. Plastic worms are favored by the diehard largemouth anglers. Wading and casting along the cattails in the northeastern corner is a favorite for hooking up with springtime bass and crappie. Bait-fishing with worms or minnows is recommended any time. The trout rise and feed at the surface at dawn and dusk, and using a boat and a fly rod or from shore with a casting bubble is the way to hook into these grownup stocked rainbow trout. Winter-stocked trout are caught by fishing on the bottom with salmon eggs. Angling at Bill Evans Lake really shines in the spring and the fall. Make sure you stay late enough to watch the red sunsets stretch across the Gila country's desert skyline.

Access to Bill Evans Lake is off U.S. 180, just south of Cliff and twenty-six miles north of Silver City. The turnoff, Forest Route 809, is paved and follows the Gila River. At the three-mile point the road passes a few ranch houses and comes to the all-weather gravel road that leads up the hill to the lake.

THE UPPER BOX OF THE GILA RIVER

The Gila River offers a wonderfully diverse fishing opportunity beginning just upstream from the village of Cliff. Sunfish, channel catfish, smallmouth and largemouth bass, plus brown and rainbow trout all swim these waters. The smallmouth, planted years ago, are now the dominant sportfish. Hellgrammites and grasshoppers are two great natural baits for the bronzebacks. Lead-head jigs, wooly worms, and small lures are also good tackle choices.

There is a paved road on each side of the river through Cliff and to the town of Gila. Both roads turn into dirt jeep trails. The one on the south side, F.R. 155, is usually driveable in a car; it deadends at the confluence of Turkey Creek and the Gila River, which is right at the Gila Wilderness

Boundary and is choice smallmouth bass country. There are no roads for almost forty miles of river upstream from the Turkey Creek confluence. You walk in, pack in, float in, or you just don't go.

The paved road on the north side of the river ends at the confluence of Mogollon Creek. Mogollon is sometimes a dry canyon at its Gila confluence, but starting ten miles upstream it becomes an excellent wild trout stream. This is a serious walk-in backpack or horseback trip ending near Mogollon Baldy Peak. Start at Trailhead 658, which is accessible via F.R. 147, an unimproved gravel and dirt road. Use the Gila Wilderness map to begin your plans. The good fishing starts upstream from Seventy Four Mountain and goes up to Trail Canyon. Trail Canyon Creek is being reclaimed with Gila trout and is closed to angling. The Mogollon and its forks offer great fishing for wild browns, mostly four to ten inches long. Contact Gila National Forest personnel to get current road and trail conditions.

The other access to the Middle Box of the Gila River is by trail, starting at the Sapillo Creek bridge, twenty-five miles north of Silver City on S.R. 15. But first a note about S.R. 15, the access road to the middle of the Gila National Forest. It is paved, steep, narrow, and not recommended for vehicles pulling trailers over twenty feet long. In fact, pulling any trailer or driving a recreational vehicle on S.R. 15 should be attempted only if you know the brakes, engine, and drive-train are in good condition. The official state highway map shows it to be forty-three miles from Silver City to the Gila Cliff Dwellings National Monument. Plan on the trip taking almost two hours in a car.

Back to the bridge over Sapillo Creek, twenty-five miles north of Silver City. The Sapillo Creek trail is six miles long, paralleling the creek to the Middle Box of the Gila River. Since Sapillo is often low on water, it offers chancy fishing. But if you're interested in an adventurous trip to an almost unfished portion of the Gila, consider a hike or a trail ride to the Sapillo Creek confluence. The water is loaded with channel catfish, smallmouth bass, chubs, and browns. Any stocked rainbow trout that get down this far are used as hors d'oeuvres by the big channel cats. The river makes miles of horseshoe curves with a pool at every bend and a riffle at every run. The bait-fishing is great, and lure or fly-fishing is good whenever the sun is off the water.

This is not an easy one-day trip. Check out the Gila Visitors Map and talk with Gila Forest Service personnel about trail conditions on Forest Trail 247. The trail is often used by outfitters guiding horseback riders.

LAKE ROBERTS

The bridge at Sapillo Creek also marks the turnoff to Lake Roberts, a seventy-acre impoundment on Sapillo Creek, four miles east of S.R. 15 on S.R. 35. Drinking water, picnic tables, a boat rental, bathrooms, and two fee-use camping areas make Lake Roberts a busy place during vacation time. The best midday fishing is before Memorial Day or after Labor Day. Catchable-size rainbow trout are stocked in the fall, winter, and spring, but after the summer sun arrives the water chemistry (high pH values) makes the lake unsuitable for stocking trout.

Worms are a favorite trout bait at Lake Roberts, and a productive way of presenting nightcrawlers is by trolling with christmas trees or cowbells. The lake has bullrushes along much of the shoreline, and wading the edges while casting a wooly worm has been known to produce vicious strikes. During hot summer days the trout will often be stacked up near the cold, underwater feeder springs. Try getting your worm deep off the dry canyons coming down to Lake Roberts; that's where the springs are. Night-fishing is the most productive technique for summer fishing at Roberts; you get to sleep while everybody else is trying to fish and you catch fish while everybody else is trying to sleep.

Fully improved Mesa Campground is on a hill overlooking Lake Roberts. The partially improved Upper End Campground is just above the inlet swamp on the east side. Bring bug spray if you stay at Upper End. Both campgrounds are fee-use areas. A good trail from Upper End Campground leads around the swamp to the bank-fishing along the south east shore line. The Lake Roberts Day Use Area has a boat launch site (no gas motors allowed), bathrooms, and a fish-cleaning station. No camping is allowed in the day-use area. Rental boats are kept here, but they must be rented at the convenience store located a half-mile below the dam.

Lake Roberts is gradually silting in. Giant thunderstorms in the lake's watershed have poured in tons of silt and the lake is slowly turning into a swamp. Bullrushes choke much of the shoreline, and the acres of shallows produce a growth of thick summer algae. Lake Roberts is losing the habitat it needs to support rainbow trout. Summer pH values are too high for stocking trout. The Special Services Division of the Department of Game and Fish bulldozed part of the shoreline to try to create an area where the bullrushes won't grow. There is no long-term solution to the high pH problem. Lake Roberts still has good fall, winter, and spring fishing. In summer, however, it can be difficult.

THE MEETING OF THE FORKS

Driving north from Sapillo Creek Bridge on S.R. 15 you begin the steep drive up the side of Copperas Peak. There is a scenic vista at the top; then it's five miles downhill to the bridge over the Gila River. The East Fork meets the already combined West and Middle forks and makes the main Gila River just a rock-throw east from the bridge. Grapevine Campground, a no-fee area with no improvements, is located off the gravel road just before the bridge. This is the perfect spot to rest your feet in the normally clear waters of the Gila River; or ask around for the location of the huge namesake grapevine; or you can hike up the East Fork, past the children splashing in the pools and around the campers' tents. Put on your sunglasses and wade up this warm little river, and you'll notice a tremendous number of small fish.

The fishing in the East Fork starts as you get upstream, past the crowds. Grasshoppers and worms are the preferred bait; cast to the head of the pools and let your tackle come slowly through the deeper water. If you hike upstream you'll find some pretty good smallmouth bass fishing, but nearer the bridge you'll still be in heavily fished water.

It's an easy walk and wade down the main Gila River from the Grapevine Campground. The birds, bugs, lizards, frogs, flowers, and warm water make this route a fun and reasonably safe hike for the whole family. Except for rain or the spring runoff, the water is wonderfully clear. The farther you go before making the first cast, the better your chances will be of hooking a brown trout, a bass, or a channel catfish. If you want to fish the Gila River away from the crowds, you've got to get a bit further from the paved road; and Alum Trail is one place to go.

Alum Trail starts about two miles south of Grapevine Campground, right off S.R. 15. This is F.T. 788 starting at Trailhead 650. Always check trail conditions at the Visitor Center before heading out. Buy a copy of the Gila Wilderness Visitors Travel Map. This is a one-mile trail that drops down a thousand feet to the Gila River. The walk in keeps the crowds out, yet it's a reasonable one-day trek. Walk down after an early breakfast, fish all day, and use the moon and a flashlight to light the trail on your way out. This is a nice trek to reach some of the best fishing on the Gila River. Expect brown trout, bass, channel catfish, and no convenience store.

The unimproved Forks Campground is just upstream from the Gila Bridge on S.R. 15. Past the campground is the village of Gila Hot Springs. You'll see a recreational vehicle park and some vacation homes, but the place to stop is at Doc Campbell's. Doc Campbell's is a convenience store, tackle shop, gas station, and information center. They also have a freezer full of the best homemade ice cream for sale in the Gila National Forest. Further up the road is the Heart Bar Wildlife Area, owned by the Department of Game and Fish. It contains more than two miles of the Gila and two small (occasionally stocked) ponds. There's some good fishing in the Heart Bar, mainly because it's a five-minute walk from the road to the little river. Most people are concentrated where the road is right next to the river.

Just up the road is the Gila Visitor Center, the place to go for maps, flush toilets, and trail and road conditions. The Middle Fork of the Gila takes off near the visitor center, and if you take the road to the Cliff Dwelling National Monument you will be following the East Fork. There are corrals for horses, improved campgrounds for the human visitors, and a lot of people in the summer.

This is roads end for S.R. 15. It is also the jumpoff point for those backpacking into the Gila Wilderness. The fishing, as you move up the West or Middle Fork, turns away from catfish to smallmouth bass and trout. The countryside changes quickly from an alpine desert to the greenery of elk country. One of the best ways to enjoy the Gila's trout fishing is to hire a professional guide for an outfitted horseback trip into the wilderness area. Check at Doc Campbell's and at the visitors center for a list of those providing this service.

THE FORKS

Of the three tributaries, the Middle Fork offers the best overall trout and bass fishing. The West Fork is good for trout, but it is a bit smaller. The East Fork is last on the list for trout, but it has some great smallmouth bass fishing. Rainbow trout fry are stocked deep in these wilderness waters by horseback. The browns are self-reproducing, as are the chubs, bass, and Gila trout. These are wild fish in a wild setting. Light tackle is the rule for good catches and there's no need to keep more fish than you can eat for dinner. Fly-fishing is often excellent, as is casting with small lures. The trout are much easier to release if you squeeze down the barbs on your hooks.

Middle Fork

Snow Lake, located on the headwaters of the Gila River, offers good access to the upper end of the Middle Fork. By a two-hour drive on a gravel road from Reserve or Mogollon (see the section on Snow Lake), and then by a ten-minute walk downstream from the dam at Snow Lake, you will be standing next to the Middle Fork of the Gila. Flying distance from here to the ice cream at Doc Campbell's is about twenty-five miles; it would take most of a week to hike it.

The Middle Fork meanders through its own little canyon, with trout, chubs, some bass, and an occasional beaver sharing this wilderness water. Iron Creek is the first major tributary below Snow Lake. The upper end of Iron is closed to fishing because the protected Gila trout still lives in its waters.

Canyon Creek is the next important spot on the Middle Fork because it offers trail access on F.T. 31 from Beaverhead Road (F.R. 142). The hike takes from two to three hours and ends where Canyon Creek dumps into the Middle Fork. Good fishing is found both upstream and downstream. Beaverhead Road, a dirt road connecting Beaverhead Ranger Station and Snow Lake, often requires a four-wheel-drive vehicle and always requires careful planning. Check with Gila National Forest personnel about road conditions and parking areas. The Middle Fork slides back into a canyon for the rest of its trip down to the confluence with the West Fork, right at the Gila Visitor Center.

East Fork, West Fork, and Wall Lake

There is no easy access to the headwaters of the West Fork, which are in the middle of the Gila Wilderness Area. The closest trailhead is T.H. 669, at Willow Creek Campground. Willow Creek is stocked with catchable-size rainbows in the campground area, and it is loaded with little wild fish just fifty feet upstream from the last picnic table. A serious hike on F.T. 151 from Willow Creek will get you to Turkeyfeather Creek, which eventually turns into the West Fork. The upper West Fork and its tributary creeks are best visited by horseback, riding up from the Gila National Monument. The lower end of the West Fork, up to Hells Hole, is stocked with fingerling rainbow trout. Enough of these little fish grow to catchable size to make the hike worthwhile.

The East Fork gets its start near fifteen-acre Wall Lake, a marginal trout pond in the northeastern corner of the national forest. The drive to Wall Lake is a long one. Head west from I–25 at the Cuchillo Exit (Exit 89) near Elephant Butte Lake. Then make a long climb out of the dry country on S.R. 52, past Chloride (which is almost a ghost town) and into the

National Forest. It's another twenty-five miles of paved road to the Beaverhead Ranger Station. Head south on gravel F.R. 61 for about six miles to reach Wall Lake. Fishing at Wall Lake is marginal, though it is stocked with catchable-size rainbow trout. Bullfrogs have taken over Wall Lake, and this is one of the prettiest spots in New Mexico to get the makings for a great frog-leg dinner. Check the current New Mexico Fishing Regulations for season and bag limits on bullfrogs.

Taylor Creek comes out of Wall Lake; follow it downstream and it runs into Beaver Creek, forming the East Fork of the Gila River. The smallmouth bass fishing can be outrageous in both Beaver Creek and in the upper end of the East Fork. A few big bass and plenty of five- to seven-inch smallmouth bass live in this part of the East Fork. But access is difficult, the fishing chancy, and you need a four-wheel-drive vehicle and most of a lifetime to find the good spots. Trout fishing is very chancy on the East Fork, conditions are much better for the bass. Check the Gila National Forest Map and get current road information before you head out.

SNOW LAKE

Travel to southwestern New Mexico and find Snow Lake, hidden in the middle of Gila National Forest. This hundred-acre lake is a two-hour drive off the pavement, so you need to start with a full tank of gas. The fishing is for rainbow trout; both fry and catchables are stocked by the New Mexico Department of Game and Fish. Snow Lake is deep enough and receives enough runoff, at least for most years, to avoid an annual winterkill or summerkill. Springtime fishing is great. Ice-fishing is out of the question because the roads are snowbound and usually are not cleared until around the first of May.

Snow Lake was formed by damming Snow Creek, an intermittent headwater tributary to the Middle Fork of the Gila River. The deepest part of the lake, which follows the old creek bed near the dam, is a good place to boat-fish the bottom with bait. There is a concrete boat ramp, but special regulations limit you to electric trolling motors or hand-powered boats. On this forest lake a canoe is the perfect fishing vehicle. Wild meadowgrass forms much of the shore, and grasshoppers are a handy natural bait. Try shining a flashlight at night into the clear shallows near the boat ramp and you'll see dozens of crawfish on the rocky bottom. The trout like these southwestern lobsters as much as you will. Boil some for dinner or use the tails for bait. Hot sunny days have a negative effect on this coldwater lake, but summer angling is good, especially at dawn, dusk, or at night. Spring and fall are better than summer, but any time the roads are passable the fishing is fine.

Camping at Snow Lake is a treat. The developed campground overlooks the lake and the view stretches eastward to the trees, hills, and mountains of Gila National Forest. This is a fee-camping area with drinking water, picnic tables, clean outhouses, and forty good tent sites open from April 1 to November 30. Quiet, no-cost, and unimproved camping is available at the south end of the lake. The roads at the boat ramp and developed campgrounds are all paved. Wheelchair access is good in the boat-ramp area.

Snow Lake is on the edge of the Gila Wilderness Area. A hundred-yard walk downstream from the dam will put you at the beginning of the Middle Fork of the Gila River. This is a small, clear stream full of wild trout, a special place to show a young person the survival moves of wilderness trout. Summer evening fly-fishing can be excellent on this upper stretch of the Middle Fork.

Access to Snow Lake is from Reserve on Forest Road 141 or from Mogollon on State Route 78. The Mogollon route is thirty miles long, but it is more prone to mud, ice, and snow (and is closed during the winter). The Reserve route is forty miles of maintained, two-lane gravel road, but watch out for logging trucks. In dry weather, both roads are passable in a trustworthy car. Stop in Reserve, fill your gas tank, and then check in at the Reserve Ranger Station for road conditions and a Gila National Forest map. Reserve is 130 miles west of Socorro on U.S. Route 60 and New Mexico 12.

MIMBRES RIVER

Forest Route 61, the dirt road from Beaverhead Ranger Station to Wall Lake, continues south along the edge of the Gila Wilderness Area. Even in dry weather this is a road for a four-wheel-drive vehicle, and it often offers an adventure. The road hits pavement again about fifty miles south of Beaverhead and ten miles east of Lake Roberts. Forest Route 61, closed to vehicle traffic in the winter, is the only access to the upper Mimbres River, the most remote stream in this area.

Water from the Mimbres never reaches the ocean. It starts and ends in a closed basin, evaporating in a desert wash. But there is trout fishing in the green meadows of the high country. Officially, the Mimbres runs through the middle of the Black Range Primitive Area. The elk, turkey, and the hunters know these waters better than the anglers. It's a strong little river, with wild trout and few fishermen.

The flash runoffs of 1984 wiped out much of the Mimbres River's stable shoreline and it will take a century for nature to rebuild the banks. But the trout survived, and the fishing in this little stream is good. From above Coney Campground, off Northstar Mesa and F.R. 150A, walk, wade, and hike upstream, casting for unstocked trout in the Black Range Primitive Area. Check road and trail conditions before you go, for you'll be the only people there.

It's obvious when the Mimbres leaves the confines of the National Forest. The river has been pushed, shoved, moved, mined, and generally wrecked from the fisheries' point of view. There's a bit of public access near the Mimbres Ranger Station next to S.R. 61, but hardly any fishing.

BEAR CANYON DAM

Bear Canyon Dam is on a little stream that feeds the Mimbres, two miles north of the town of Mimbres. There's a bait shop near the turnoff. A gravel road leads west from S.R. 61, goes up a hill, and tops out with a view of this twenty-acre lake. It's a great little fishing spot in a steep-walled canyon. Bait fishermen can leave Bear Canyon with a mixed bag of bass, channel catfish, rainbow trout, and sunfish. The trout are stocked only in winter, but bass and panfish are caught all year long. Gas motors aren't needed or allowed; a canoe or a rowboat is perfect for casting around the edges of Bear Canyon. Camping is allowed but difficult; there are no improvements, not much flat ground, and a recreational vehicle would have a hard time getting around the narrow roads. Don't bring in a trailered boat.

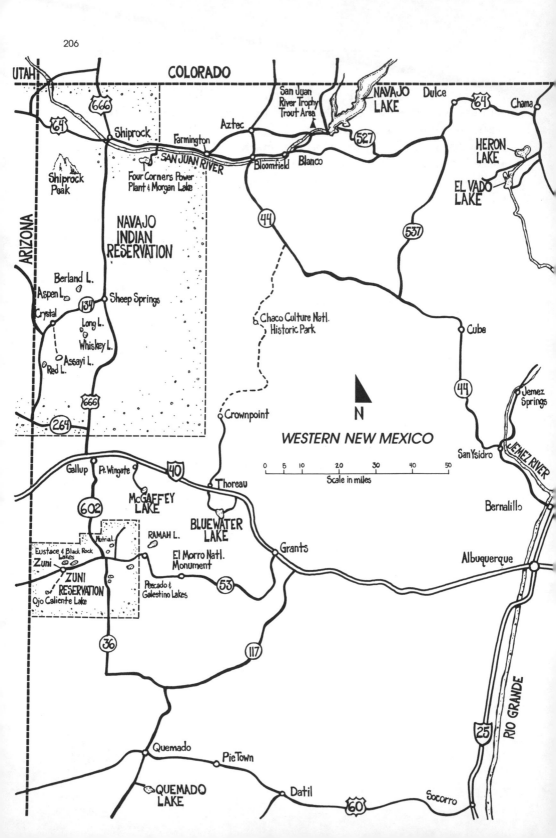

UTAH

COLORADO

ARIZONA

666

64

Shiprock

San Juan River Trophy Trout Area

NAVAJO LAKE

Dulce

64

Chama

527

Farmington

Aztec

HERON LAKE

SAN JUAN RIVER

Bloomfield

Blanco

Shiprock Peak

Four Corners Power Plant & Morgan Lake

EL VADO LAKE

NAVAJO INDIAN RESERVATION

44

537

Berland L.

Aspen L.

134

Sheep Springs

Chaco Culture Natl. Historic Park

Cube

Crystal

Long L.

Whiskey L.

Assayi L.

Red L.

666

N

Jemez Springs

264

Crownpoint

WESTERN NEW MEXICO

44

San Ysidro

0 5 10 20 30 40 50
Scale in miles

JEMEZ RIVER

Gallup

Pt. Wingate

40

Thoreau

Bernalillo

602

McGAFFEY LAKE

BLUEWATER LAKE

Nutria

RAMAH L.

Grants

Albuquerque

Eustace & Black Rock Lakes

Zuni

El Morro Natl. Monument

ZUNI RESERVATION

Ojo Caliente Lake

Pescado & Galestino Lakes

53

36

117

RIO GRANDE

25

Quemado

Pie Town

QUEMADO LAKE

Datil

60

Socorro

Western New Mexico

QUEMADO LAKE

Early spring, immediately following iceout, is one of the most productive times to fish Quemado. In springtime this lake is a consistent producer of thirteen- to eighteen-inch rainbow trout that can put a deep bend in the stoutest fishing rod. The fish will be scattered all around the lake; lure, fly, or bait all produce. Good angling continues until the hot days of summer.

Nutrient levels are very high in Quemado, making for good growth rates in the stocked rainbow trout. But the same high nutrient levels also promote a very heavy summer growth of aquatic plants. The combination of plants and algae, high water temperature, and the high nutrient levels in Quemado often make the water chemistry unsuitable for stocking trout. The lake can become extremely alkaline in the summer with a pH greater than 9, which is well over the limit that trout need to thrive. So watch the weekly fishing reports if you plan a midsummer trip to Quemado; in some years it's tough fishing, but other summers offer fine fishing right through the hot season.

The New Mexico Department of Game and Fish have stocked sterile grass carp in Quemado Lake in an effort to alleviate this problem. The plan is for the carp to feed on the algae and aquatic vegetation, thus helping to balance the lake's water chemistry. The carp, because they are sterile, cannot reproduce. If you catch a carp in Quemado Lake, carefully release it. The carp are making the lake more productive for the trout as well as for the trout fisherman.

Fall—a good time to fish Quemado Lake—brings cooler weather and maybe an early snow squall. The trout are active during midday, putting on fat for their long winter siesta. Winter might also bring a good coat of ice to Quemado (or it might not), but even if it does iceover there's no guarantee that it will be thick enough for ice-fishing. In some years a four-week period in January or February offers good ice-fishing. The roads are usually cleared within a week of any major snowstorm.

Quemado Lake covers 130 acres after the spring runoff. The two feeder streams are tiny and intermittent, and the summer rains compete with evaporation to keep the lake at its full level. A steep hillside borders the lake's long southern shore. To fish this shoreline, park at the boat launch area, pack a lunch, and hike across the dam to the spot that fits your fancy. The north side and inlet areas are reached by parking alongside the gravel access road and walking downhill to the lake. Anglers wishing to fish along the rocky shoreline of the dam will soon become aware of the many snakes—mostly garter and bull snakes—living in the rocks just above the water line.

Bait-fishing from the shore at Quemado is very successful once you find an area where the trout are feeding. Small marshmallows are a local favorite, or try cracking the shells of a few of the snails found in the lake, using the meat for bait. Regardless of your bait, remember to keep checking your hook and recasting to different spots. There is a small island near the inlet area which is a popular spot for bottom-fishing, but you'll need a boat to get there.

The fly-rod fanatic should bring extra dragonfly and damselfly nymphs. The dragonfly hatch (around Memorial Day) is fantastic, especially when fished from a float tube. There are no wadeable flats in Quemado, but wading the shoreline and casting along the edges is effective. Bring some Zonkers or other black and white minnow imitations that will match this lake's baitfish. Streamers are effective if worked from any of the shore points, especially at dusk. Flies that imitate scuds also catch rainbow trout in Quemado Lake.

The lure fisherman should come ready to cast, since trolling shallow running lure in Quemado often catches more weeds than trout. Keep casting; each retrieve allows you to see if you've foul-hooked a weed. Make sure your selection of lures includes those that will run at different depths; and if you're new to this lake, concentrate your fishing around the shore points, which are next to both shallow and deep water, allowing you to cover different depths from one casting position. If the rainbow trout are hitting on top, consider casting a fly on a casting bubble. A small wooly worm or gray-hackle peacock is effective whenever these trout are taking insects near the surface.

Quemado Lake is situated on the high desert plateau between Grants and Silver City; the turnoff to the lake is about fourteen miles south of Quemado on S.R. 32. From I–40, turn south just east of Grants on paved S.R. 117. This is a dramatic drive: to the west are the ancient lava flows of the malpais; to the east you'll see striking sandstone cliffs filled with natural bridges, arches, and caves. S.R. 117 leads right to the town of Quemado, and this is the best route for the Albuquerque-area fisherman. Another route to the lake is from Socorro; turn west on U.S. 60 and continue west to the town of Quemado. From Silver City, head north on

U.S.180 to Reserve; then take N.M. 12 to Apache Creek and turn north on N.M. 32. The marked Quemado Lake turnoff is twenty-seven miles north of Apache Creek.

Access to the lake is via four miles of paved and well-maintained gravel road which leads right to the concrete boat ramp. Boats are limited to electric trolling motors. Camping (with no fee) is allowed in the large parking area near the boat ramp. Garbage cans and clean outhouses are provided by the U.S. Forest Service. A gravel road follows the hillside along the northern shore and then drops down to a nice forest service campground (no fee) on one of the little inlet streams. It is a twenty-minute walk from this forested campground to the inlet bay of the lake.

Snuffy's Tackle Shop is a small convenience store located right off the paved access road on the way to the lake. Snuffy's rents boats and trolling motors and offers camping and recreational vehicle hookups in their improved campground. They are always ready to share the latest fishing information.

ZUÑI INDIAN RESERVATION WATERS

Located in west-central New Mexico on the Arizona border, the little-known Zuñi Indian Reservation offers some very good trout, catfish, large-mouth bass, and northern pike fishing. There are seven stocked lakes open year round, twenty-four hours a day, to public fishing (as long as you first purchase a Zuñi fishing permit). Boats are allowed on Zuñi waters. Summer temperatures are moderate, the angling rarely crowded, and the lakes lie in broad valleys defined by miles of red-rock mesa.

The town (and Pueblo) of Zuñi is roughly in the center of the reservation. Zuñi is a fairly large community with grocery stores, schools, hospital, gas stations, restaurants, and hardware stores, but no motel. Access is on paved roads south from Gallup or Grants, or north from Quemado. There are two main highways on the reservation, S.R. 53 runs east-west from Grants to St. Johns (in Arizona) and S.R. 32 runs north–south from Gallup south toward Quemado. These two highways intersect just east of the town of Zuñi.

There are seven lakes as well as some stream-fishing on Zuñi lands. Daily or annual fishing permits are available at Zuñi Tribal Headquarters, at gas stations in Gallup and Zuñi, and in Albuquerque at Charlie's Sporting Goods. Zuñi fishing regulations forbid the use or possession of minnows, either live or dead. It is illegal to use fish parts as bait. Boating is allowed;

Zuñi Indian Reservation Waters

electric trolling motors are okay, but gas motors are not. Camping is allowed at some of the lakes. A Zuñi Conservation Officer will stop by to collect the camping fee.

Black Rock Lake is a shallow, good-size reservoir on Nutria Creek. Head east of Zuñi on S.R. 53, past the schools, and turn north at the sign pointing to the new BIA Hospital. After driving through the Blackrock housing development, you'll soon be at the lake. There is a dirt road pull-off for fishermen or you can continue on to the dam. Those with a canoe or cartop boat should park and launch at the dam. A trailered boat would be difficult to launch at Blackrock. Use safety-pin spinnerbaits for the northerns; crankbaits and spoons will work, but you spend too much time clearing weeds from the treble hooks. Much of Blackrock's shoreline is lined with bullrushes and water weeds, which makes good habitat for the northerns and decent habitat for the trout. The rainbows and cutthroat show good growth rates and can be taken on salmon eggs, flies, or Mepps-style spinners. Since the big pike feed on newly stocked trout, consider casting a five-inch floating Rapala in rainbow trout colors. And bring a good net. Summer shore-fishing is tough with all the water weeds. Try bank-fishing in the late fall, winter, and spring, when the aquatic vegetation dies back. In summer, use waders and work the shoreline or fish from a small boat. Blackrock Lake is one of the few places in New Mexico where you can try for both northern pike and trout.

Eustace Lake is the next lake below Blackrock Lake on Nutria Creek. Located just north of the Zuñi Fairgrounds, between Zuñi and Blackrock, Eustace grows largemouth bass, northern pike, sunfish, and channel catfish. Except for the last one hundred yards, access is on paved roads. Eustace is deeper than Blackrock, but it still has plenty of shallows, bullrushes, and water weeds. Possibly because this lake is not stocked with trout, Eustace doesn't get fished as often as Blackrock; yet it offers good warmwater fishing.

Galestino No. 1 and No. 3 are trout lakes located just east of S.R. 32, about eight miles south of S.R. 53. The dirt access road is good when dry. In years of limited rain and snowfall these two lakes don't hold enough water to be good trout lakes. But normal years produce good growth rates in the stocked rainbows. These lakes are not as popular as the next two on our list of Zuñi fishing waters; but don't discount the Galestino Lakes, especially in the spring and fall. Try damselfly nymphs if you are a fly-rodder, or cast a dark squirrel tail dressed Mepps-style spinner.

Nutria lakes No. 1, No. 2, No. 3, and No. 4 are located north of S.R. 53 and east of S.R. 32. Low earthen dams back up the waters of Nutria Creek, creating acres of marshes and two good trout and catfish lakes.

Except for a five-week period in January and February, the trout can be caught year round by casting flies. There is a heavy dragonfly and damsel fly hatch in the spring, and good mayfly, caddis, and midge hatches throughout the warmer months. Salmon eggs and garlic cheese and worms catch trout, but you are more likely to hook into a nice bunch of one- to two-pound channel cats. Fishermen argue whether Nutria No. 4 or Nutria No. 2 is the best of the series; No. 1 and No. 3 are marshes. The best access is attained by driving east on S.R. 53 from Zuñi, past the S.R. 32 intersection, and then turning north on the paved road marked with a "Nutria Lakes" sign. Drive about seven miles north and then turn west (you can see the lakes) on a dirt road. This road gets difficult after a rainstorm. You drive over No. 3 dam and then over No. 4 dam to reach the shoreline of No. 4. There is a campground at No. 4. A dirt road heads south for four miles, connecting No. 4 to No. 2. The other access is by driving north on S.R. 32 from S.R. 53. Turn west on Zuñi Route 7 just after crossing little Nutria Creek. This dirt road follows the creek for four miles to No. 2. It is impassable when wet. Though the thick bullrushes close off much of the shoreline, excellent catches of trout and catfish are made by casting from the open areas of the lake shores. Both lakes are great spots for canoeing. Camping is a treat at Nutria, you'll meet very few people, the fishing is wonderful, and the sunsets light up this red-rock mesa country with incredible hues.

Ojo Caliente is a trout and catfish lake located south of Zuñi. From the four-way stop on S.R. 53 in the middle of Zuñi, turn south. After crossing the bridge over the little Zuñi River, the road comes to a junction; bear to the right and head southwest on Zuñi Route 2. The road turns from pavement to an all-weather gravel road. In about ten miles, just past a small village, you turn west on a dirt road marked with an "Ojo Caliente Lake" sign. You can see the lake and a marsh from the road. There is a camping area at the Ojo Caliente. This lake has good (some say very good) fishing for trout and channel catfish. Expect catches of eight- to twelve-inch fish and a good chance for a pair of sixteen- to twenty-inch fish, both trout and channel cats.

Pescado Lake is the easternmost reservoir on the Zuñi Reservation. Located just south of S.R. 53, the turnoff is about seven miles east of the S.R. 53 and S.R. 32 intersection. Pescado is stocked with largemouth bass and fishing here offers good chances for one- to three-pound bigmouths. A few trout work their way to Pescado from Ramah Lake, five miles upstream. Pescado Lake also holds plenty of bluegill and a few channel catfish. Right below Pescado Dam, a series of marshy ponds and creeks sometimes offer northern pike fishing. These predators move upstream from Blackrock Lake during the spring runoff.

Fishing on Zuñi waters is a treat: no crowds, no water-skiers, no power poles. These are relatively unknown waters in a rarely visited part of New Mexico. Fishing permits, either one day or annual, are reasonably priced. The drive from the Albuquerque area is a pleasant two and a half hours. Bring a canoe and you can cast to areas rarely, if ever, fished. If some of the dirt roads are muddy, you can fish the lakes with paved road access. All the lakes are near marshes and the birding is great. Ducks and herons are everywhere. You are likely to find an old piece of pottery or an arrowhead. Leave these artifacts where you find them. That is the law. The Zuñi people have been living along these creeks for thousands of years. Enjoy their country and don't litter.

RAMAH LAKE

Ramah Lake is an old irrigation reservoir, yet it is one of New Mexico's newest public fisheries. Located in western New Mexico, the little town of Ramah was established by the Mormons in the late 1800s. They put an earthen dam across Cebolla Creek, just north of town, to collect spring runoff for summer irrigation use. The reservoir they created—Ramah Lake— is about one thousand feet wide and a mile long.

For years, this lake was privately stocked (with bass, bluegill, and oc- casionally trout) and open to fishermen for a trespass fee. But in 1987 the New Mexico Department of Game and Fish leased public fishing rights to Ramah Lake. Fisheries personnel electroshocked the lake and found a good population of bass and bluegills as well as a few trout. Management of Ramah is centered around the bass and bluegill fishery. Catchable-size trout are also stocked.

Ramah is an old reservoir, and much of the lake is shallow and silty. In fact, the upper end of Ramah is more suited for ducks than for fish. The acres of silty shallows make for a heavy summer growth of aquatic vegetation, weeds that make it tough for the shoreline fisherman. You need a boat to take advantage of much of Ramah's shoreline.

Catching Ramah's bass means imitating their chief food supply, little bluegills. Crankbaits will work, but unless you run these treble hook lures at the right spots, you are going to collect a lot of weeds and very few largemouth. Better to use a spinnerbait, the type with a V-shaped wire. A lead-head hook covered by a plastic skirt rides point-up on the lower end, and a blade spins on the upper end. At the point of the V you attach your ten-pound test line. This rig, which is reasonably weedless, does catch largemouth. Texas-rigged plastic worms are another good weedless tackle choice. The bluegills are caught on smaller gear; cast a fly or use bits of worm and a bobber.

Though a good part of Ramah Lake is shallow, silted in, and overgrown with water weeds, there are areas of Ramah with rocky structure. Ramah Dam was built where Cebolla Creek goes through a steep-walled canyon. Fishing from a boat, you can drift along the rock walls working your lure in deeper (twelve-foot) water. So you have three options for boat-fishing at Ramah: work the shallows, the deeper water, or the transition zone between the two.

Shore anglers have one opportunity to fish in deeper waters. Park and walk across the dam and work the south shoreline just east of the dam. Nightcrawlers are a good bait choice, especially if you use a large (2/0) hook and a bobber. Don't strike at the little nibbles; those are the bluegills snacking on your big worm. Wait until you get a good strike from a largemouth.

Spring is spawning time for both bass and bluegill, and the water weeds haven't yet choked out the shallows. Plastic worms, pig-and-jig combinations, or Flatfish are good choices for bass. For bluegills use wet flies; try green wooly worms to imitate the dragonfly and damselfly nymphs. Summer's best bass fishing is early and late in the day; try quiet surface lures over submerged weedbeds. Bluegill are caught by still fishing with small hooks covered with bits of worm, or by jigging little plastic tube-jigs. Wet flies are always good. Bluegill fishing is best in clearings in the water weeds. Late fall and early winter finds the weed growth dying back and midday fishing is good. For bass, work the middle depth of water between the canyon wall drop-offs and the shallow coves. Winter slows the fish and the fishing. Ice fills the shallows, but is rarely safe enough for ice-fishing. Bass can be caught in deep water with plastic worms, bluegills with white grubs, and the trout go for salmon eggs. Most anglers wait for spring.

Ramah Lake is located just north of the little town of Ramah on S.R. 53. From Grants, take Exit 83 off I-40 and head south on S.R. 53. You'll drive past the Ice Caves and El Morro National Monument (Inscription Rock). About fifty-five miles from the freeway you reach Ramah. A large sign, "Ramah Lake," points the way to the reservoir, a mile north of town. The last quarter-mile is dirt and used to be impassable after a rain shower. The Department of Game and Fish has upgraded the road and added parking

Ramah Lake

Sunfish are great fun on light tackle.

and outhouses. There was once access to the north end of Ramah Lake through the Timberlake Ranch Subdivision, but this route is now closed to public use.

BLUEWATER LAKE

Bluewater Lake State Park is one of New Mexico's most popular fishing destinations. Its sixteen hundred acres of water consistently produce twelve- to sixteen-inch rainbow trout. Catchable-size hatchery rainbows are usually not stocked in this reservoir. Instead, the Department of Game and Fish regularly stocks three- to four-inch fingerlings. Bluewater has the conditions necessary to grow big trout from little trout. It's not only less expensive, but in this lake it's more productive to stock fingerlings. Catch rates are higher here than in most put-and-take lakes.

Located just south of I–40 between Albuquerque and Arizona, Bluewater Lake is actually an irrigation reservoir. It was formed in the late 1920s by a big concrete dam between the sheer rock walls of Bluewater Canyon. Although it is partially fed by springs, it is the summer rains, the spring runoff, and the irrigation drawdowns that determine the lake's size. The reservoir has been nearly full in the 1980s, covering about eighteen hundred surface acres. A dry year, like 1977, can bring it down to four hundred acres and mudflats.

The food chain at Bluewater Lake starts in the extensive shallows found in the Cottonwood arm. These shallow shoals are important because a lake only grows as many fish as it can feed. Cottonwood is the entire western part of the lake and offers great fishing in both the spring and fall. In the middle of summer and the dead of winter, the rainbows head for the deeper water of the main lake. Depths of thirty to fifty feet, the deepest in the lake, are found north and south of the dam.

Good shallows and adequate depths create a good food chain and great trout habitat, which makes for an excellent sport fishery. Channel catfish grow to three pounds, and often larger. Rainbows have been caught (and weighed) in the seven- to eight-pound class; a state-record rainbow trout was caught here in 1986 by using a crayfish as bait. Crayfish are found here in abundance. The main inlet stream supports a naturally reproducing population of little rainbow trout, and during the spring runoff there is a spawning run of big rainbows up the stream. And below the dam, Bluewater Creek is a good little brown trout stream.

That's the good news. The bad news is the number of suckers found in this lake. They were introduced, years back, by a bait fisherman emptying his minnow bucket at the end of a day's fishing. Although Bluewater is very good at growing big trout, it's also very good at producing huge populations of white suckers. The lake is rotenoned (poisoned) every ten to fifteen years, most recently in 1977. It's impossible to kill all the suckers with this procedure, and the Department of Game and Fish is working on other solutions.

Bluewater Lake is located west of Grants and a few miles south of I–40. Two exits lead to the shores of Bluewater and the one you choose depends on the time of year and your personal style of fishing. Take the Prewitt exit, fifteen miles west of Grants, and then go south on S.R. 412 to reach lower Bluewater Creek, the entrance to the state park, the improved campgrounds, the convenience stores, a good boat ramp, boat rentals, the North Bay, the dam, and the dirt and gravel roads that parallel the deeper waters along the northern and eastern shores. There are plenty of little points and private bays along the north shore. The water drops off fairly quickly from this side, and a decent cast will put your bait into ten to twenty feet of water.

The other way to reach the shores of Bluewater is from the Thoreau exit, twenty-four miles west of Grants. Head south from the freeway on the paved road, which climbs up a steep ridge and then drops down to pass over the eroded banks of Cottonwood Creek. There's no public access here, but you can see the Cottonwood arm (the entire western side of the lake). The road continues on, following the southern shoreline of the Cottonwood arm. Public access to the shore is on dirt roads. This land is subdivided; and quite a collection of little convenience stores, homes, churches, and fishing shacks checkerboard the landscape. There is a fee-use state-park area near the main body of the lake (look for the bathrooms, paved parking area, picnic tables, and the boat ramp). Just past the lake the paved road turns into the maintained gravel F.R. 178, which follows the inlet, Blue-water Creek, for about three miles before the two separate. The little inlet stream heads west, up against the Continental Divide, and F.R. 178 turns to dirt and continues south to S.R. 53 east of El Morro National Monument.

Bluewater Lake is fishable just about year round. Ice-fishing, from January to the end of February, is usually limited to the North Bay and to the Cottonwood arm. The main body of the lake rarely freezes solid enough for safe ice-fising. Open-water fishing is good in March, as soon as the sunshine melts the ice and the spring winds stir up the water. By middle to late March the lure, fly, and bait fishermen are all catching rainbow trout in five to ten feet of water.

The runoff draws large spawning rainbows up Bluewater Creek, and the fishless angler should consider using light spinning tackle tipped with a single splitshot, a little gold hook, and a salmon egg. Drifting that egg along the bottom of the creek's pools and runs could tie you into some sixteen- to twenty-inch trout. April weekends find Bluewater Creek crowded with anglers, all pursuing spawning rainbows. Park on state park land near the inlet and work your way upstream. Or continue on F.R. 178, past the lake. The road drops back down to stream level and you can fish upstream or down, without the crowds.

Fishing the shallow shores of Bluewater with bottom baits of corn, cray-fish, marshmallows, worms, or salmon eggs continues to catch trout until the middle of May. The fish are feeding in water easily reached by the shore-bound angler. When summer arrives, however, the trout are forced to deeper water, and the shoreline anglers need to put their bait into the cooler depths. That's why the north shore and the area around the dam, with its steeper dropoff, can offer better bank-fishing in hot weather.

From June to the end of September the angling at Bluewater is difficult for the boatless angler. The midday shoreline angler, especially on the south side, will continue to have problems getting his bait to the level where the trout are holding. Consider going to heavier tackle, bigger hooks, and large

Bluewater Lake

Springtime fishing for big trout does not always mean catching one. This little rainbow was caught and released on Bluewater Creek above Bluewater Lake on April Fools' Day.

pieces of bait. Bluewater's catfish are suckers for crayfish tails, especially during July and August in the Cottonwood arm.

Summer days are the time to troll deeply for hot-weather trout. Cowbells and christmas trees are built to get your bait down, but a small downrigger will get your bait or lure deeper. The rainbows will be twelve to twenty feet deep from 9:00 A.M. until 6:00 P.M. Hot-weather, midday trout fishing at Bluewater Lake is typical of all New Mexico's better trout lakes. Get your lure to the level where fish are holding. The rainbows are in good shape and still feeding. Dawn and dusk are the better times for the angler willing to cast or drift with wooly worms or small lures. Those few anglers willing to fish from 5:00 A.M. until 8:00 A.M. will see plenty of rising fish. Anglers night-fishing with bait will also come close to catching their limit of rainbow trout.

Sometime in October the fishing starts to pick up, because the autumn feeding spree has started. Anglers casting from the shoreline can fill their stringers during the middle of the day. Larger fish start showing in shallow water. The trout are putting on a layer of fat sufficient to get them through the colder and shorter days of winter. They're hungry and their food supply is disappearing.

A nine-pound rainbow was caught near the main boat dock in the fall. October's weather in western New Mexico is gorgeous. These are two reasons why autumn is an excellent time to make the trip to Bluewater State Park. There is no need to fish deep. Lure, bait, or fly will all catch fish. The hot actions slows as the water temperature drops to around forty degrees, usually in December. But bait-fishing, especially in the deeper water by the dam, is still good at Christmas.

No matter what you call them—crayfish, crawdads, or crawfish—these freshwater crustaceans are an important part of the food chain at Bluewater. The small ones are a valuable part of the trout's springtime diet. Remove and shuck the tails from the larger ones, and you've got the perfect catfish bait. A trap worked in the shallows of the Cottonwood arm can collect a bunch of these southwestern lobsters, which are most active at night. Boiled in water with red chili or crab seasoning, crawfish is a luncheon delight.

Every few years a style of angling is rediscoverd at Bluewater Lake that accounts for a lot of rainbow trout. The secret is slow trolling or just drifting with wooly worms. The slow troll catches the most trout, while the drift technique brings in the largest fish. At a slow troll you're using a motor or oars to move the boat; drifting is just moving with the breeze. This is an extremely productive method when the big rainbows are cruising the shallows, at dusk in the summer or all day long in the spring and fall. The key to a good drift is picking a spot where the wind will move you gently along the shoreline. Use big wooly worms with sharp hooks and a reel with a good drag, and carefully release the big fish you don't intend to keep. Once you learn the subtleties of this technique, you'll get into some large trout. Big rainbows are much too valuable to be caught only once.

It can be frustrating if you've made the drive to Bluewater only to have the nice breeze turn into a minor gale. Try the creek below the dam. The stream is in a steep canyon that blocks out much of the wind. This part of Bluewater Creek is stocked with brown trout fry. The few that make it to catchable size are wild, wily, and easily put down. Use light tackle and stealth or bottom bait and patience. If you don't get any hits in the stretch below the dam, try the fishing farther downstream. The best access is by turning south on the last dirt road after the convenience stores and before the state park entrance, but don't take this road after a rainstorm or in the winter. You'll need a four-wheel-drive vehicle or a pickup in dry weather. Or park near the mailboxes and walk down; it's not more than a fifteen-minute trek. The fishing gets better as you move downstream. You can also hike down from the dam overlook, but be careful, for this is a steep hill. Winter flows out of the dam are next to nothing; the best water flows are in spring, summer, and fall.

McGAFFEY LAKE

Little McGaffey Lake is a two-and-a-half-hour drive west of Albuquerque. The tall pines beside this mountain pond will soon soothe the freeway drive. With only fourteen surface acres when full, McGaffey is a personal-size lake. The road is paved to within a mile of the lake, and a well-maintained gravel road leads right to the eastern shoreline. The fishing is for rainbow trout, which are stocked each year by the thousands.

This is a fine lake for any kind of fishing. Casting small lures is most effective, especially off the middle of the eastern bank. Trolling lures or big flies also produce. Gas or electric trolling motors are not allowed here, but you certainly don't need anything but armpower on such a small lake. The water level will drop during hot and dry summers, and this can hurt the fishing. Watch the weekly fishing reports if you are thinking of a midsummer visit. At McGarrey the fly-rod is most effective; you can cast small streamers or wooly worms from shore or match the hatch when the trout start rising. The inlet area is full of cattails and water weeds, but it's also loaded with trout. A pair of waders or a float tube will put you into an afternoon of enjoyable fishing in these weedy shallows. The almost daily insect hatches, especially in the evening, bring the trout to the surface, this is the best time to cast a clear bobber trailing a wooly worm or gray-hackle peacock. It's a great way to beat the fly fishermen at their own game.

The bankside bait fisherman can chunk and chance it while enjoying the hillside view. Watch for the long-eared, gray-tassel squirrels; they are very good at stealing your corn or salmon eggs. You will have better luck with bait by changing the location of your cast every ten minutes, looking for the spot that puts your hook at the level where the trout are feeding. The outlet stream, just below the dam, is a good place to get hellgrammites for bait. This is an easy lake to walk around, fishing as you go. If the east bank is a bit crowded, try the west side with a small flashy spinner.

The best time to catch larger fish at McGaffey is late in the year; the vacation crowds have disappeared and those thin stockers have grown to be fat thirtee-inch trout. Good, autumn tackle choices include a wooly-bugger or a Super Duper lure.

Ice-fishing at McGaffey is chancy. The lake's small size, its shallow depth,

McGaffey Lake

A fat, healthy rainbow caught on a #10 damsel-fly nymph wet fly near the marshy inlet of McGaffey Lake. These are hatchery-raised trout.

and its eight-thousand-foot elevation can produce a severe winterkill. It is different every year, with occasional fifteen-inch rainbows putting smiles on the winter fisherman's face.

Camping is not allowed on the banks of McGaffey, but two good campgrounds are just a five-minute drive away. Quaking Aspen (not as crowded) and McGaffey (closer to the lake) campgrounds are national forest fee areas, and both have marked tent sites, picnic tables, garbage cans, water spigots, fireplace grills, and nice outhouses. These fine facilities are open from mid-May to mid-September and have a total of eighty camping units. The campground roads are maintained gravel.

McGaffey Lake is ten miles south of I–40. Take the Red Rock State Park exit (S.R. 400) and head south past Wingate High School. There is a full-service convenience store just past the school. The turnoff is 124 miles east of Albuquerque, just 12 miles west of Gallup.

NAVAJO NATION FISHING LAKES

The Navajo Department of Fish and Wildlife has developed in New Mexico four mountain trout lakes, a northern pike and bass lake, and a unique bass and bluegill reservoir. Their tribal lands are in the northwestern corner of the state, from Gallup north to the Four Corners area. A state fishing license is not required. Navajo fishing and boating permits are available in Albuquerque at Gardenswartz Sportz, in Farmington at Ross's Sporting Goods, in Gallup at Yellow Front Stores and at Swift Sporting Goods, and in Navajo at Griswald Convenience Store.

Morgan Lake

Morgan Lake is the cooling reservoir for the big Four Corners Power Plant, the complex is located between Farmington and Shiprock. This is a twelve-hundred-acre largemouth bass lake, with bluegills as the main forage fish. Access is south from U.S. 550, near mile-marker 18. The turnoff is marked with a "Four Corners Power Plant" sign. Stay on the paved road as it goes over the San Juan River (no sportfishing here). The road heads south and west; your landmark is the tall stacks of the power plant, visible in the distance. Turn off the pavement right as you get to the lake. There is no public access if you continue over the dam to the power plant.

The roads are barely improved, just dirt and sandy tracks around the northern and western sides of the lake. A four-wheel-drive vehicle is a must after a big thunderstorm, but a passenger car is fine if the roads are dry. Most of the lakeshore is thick with brush, and side trails lead off the perimeter road to the shoreline. There's a concrete boat ramp hidden by trees on the north side.

A quiet bay, complete with good parking and picnic tables, is right at the northwest corner of Morgan Lake. This is a perfect spot for a family picnic and an afternoon of good bluegill fishing. Worms and small hooks are the key to catching this lake's bluegills, but keep handy a rod rigged with a chartreuse crankbait. Bass will often move in and chase a hooked bluegill. Let the kids reel in the bluegill while you cast the crankbait.

Winter weekends are tournament time at Morgan. Occasionally a small flotilla of bass boats will be slowly cruising the lake, with anglers casting for a winning limit of largemouth bass. Winter fishing is good because of this lake's ties to the power plant. The water stays warm, which keeps the bass and bluegills active. Chartreuse spinnerbaits or crankbaits are favorite lures because they imitate the bluegills.

Channel catfish and bullheads also inhabit the lake, but most of the fishing action is centered around the bass and bluegill. The sunsets at Morgan are often dramatic. Hundreds of electric lights dot the power plant,

Navajo Nation Fishing Lakes

A stormy spring sundown at Morgan Lake. The Four Corners Power Plant is on the far shoreline. A Navajo Tribal fishing permit is required at this bass and bluegill lake.

while red skies, setting sun, and evening thundershowers frame sacred Shiprock, the lone mountain jutting up from the dry plains twenty miles west of Morgan Lake.

The Chuska Mountain Lakes

U.S. 666 is the paved highway running down the center of the Navajo Indian Reservation in New Mexico. To the east lie the great dry plains holding the secrets of Chaco Canyon. To the west, climbing quickly out of the dry plains, are the Chuska Mountains. While the lowlands are the color of a tan dust, the Chuskas are green with trees and shrubs. Their nine-thousand-foot elevation catch the clouds, wringing out rain and snowstorms. Berland, Aspen, Whiskey, and Asaayi are destinations for the fisherman; these are trout lakes of the Chuska Mountains, developed by the Navajo Department of Fish and Wildlife.

Access to these lakes starts at Sheep Springs, a small rural outpost with a gas station convenience store on U.S. 666. Turn west at Sheep Springs on paved S.R. 134 and in eleven miles you have climbed almost thirty-five hundred feet in elevation, reaching the summit at Washington Pass. By taking the first turn north, you're on the dirt road to Berland and Aspen; both are stocked with catchables and are three to seven acres in size.

One mile off the pavement you will catch a glimpse of Todacheene Lake, a beautiful lake with absolutely no fish. Past Todacheene, the road switchbacks up a steep hill and the turnoff to Aspen (a left turn) appears just after you finish the switchbacks. If you pass the Aspen Lake turnoff, you drop down and cross a creekbed, and then it's a mile and a half farther to Berland Lake. This route requires a four-wheel-drive vehicle when the roads are muddied. A trustworthy pickup is okay if the roads are dry.

If you take the dirt road south at Washington Pass, you will be heading toward Long and Whiskey Lake, about seven miles from the pavement. You drive past Long Lake at the six-mile point, and Whiskey is just down the road. Long was recently opened as a managed trout lake. If it performs anything like Whiskey, then it will be a great fishery.

In the 1980s, Whiskey Lake has been the star performer of the Navajo trout waters. This 270-acre lake is producing a lot of big trout. It doesn't have a winterkill problem and is stocked, like all these lakes, with catchables. These little eight-inch rainbows grow quickly in Whiskey Lake, making fifteen- to twenty-inch trout available to the Chuska Mountain angler.

Asaayi Lake is located west of Long and Whiskey. You can drive there from Whiskey Lake, but you will need a good map and current logging road information. It's better to stay on the pavement at Washington Pass and to continue six miles west on S.R. 134 to the little village of Crystal. Head south on the marked dirt road for six miles and you're at Asaayi Lake, thirty acres of prime trout water on Bowl Canyon Creek. Another good access point (some say the best) is from the small town of Navajo, right on the Arizona border. Stop at Griswald's Store for fishing permits and road information.

Red Lake is located just outside of Navajo, right on the Arizona border. Red is a bass, bullhead, catfish, and northern pike lake of two hundred acres, with a good gravel access road right off the highway.

There is great beauty in these remote lakes, especially after the drive from the dust of the valleys up to the cool aspens of the high forest. The Chuska Mountain Lakes are a long way from telephones, tackle shops, towing services, and grocery stores. Take a trustworthy vehicle and bring what you'll need. There is a daily camping fee collected at the lakes. Expect snow squalls in May and thundershowers on summer afternoons. The best maps for planning a fishing trip in the Chuska Mountains are the USGS 1:100,000 Toadlena and Gallup maps.

The Navajo Fish and Wildlife Department is headquartered in Window Rock, Arizona. For current fishing information, call them at (602) 871-4941. They have just completed their own trout hatchery, a big step forward in Navajo fishery management efforts. There are a number of Navajo bass and trout fishing lakes in Arizona. Tsaile and Wheatfield—both just over the border—are the top producers.

NAVAJO LAKE

Navajo Lake is located about forty miles east of Farmington, off U.S. 64 in northwestern New Mexico. Completed in 1962, the dam backs up water deep into the canyons of the Pine and San Juan rivers. If you stop at the Pine River Visitor Center you look out at the main body of the lake, which is about a mile wide and two miles long. Branching out like a big V, the Pine River and San Juan River canyons reach north about fifteen miles to Colorado. Dozens of side-canyons and coves add character to this ten- to fifteen-thousand-acre lake.

Easy access makes the dam and the boat-ramp areas popular for the bank fisherman, but it is definitely those anglers with boats who can take full advantage of this huge lake. Since this is both a warm- and coldwater fishery, you never know what you're going to hook—smallmouth bass or kokanee salmon; northern pike or brown trout; largemouth bass, channel catfish, and rainbow trout; or crappie, bluegill, carp, suckers, and bullhead catfish. One or more of these sportfish are active nearly any day of the year.

The most productive anglers change their tactics with the seasons, concentrating on the hot action for that time of year. Summer can mean deep trolling (from thirty to sixty feet) for trout and kokanee in the main body of the lake, or working the shorecliff drop-offs with lures for smallmouth and crappie. The bass boaters fish the coves with spinnerbaits, buzzbaits, and plastic worms.

Fall brings the trout near the surface, and trolling a shallow-running lure is best for browns and rainbows. Big northern pike are possible when trolling along the rocky points with deep-running lures (from eight to eighteen feet). In late fall, when the kokanee are spawning, snagging is best around the dam area; the run peaks in November. When the kokanee are spawning, try bait-fishing for trout with yellow salmon eggs.

Winter rarely freezes the main body of Navajo Lake, and any nice February afternoon can find the fishing still decent, either from the bank or by trolling in the arms at the edge of the ice. Crappies, northern pike, and bass all spawn in the spring, and shallow-water fishing in the coves is very productive. March is also the time to troll for big browns.

Navajo is the second most popular boating lake in New Mexico. Pine, Sims, and Arboles (Colorado) recreation areas all offer excellent boating and camping facilities. Pine, just north of the dam, supports a large boat ramp and parking lot, 180 improved campsites with overflow primitive sites, recreational vehicle hookups, bathrooms, and a full-service marina with boat rentals, gasoline, and a convenience store. Sims Recreation Area is reached on a paved road heading north off N.M. 64 between Dulce and Bloomfield. There are sixty campsites, a marina, a convenience store, and a good boat ramp. Arboles, in Colorado, is also a complete boating and camping facility. These are all fee-camping areas with no charge for launching a boat. Slips and moorings are available at the marinas.

A well-equipped boater can scout the shores of Navajo for a quiet campsite away from the developed areas. All the New Mexico shoreline is open for camping. Dirt and gravel roads provide access to some of Navajo Lake's shoreline. Get a free map and check current lake and road conditions at any of the visitor centers. These roads, even those listed as "improved," can lead to a misadventure in mud instead of an adventure in fishing.

Bass tournaments have demonstrated the potential for largemouth bass fishery at Navajo, but the lack of extensive shallows have kept this reservoir from exploding with bigmouth bass. It's a different story for the smallmouth. Rocky shorelines and good spawning cover have turned the lakeshore into a smallmouth factory. Don't expect many big smallmouth bass, but there are a lot of six- to twelve-inch smallmouth. While the largemouth angler works the coves, the smallmouth angler works the rocks and canyon walls, casting lures right against the cliffsides. Crayfish imitations are a good bet since they match one of Navajo's best fish foods.

Crayfish lures, buzzbaits, and spinnerbaits are common bass lures, but they are also very effective for this lake's northern pike population. Bring a big net and try the rocky points up the San Juan arm. In spring, the pike are in shallow water for their spawning maneuvers. Midday summer and fall anglers often need to get their northern lures deep, so make sure you have a few spoons and heavy spinners that will dive down eight feet. In the late afternoon, try casting to submerged grass along the shoreline. Pike often hold in shallow-water feeding lies, just waiting to take a stab at a wounded minnow imitation. Northerns are usually incidental catches for

Navajo Lake

Navajo Lake is the second most popular boating lake in New Mexico.

the Navajo Reservoir fisherman trolling a Rapala-type lure for trout. The few anglers who concentrate on pike use very heavy tackle. Thirty-pound northerns have been caught and larger ones lost.

Kokanee catches peak during the legal autumn snagging season, from September 1 to the end of December. The actual spawning usually culminates in November. Because kokanee salmon die after spawning, the bag limit is increased to twenty-four per day, with no possession limit. The best spot for snagging kokanee is at the dam. In summer, spring, and fall, kokanee fishing is a deep-water affair. Leadcore and christmas trees will get your kokanee lure deep, but a downrigger is the best way to go. These freshwater salmon have a very rich flesh and are fabulous when smoked. Rainbows, browns, crappie, and smallmouth bass move in to feed on the kokanee spawn in November, and bait-fishing is great with yellow salmon eggs or corn.

Crappie catches peak every spring at spawning time, in May or June, and always in shallow water. Frances and La Jara canyons are good producers. Channel catfish will hit lures cast for smallmouth bass, but the best fishing is with minnows, especially up the Pine arm and near Arboles in Colorado.

Stout tackle and big nets are handy when hunting these big fish. Several large catfish have been caught which were close to both New Mexico and Colorado state records.

Brown trout aren't stocked in Navajo, but they continue to be caught, especially in spring and fall when trolling shallow-running, minnow imitations. Rainbows, which are stocked in huge quantities, provide the best sport for the bankside fisherman. The boat ramps and dam areas are favorite spots any time of the year. Large rainbows are occasionally caught way up the Pine River Arm. Access is about a mile south of the Colorado border on a dirt road heading east from S.R. 511.

Spring winds are common at Navajo, and the boater must use caution. Get your craft out of danger before the whitecaps get serious. Autumn is the most enjoyable time at Navajo because it isn't crowded, the winds are calm, and the cool weather puts all the species on a prewinter feeding spree. Try trolling an orange Rapala around Big Island. This is a large island between the Pine and Sims recreation areas (it is underwater at high water levels). It is easily located at the east end of the Pine Marina boat-mooring lines.

Up-to-date fishing information at Navajo Reservoir can be obtained at any of the visitor centers and at the marinas. Another good spot is the boat ramps, especially in the evening when the anglers bring their boats back in. Jim's Sporting Goods in Bloomfield and Abc's Tackle Shop on the San Juan River below the dam always have current information. The state park Boating Officer at Navajo Lake, based out of the Pine River Visitor Center, often has the best information on catching fish in Navajo Lake.

PART TWO

Sportfish in New Mexico

Coldwater Species

RAINBOW TROUT

Rainbow trout are the backbone of New Mexico's fisheries. More money is spent in raising, stocking, and managing rainbow trout than for any other species of fish. For most of the fishermen in the Land of Enchantment, when you talk about fishing you're talking about rainbow trout, and these sparkling fish are stocked just about everywhere there is cold water. Production from New Mexico's six hatcheries is over a half-million ten-inch rainbows per year and almost four million fry and fingerling.

Rainbows are the fish manager's choice of a trout that's reasonable in cost, easy and fun to catch, and hardy enough to live until it's caught. Most hatchery-raised rainbows are far removed from their wild genetic backgrounds. As domestic turkeys have little or no relation to their wild and wily counterparts, so the catchable-size hatchery rainbow trout has lost much of its ability to survive the test of a wild New Mexico stream. But catchable-size rainbows thrive when stocked in New Mexico's lakes.

The key to identifying a rainbow trout is the reddish band marking their silver sides. In clearwater lakes, the red slash can fade to a faint pink tinge. In New Mexico's best streams, like the Rio Chama, rainbows take on their full colors, with dark backs changing to polished silver sides, a deep red band along the lateral line, a hint of green and blue in the sunlight, and black pepper specks showing from teeth to tail.

The old state record rainbow, caught on a dry fly in the San Juan River, weighed a little less than twelve pounds. The current record, caught at Bluewater on a crayfish, weighed sixteen pounds. But the normal catch is either a thin, ten-inch stocker just out of the hatchery truck or a fat and sassy twelve- to fourteen-incher that leaps and fights against the sting of the hook. If you are after a fish that strains hard against your rod, then look for those lakes and streams stocked with fry and fingerling.

New Mexico's best trout lakes grow big trout from stocked fry and fingerlings. Eagle Nest and Bluewater lakes are both in this category. Canjilon and Fenton are prime examples of lakes that receive very heavy fishing pressure and that are stocked with catchables. Some lakes in southern New Mexico have summer water temperatures too high for trout survival, and catchable rainbows are stocked only in the winter; the same is true for many of the stocked drainage ditches.

Fishable populations of naturally occurring rainbows are rare in New Mexico. Rio Grande cutthroats and Gila trout are New Mexico's native trout; rainbows were introduced from their home rivers in the Pacific Northwest. Most of this state's smaller streams contain self-reproducing populations of brook, cutthroat, or brown trout. Bluewater Creek above Bluewater Lake is an exception. The Pecos above Terrerro holds a good wild rainbow population. There is a small population of wild rainbows in the East Fork of the Jemez, just up from Battleship Rock. Certainly there are dozens of other little spots that harbor wild rainbow trout, but they are the exception, not the rule.

The best New Mexico streams for catching rainbow trout are the San Juan River below Navajo Dam; the Chama River, above and below El Vado Lake; and the Los Pinos River. Rainbows averaging over sixteen inches long, with many measuring over twenty inches, live in the trophy section of the San Juan. The Chama above El Vado is a big, wild stream, and not easy to fish, with El Vado Lake acting as a downstream ocean. Access is easier below El Vado Dam; here the Chama may be the most consistent producer in New Mexico for the bait fisherman. The Los Pinos has just the right mix of riffle, pools, and runs to support the hatchery-raised rainbows.

Trash left by fishermen around the state's popular trout-fishing spots proves that salmon eggs are the first choice for trout bait. Corn and yellow salmon eggs are selected whenever trout are keying in on kokanee spawn. Medium-size spinners, lures, streamers, or bucktails are the right choice when trout are after minnows, which occurs often in the spring, just after iceout. Wooly worms are a favorite anywhere trout are. Small marshmallows seem to be an excellent choice where snails are. Fly fishermen score by matching the hatch: they tie on a fly that matches what the trout are feeding on; a good selection includes elk-hair caddis dry flies, gold-ribbed hare's ear nymphs, and adams dry flies, all in sizes from No. 10 down to No. 18., plus some No. 10 woolybuggers. And don't forget the can of worms. Garden hackle is especially effective after the runoff has peaked and just when the water starts to drop. The best autumn bait for many of our trout waters is free for the taking. Trout love to smash grasshoppers.

BROWN TROUT

The brown trout is one of the angler's favorite fish. More difficult to catch than other trout species, browns were first introduced to New Mexico around 1926. Catchable-size browns are not raised by the Department of Game and Fish. Only fry are stocked in New Mexico's waters, and many trout streams hold naturally reproducing populations. The brown trout you catch is a trout raised in the stream, not in the hatchery. Fishing for browns requires that you be quiet, cast accurately, and create your own good luck. Fooling and then landing a good-size brown trout is a significant event in any fisherman's life. This Land of Enchantment is loaded with excellent opportunities for tangling with wily brown trout.

Browns are named after their body color, an olive brown with a golden tint. Black and orange or reddish spots dot the sides. The belly is yellow or cream colored. Browns do quite well in water that is warmer, siltier, and less turbulent than the clear riffle waters preferred by other trout species. But brown trout are also found in the upper, middle, and lower stretches of New Mexico trout streams. Sometimes they do too well, reproducing to the point of crowding out their own food supply; this results in the hundreds of stunted browns found in some of the little high-country trout streams. Brown trout thrive in a lake, especially if there's a good feeder stream for spawning purposes.

Definitely a predator fish, browns eat a lot of little fish. In fact, they've eaten and crowded many native fish out of existence. Big browns will still pick hatching mayflies off the surface, just as they did when they were little fingerlings. Larger brown trout feed heavily in the morning, evening, and at night, which is one reason why good-size browns still survive in even the most heavily fished streams. Three-, four-, and five-pound brown trout are caught every year in the Pecos and Jemez watersheds right next to the highway.

You can see the state record brown trout. This monster hangs on the wall of the tackle shop at Cooper's El Vado Ranch, on the Chama River below El Vado Dam. It was caught in 1946, weighed twenty pounds, four ounces, and was caught on a live chub. The Chama is still a good brown trout river. A sixteen-pounder was caught here in 1986.

New Mexico is loaded with excellent places to fish for brown trout. The best summer river fishing might be on the San Juan River Fishing Easement below Abe's Bridge. This is bank- or wade-fishing, and is best from late evening into the night and when using a large elk-hair caddis fly or a shallow-running lure. Navajo Lake Reservoir is superb in late spring or in midautumn, and when trolling a floating orange Rapala. Three of the best small streams for brown trout are the Rio Guadalupe, the Chama River above the town of Chama, and the Mora-Pecos River. Use weighted nymphs or small Mepps-style spinners. The best autumn adventure for brown trout would be a November weekend hike into the Rio Grande Gorge at or below the junction of the Red River; this is definitely the right place to cast black marabou streamers or silver and black bucktail Panther Martins. Santa Cruz Lake is good when trolling worms or a black/white Rapala in the spring or the fall. The Cimarron River below Eagle Nest Dam is a great place for spring fishing with stone fly nymphs or wooly worms; use ultralight spinning gear or a fly-rod. The Pecos is super from mid-June until the first snowfall. On a warm day in February, you can cast little jigs or dry flies to rising browns in the Corrales Clear Ditch in Albuquerque. The list could go on for another three pages, for New Mexico is loaded with excellent opportunities for the angler to pit skill and stealth against the wily brown trout.

BROOK TROUT

Brook trout are a rare catch in New Mexico. These trout need a consistent supply of cold, clear water in an area free of competition from other trout. This type of habitat is a rare commodity in the Southwest. Widely stocked in the first half of the century, this colorful fish has been supplanted by stockings of brown and rainbow trout. While there isn't much room for brookies in our watersheds, a few self-reproducing populations still remain in New Mexico.

Sacramento Creek and Dam, near the Sunspot Solar Observatory south of Cloudcroft, supports a good little brook trout fishery. Cabresto, Hopewell, and Bonito lakes all have good spring and fall brookie fishing. The Blue Hole, a spring-fed sinkhole on the feeder creek to Bonito Lake, is a tiny, gin-clear pond loaded with brook trout. Bonito Creek, upstream from Bonito Lake, sustains a small brook trout population. Eagle Creek and the Agua Chaquita, both in the Lincoln National Forest, have good numbers of brookies. Osha and Soldier creeks, both little tributaries to Cow Creek on the Pecos Watershed, used to have brook trout, and maybe they still do. Six miles upstream from the town of Red River, the upper Red River and its East Fork have brook trout. The best brook trout fishing in the state is found on the Vermejo Ranch high-country lakes near the Colorado border. The current state record was caught here, in Long Lake (part of the Glacier

Lakes above Costilla No. 1), in June 1979, on a black gnat fly—the brook trout was over eighteen inches long, weighing four pounds, six ounces.

Brook trout are a sight to behold. A wavy crosshatch of black green lines marks the back of this pretty trout. Red on blue spots dot the sides. They cannot survive summer water temperatures much over 70°F and they need water below 65°F to thrive and reproduce. Brooks are fall spawners; a ten-inch female will lay about five hundred eggs. Only seven will live three years. A four-year-old brook trout is rare indeed.

Hopewell and Cabresto lakes offer the best public brook trout fishing. Iceout and midautumn are prime times. Scuds abound in Cabresto, and a No. 12 fresh water shrimp pattern fished slow and deep works well. Dawn and dusk are ideal times for fly-fishing. Dark lures seem to work best for the spinning rod angler. A twelve-inch fish is a superb catch, and anything larger is a prize to remember. For summer angling, fish the deep, cold water—that's what brookies like best.

CUTTHROAT TROUT

Named after the distinctive bright red marking under each side of the jaw, cutthroats are one of New Mexico's two native trout. Logging and grazing practices in the 1900s ruined hundreds of cutthroat streams, and the stocking of brook, brown, and rainbow trout finished off most of the original species. Cutthroat hybridize with New Mexico's most common hatchery trout, the rainbow. Thus, most cutthroat in New Mexico are actually cutbows—a cutthroat crossed with a rainbow. Some look like rainbows, but with the cutthroat's characteristic red mark on its jaw. Others resemble pure cutthroats, with maybe a hint of a rainbow's coloring.

The Rio Grande cutthroat is the official state fish of New Mexico. Pure strains of these trout still exist in the Costilla and the Vermejo watersheds. The New Mexico Department of Game and Fish has reclaimed Nabor Creek and Nabor Lake in the Sargent Wildlife Area with Rio Grande cutthroat. Other creeks, like Peralta Creek, the upper Rio las Vacas, and the Rio Frijoles, all in the Jemez Mountains, will receive the same treatment.

Catching cutthroats is not much different than angling for the other trout species. They feed mostly on underwater insect nymphs and are caught on lures, bait, and flies. Cutthroats are considered to be the easiest trout to catch. The Costilla and the Santa Barbara are New Mexico's two best public-access cutthroat streams. The big Rio Grande and the little Chamita support good populations of cutbows. The best stillwater fishing for big cutthroats is found in the Latir lakes, this is fee-fishing on Rio Costilla land and Cattle Company land. The state record came out of the Latirs in 1981, weighing ten pounds and two ounces.

The Vermejo River (private fee-fishing) has excellent, maybe pure Rio Grande cutthroat fishing. Cabresto Lake and the high Sangre de Cristo (Pecos) lakes have good fishing for cutthroats, as do the Jicarilla Apache and Navajo Indian lakes. Heron Lake, Eagle Nest Lake, and the San Juan River are heavily stocked with Snake River cutthroats. Many of the tiny headwater tributaries in the Pecos, Jemez, Chama, and Red River watersheds have good fishing for little cutthroats.

LAKE TROUT

The New Mexico Department of Game and Fish stocked lake trout in Heron Lake in 1978. Heron has the habitat that lakers need. The reservoir is a big, deep, and clear lake with plenty of oxygen at great depth and a good supply of forage fish. Although a few smaller lake trout have been caught, it's doubtful that many of the lake trout are successfully reproducing. Lakers have a strongly forked tail, a blue-gray or bronze body, and are covered with small yellow splotches. Most lake trout caught at Heron are about two feet long.

Angling techniques vary with the time of year. In spring, just after the ice clears out (Heron doesn't always freeze), the lakers will be cruising all over the lake. Lake trout feed exclusively on smaller fish, and in Heron that means kokanee and rainbow fingerlings. Catches from the bank are possible at Heron Dike, west of the dam. Shallow trolling along the shoreline or deep trolling at thirty feet in the main lake is the most effective technique. Brightly colored Z-Rays are the favorite lure choice. In summer the lakers often go deep, real deep. Heron has depths aproaching two hundred feet, and though anglers with sonar units have pinpointed big fish, few have been caught. Autumn brings on spawning maneuvers in somewhat shallower water. Trolling the shoreline with a big lure is again effective. The state record is broken most every year (about thirteen pounds as of 1988) as the originally stocked fish keep getting bigger.

KOKANEE SALMON

Kokanee salmon are dwarf landlocked sockeye salmon. They are almost exclusively plankton eaters, and have a three- to five-year lifespan. Kokanee are inexpensive to stock and can be relatively easy to catch, thus providing ideal conditions for both fishermen and fisheries managers. Since trout don't eat plankton, the two species can coexist in the same lake without competing directly for food. Heron, Navajo, and Eagle Nest are New Mexico's best kokanee waters. El Vado Lake and the Chama River above El Vado are also stocked.

New Mexico's kokanee salmon start out as fertilized eggs in Parkview or Red River Hatchery. The eggs are from Eagle Nest or Heron Lake kokanee caught in nets at spawning time; eggs are also obtained by trade from neighboring states. The little salmon are stocked as soon as they lose their egg sacks. Annually, about two million are put in New Mexico waters. The fry grow into fingerlings, and the fingerlings develop into little kokanee salmon. Anglers don't get to see the four- to twelve-inch fish because they're not fooled by the fisherman's hook. But kokanee salmon will hit a lure during the summer of their third or fourth year. These fish will be from twelve to sixteen inches long; their size varies from year to year, but most age-class fish will be the same size. The state record kokanee weighed three pounds, ten ounces, and was caught in autumn at Navajo Lake.

Fishermen after kokanee have learned to fish deep because that's where the salmon are. Big schools of kokanee cruise at the level which has the right combination of oxygen, plankton, temperature, and daylight; and in New Mexico's lakes that means twenty to forty feet in spring and fall, thirty to sixty feet in midsummer. Leadcore line, down-planners, christmas trees, cowbells, or six ounces of lead will all get your kokanee lure to the right depth; but there is nothing like a down-rigger to get the job done efficiently.

Lure choice is easy, because anglers have found that the Kokanee Killer—type lure catches fish. These are silver spinner lures with fluorescent red accents and one treble hook. Kokanee have soft mouths, so it's easy to jerk the hook out. A light setting on the drag will solve that problem. You can also buy a rubber snubber, which goes between the line and the lure; it's no more than a fancy rubber band that smooths out the sharp tugs while you try to land the fish.

Kokanee spawn only once, at four years of age, and then die; and that's why it is legal to snag kokanee from September 1 to December 31. New Mexico's fisheries managers want a good return-to-creel of sportfish, and snagging is the last chance to get these soon-to-die fish to the public. In November and December, large schools of kokanee are concentrated near the shoreline, often in the same area where they were stocked. The males trade their silver color for a brilliant fluorescent red, and their jaws develop a distinctive hook (kype). The females turn steel gray. Anglers cast leaded treble hooks with heavy test line and then jerk and retrieve the hooks back to shore. Bag limits are increased to twenty-four during the snagging season, when there is no possession limit. The peak kokanee run changes from year to year at different lakes. Check the weekly fishing reports, starting in September, for current conditions.

Kokanee feed predominately on plankton, a diet that loads their flesh with fish oils. Clean them quickly and get them on ice as soon as you can, because their flesh spoils easily. Many people say that freshly caught walleye fillets, when batter-dipped, seasoned, and fried in hot oil, are the best tasting freshwater fish in existence. Maybe yes, maybe no. However, there is nothing comparable to smoked salmon. New Mexico kokanee are absolutely superb when kippered—soaked in brine and then smoked over mesquite.

Warmwater Species

BLACK BASS

Black bass is a term referring to part of the sunfish family, which for New Mexico waters means largemouth, spotted, and smallmouth bass. Spotted bass occur in Cochiti Lake and in the lower Pecos River Watershed, specifically in Lake Sumner, and are usually incidental catches; however, the other two species offer some of the finest sportfishing in the state. You can tell the difference between a largemouth and a smallmouth bass by looking at how far the rear of the upper jaw extends past the eye of the fish. Smallmouth have an upper jaw that goes to but not beyond the eye, while the upper jaw of a largemouth extends well beyond the eye. Smallmouth are a more brown or bronze color (bronzebacks) and they have distinct vertical markings. Largemouth are more silver, black, and green in color, and have a dark and hazy horizontal mark from head to tail.

SMALLMOUTH BASS

Good smallmouth bass fishing is found in New Mexico's reservoirs and in the Gila River, the state's bronzeback stream. Ute Lake in 1972 was the site of the state record of six and a half pounds. Since that trophy was caught, extensive work on the dam has doubled the size of the lake. Ute is better than ever and is still the best place to go for big smallmouth bass in a reservoir situation. Navajo Lake's rocky shoreline is a perfect habitat for many little smallmouth. Larger bronzebacks are few and far between, because Navajo doesn't have the nutrients to support the food chain that would grow many big smallmouth bass. Abiquiu Reservoir supports a good population of medium-size smallmouth, as does Conchas Reservoir. Elephant Butte and Cochiti also have smallmouth bass, but other sportfish are more abundant.

The Gila River and its forks offer the only dependable river fishing for smallmouth bass in New Mexico. Stocked many years ago, smallmouth now reproduce and prosper in the entire Gila Drainage. Some of the best fishing is in the Middle Box of the main Gila River, from Turkey Creek upstream to the confluence with the Middle and West Fork. Fisheries biologists have also found bronzebacks all the way up the East and Middle forks. Although the Rio Grande around Velarde is listed as smallmouth water, confirmed catches are rare.

Hellgrammites and dragonfly larvae are two favorite river baits for smallmouth. Top spots for river fishing are the deep runs just below the fast water of riffles. Small crayfish are an excellent bait anywhere. In-line spinners, such as the Sonic Roostertail, are consistent bass catchers. Smallmouth eat crayfish, minnows, and large aquatic insects. Imitate these natural baits with plastic or with feathers and you will have a chance to catch these formidable fish.

Reservoir smallmouth prefer rocky shorelines in the summer. Winter finds these bass in a waiting state. They almost hibernate in water temperatures less than 45°F. Bass spawn in the spring when the water gets over 60°F. Nests are built at depths dependent on water clarity; they are fairly deep in clear water (at Navajo) and fairly shallow in turbid water (at Abiquiu). Crappie and bluegill follow a similar spawning schedule. This concentrated activity is the reason why April, May, and June are such good months for smallmouth bass fishing. Try casting a minnow imitation, lure or fly, past submerged brush in two to five feet of water at Abiquiu and you may just hook up with a twelve-inch smallmouth. The results will be immediate. Important concerns of the work week will be lost in a spray of water and a strong test of tackle. Inch for inch, smallmouth bass are the strongest fighters of all New Mexico's gamefish.

LARGEMOUTH BASS

Largemouth bass are one of the most important sportfish in New Mexico. These bass have big mouths: you can easily put your fist in the mouth of a three-pound largemouth. Bass eat ducklings, mice, waterdogs, small birds, bugs, frogs, and crayfish; but mostly they eat other fish. Bigger bass feed less frequently but prefer larger morsels. State record largemouths have come from Ute Lake (1975 at eleven pounds) and from Bill Evans Lake (1988 at 12.58 pounds). The next record will most likely come from Elephant Butte, New Mexico's premier bass fishery. Elephant Butte is listed as one of the top ten largemouth bass lakes in the United States.

Spring, summer, and fall find largemouth in areas near submerged vegetation or other underwater structure. New Mexico's best bigmouth reservoirs have miles of shoreline dotted with underwater trees, brush, or bullrushes. Usually caught in water less than twenty feet deep, largemouth bass can smash surface lures, quietly engulf a plastic worm, or make a lightning strike at a spinnerbait.

Winter is a slow time for largemouth. Spring brings warmer days, and as water temperatures approach 50°F the bass start to feed in earnest. Once the water is above 60°F the spawning urge takes over. All this springtime activity makes April, May, and June prime months for the bass fisherman. Summer angling is a bit more difficult because largemouth get sluggish when the water rises above 70°F. But as autumn arrives the water cools, and the fishing gets easier.

Lures for catching largemouth include just about anything with hooks attached. A favorite in New Mexico is a salt-impregnated plastic lizard. Others favorites are pig-and-jig combinations, crankbaits, spinnerbaits, and plastic worms. Soft plastic lures fitted with a single hook are best when fishing in heavy cover. Crankbaits or spinnerbaits are good choices when casting over or around the cover.

Cover, often called *structure*, is important to the largemouth fisherman; these terms refer to the objects which attract and hold bass. Boat docks are a good example. Largemouth often hold under the boats, docks, buoys, and all the mooring equipment found around the improved boat ramps at New Mexico state parks. These fish are often overlooked, for most anglers crank up the outboard as soon as they clear the marina buoys. Natural structure would include submerged cedar, juniper, piñon, and cottonwood trees; flooded road beds; and rock ledges or drop offs. Bullrushes (at Ute Lake or at McRae Canyon in Elephant Butte, for example) are another favorite hideout.

Largemouth bass are New Mexico's money fish. More cash is won by fishing for bass than for any other sportfish. So many bass tournaments are held at Elephant Butte that the New Mexico Bass Federation has to co-ordinate who can have what tournament and when. There are over two thousand bass-club members in New Mexico. Their main purpose is to promote and protect largemouth bass fishing through the enjoyment of tournament fishing. All bass fishing contests require live fish to be brought to the weigh-in point; and afterward the fish are released. Anglers interested in this type of competitive fishing should join a bass club. Some clubs are big-money, hardcore tournament organizations, while other clubs concentrate more on family fishing fun. The larger clubs hold yearly bass-fishing clinics, an excellent place to develop the hobby of fishing for largemouth bass.

Largemouth Bass

Nationally recognized Elephant Butte is the best largemouth fishery in the state. Ute, Conchas, and Caballo are very good, while Lake Sumner, Santa Rosa, and Navajo Reservoir also have some good largemouth spots. Bill Evans, Bosque Redondo, and Stubblefield are small trout and bass lakes. Morgan and Jackson are medium-size bass lakes in northwestern New Mexico.

Catching largemouth can be as involved as hauling a 16,000-dollar bass boat for two hundred miles to flip a Texas-rigged (pegged quarter-ounce bullet sinker with a 1/0 TruTurn hook), electric blue, super-sparkled, and salt-impregnated plastic lizard on the southeast (shaded) side of submerged salt cedar in three to six feet of water, using twenty-five pound copolymer monofilament with a 112 dollar flipp'n stick and an 87 dollar flipp'n reel. And catching largemouth can be as easy as watching a red and white bobber while snoozing on the shoreline. Most importantly, though, both anglers are having fun.

If you are interested in the science and art of largemouth fishing, check out the writings of Ken Schultz in *Field and Stream* magazine and in his book *Bass Fishing Fundamentals*. Advanced bass fishermen can keep up with the latest techniques by reading the *In-Fisherman* magazine. Professional guides are available at Elephant Butte. Fees run about $175 a day for two anglers. That includes tackle, boat, and a professional who knows the productive techniques and locations for good bass fishing at Elephant Butte, New Mexico's finest warmwater fishery.

WHITE BASS

Fishing for white bass is a feast-or-famine proposition. Whites tend to stay in large age-class groups, which are big schools of fish of the same size. When you find a school of whites, it's nonstop action; until you find them, it's little or none at all. They feed on small forage fish, and threadfin shad are their mainstay; find the shad and you've found the whites. The type of lure you'll need is one that matches the shads' two- to three-inch size and silver color. Whether you cast and retrieve or troll, choose a selection of metal and plastic lures that work at different depths. A heavy fly-rod working a sinking line and a big white marabou streamer really does the trick when they're feeding anywhere near the surface.

While largemouth are actually members of the sunfish family, whites are members of the true bass family. White bass have a silver white body with dark stripes running from the gill covers to the tail; its body is deep, more than one-third its length. That large flat portion of its body lets it bend your rod with a strong sideways pull. When a white bass strikes, there is no need to rare back and set the hook; if your hooks are sharp the white bass will hook itself. Be careful when removing your lure. The white bass has gill-covers that are razor sharp. Use needle-nose pliers to hold its gill plates while removing the hook.

White bass meat is fantastic, but only if you fillet it soon after capture. It is easy to catch a dozen when you get into good school of these tasty fish. Anglers with boats equipped with a live-well can keep their catch alive until the end of the day. Those without live-wells should clean their catch as soon as the fishing action slows. A stringer-full of whites can turn into a bunch of mushy fillets if left till the end of the day. The white bass has a set of glands, located along its backbone, which can make the flesh greasy. Take a break and get those fillets on ice as soon as possible. They freeze just fine, and they make a great winter treat when thawed and dipped first in egg batter, then coated with seasoned cornmeal and deep-fried.

White bass spawn from mid-April to mid-May, and a female can lay as many as a million eggs. Although the survival rate is small, the big numbers involved offer the potential for a large population. Catching and keeping white bass (the daily limit is forty) does not hurt the population. Changing water levels in New Mexico's big reservoirs can wipe out the spring spawn, stunt the yearly fingerlings, or kill off the forage fish. This hurts the white bass population much more than heavy angling pressure.

Yearling white bass are six inches long. After their first year, they depend on small baitfish for food. Threadfin shad are a favorite, and if you find the shad in New Mexico's big reservoirs you've also found the whites. From late spring through early fall, the bass often corral the shad on the surface or bunch them against the shoreline. This feeding frenzy is nearly impossible to miss: hundreds of little shad leaping out of the water with dozens of bass boiling the surface. Gulls often flock overhead, diving down to snack on the stunned threadfin. It's a sight to see when you have a good rod in your hand; any silver or light-colored lure will catch white bass when cast into this feeding spree.

The state record white came from Bill Evans Lake in 1983, caught by using a Model A Bomber, which is a good bass lure anywhere. The fish weighed four pounds, thirteen ounces; but a bigger white bass should soon be caught in Elephant Butte Lake. Bill Evans Lake is not stocked with white bass, so no one knows how that record fish got there.

On bright summer days, and again in the fall, the whites tend to go deeper, where the baitfish are, and jigging does the trick. If you are trolling or casting, remember to keep trying different depths. Since they stay in schools, it is likely that the first one caught signals the presence of a large group. The most important tip for catching white bass is to fish your lure at the right depth. Work deep water carefully, jigging at different depths instead of trying to cover a large area with long casts.

High water levels during the early and mid-1980s really helped both New Mexico's white bass and the shad they depend on. Boats concentrated in one area usually signal a school of feeding whites, so join in the fun. A fourteen-inch white bass will weigh more than a pound, and a sixteen-incher will double that figure. When you catch them, get those fillets quickly on ice; that's the way to enjoy these scrappy New Mexico fish.

Elephant Butte has the best white bass population in the state. The north end of the lower lake, where the lake opens up below the Narrows, is a favorite spot for the boat fisherman. Shore fishermen should drive the westside gravel-access roads, looking for casting spots off the many rocky points. The Rock House is a good starting spot. The two accessible bays on each side of the Damsite Marina, on the south end of Elephant Butte, can be productive on summer evenings.

Ute Lake has good white bass fishing, as does Lake Sumner. Cochiti Lake was stocked with white bass in the mid-1980s. Early reports look good, but it remains to be seen if Cochiti's whites will grow and prosper. Brantley Dam should be a good white bass fishery, but it's too early to tell on this brand-new Pecos River reservoir. The Pecos River has a strong spring run of white bass up from Red Bluff Reservoir in Texas. Carlsbad is the center for this action, and white bass catches are good in the summer right in the middle of town. Caballo Lake, just below Elephant Butte, produces excellent catches of whites. Watch the weekly fishing reports—especially in late spring and early summer—for the best white bass spots.

STRIPED BASS

The first run of a hooked striped bass is unstoppable. What you do after an Elephant Butte striper hits your shad imitation is easy to remember— hold on. If you've set the drag correctly and your tackle holds, only then can you use the bend in your rod to gain line and start thinking about landing one of these three- to forty-pound East Coast imports. Elephant Butte is New Mexico's only reservoir appropriate for stripers, for they need big water with plenty of forage fish.

Though it's doubtful that striped bass can successfully reproduce in Elephant Butte, what they can do is grow and prosper. Elephant Butte is full of gizzard and threadfin shad, which are good forage fish for the stripers. Find the shad in open water (on a sonar graph unit), and you've found a likely place to cast for striped bass. To keep these big sportfish in good supply, the Department of Game and Fish has continued to stock striper fry.

Stripers feed early and late near the surface, and deeper at midday. They follow the shad, their main forage fish at Elephant Butte. Fifteen- to twenty-five-pound line is adequate for striper fishing, but the actual choice of equipment is determined by the type and location of the fishing. Jigging heavy lead-head lures in deep water over submerged cottonwood trees requires the stoutest tackle, and twenty-five-pound test is not unreasonable. A rod and reel combination capable of handling fifteen-pound test line is okay for casting a big crankbait in open water to surface-feeding striped bass. In either case, if the drag is set too light, the fish will swim into the next county. If the drag is set too heavy, these fish will break the line or destroy the reel.

The state-record striped bass weighed almost forty pounds and was three and a half feet long. Big stripers have also been caught below Elephant Butte Dam, especially in the spring. Ash Canyon produces a few hookups for the shore fisherman, and February is a good month to try. Elephant Butte Dike, west and north of the dam, is another spot for the bank fisherman.

The boat fisherman can try for early morning jump-fishing, watching for shad to break the surface as stripers go on a feeding spree. Or you can use a sonar unit and look for the big fish in deep water. Most striper fishing is done on the east side of the Butte, north of Kettle Top. (Check the chapter on Elephant Butte for complete information.)

Small stripers are often mistaken for white bass, and it is important to know the difference. The limit on whites is forty fish, while the striped bass limit is only four. Both stripers and white bass have silver bodies with black stripes running the length of the body, but on a striper three or four of the stripes go all the way to the tail. On a white bass, only one of the stripes goes to the tail.

WALLEYE

Walleye are named after their big eyes, eyes made for feeding at night. Bright sunshine and calm water send these predatory fish-eaters deep, below twenty feet. The best time to fish for walleye is when the sun is off the water. Considered to be one of the finest eating fish, walleye have thrived in many New Mexico reservoirs. Actually members of the perch family, walleyes need plenty of ten- to forty-foot-deep water and a good population of forage fish.

Walleye are a long, round bodied fish with two tall dorsal fins, the front one made up of hard spines. Walleye have a cream-colored belly, olive green sides and a half-dozen hazy bands going over the back. A silver spot marks the bottom rear tip of their tail, and they have a mouth full of small sharp teeth.

Historically, Ute and Conchas have been New Mexico's best walleye waters, though the Elephant Butte, Rio Grande, Caballo complex also supports a good walleye fishery. Previous state records came from Clayton Lake and Caballo, but the current record was caught from the Rio Grande below Elephant Butte Dam in the spring (March). It weighed fifteen pounds and twelve ounces. The state's other good walleye reservoirs are Lake Sumner, Santa Rosa, and Cochiti.

To make up for poor natural walleye reproduction, the New Mexico Department of Game and Fish makes a big effort each March to collect millions of walleye eggs. Ten to forty million eggs are hatched in Rock Lake Hatchery and then stocked as fry in all our walleye waters. Most of the eggs come from Ute Lake, and Ute gets back about five million little walleye each year.

Walleye spawn in the springtime, with March being the prime month. Although they can be caught in winter, the best action comes in April and May, just after the spawn. Walleye eat two- to five-inch fish. Roostertail-type spinners and crankbaits are good lures to troll or cast in five to fifteen feet of water. A quarter-ounce lead-head hook with a yellow curly-tail grub is a favorite for both deep and shallow fishing. Tipping your hook with bait, whether worms or a piece of baitfish, usually increases your hookups. Walleyes rarely smash a lure, and the take is subtle and requires concentration to detect.

One- to four-pound walleye are usually found in schools, so catch one and cast again, because the same technique will often produce more action. Fish near the bottom, which is where the walleye normally hold. Fish slowly and concentrate on detecting strikes, these fish rarely attack, they nibble. If possible, fish on a cloudy, slightly windy day, for walleye are more active when the sunlight is off the water. Walleye fishing is quite good along the riprap of the dams and dikes of all our reservoirs.

One style of walleye fishing that does draw smashing strikes is practiced after the sun goes down. Shore-fishing at night can be very productive, especially for fooling large walleye. Cast a five- to seven-inch, shallow-running crankbait. Scout good locations in the daytime; you are looking for water two to seven feet deep that is full of perch or bluegill and yet still near deep water. Wear chest waders, fish quietly, and bring a big net. This technique can be very effective near the dams of our better walleye reservoirs.

NORTHERN PIKE

One look at the front end of a northern pike and you know why these fish are called voracious predators. Their mouths are full of very sharp teeth. It takes a lake full of forage fish to support a population of northern pike, and on an all-meat diet they get big very quickly. The state record is a tie between two fish, both weighing thirty-six pounds, caught in Miami Lake (now private) and Springer Lake. Larger northern pike have been caught in Navajo Lake. Cochiti Lake, Lake Sumner, the upper Rio Grande, and one of the Zuni Indian lakes (Black Rock) all have good northern pike fishing.

Besides the mouth full of teeth, northern pike are an elongated fish with a dark green back. The coloring gradually changes to light green on the sides and a golden white on the bottom. There are irregular yellow and white splotches on both the sides and the back. New Mexican pike spawn in the spring, usually in March. Pike are daytime feeders, normally in the morning and again in the afternoon. They eat rodents, waterdogs, lizards, ducklings, and birds, but mostly they eat smaller fish. A twenty-four-inch, three-pound northern pike is going to be about two and a half years old. Those thirty-six-pound state records had been dodging lures for around fifteen years.

Bait fishermen catch northerns by still-fishing with a bluegill or a big minnow. The casting or trolling angler uses plugs, spinnerbaits, big flies, or spoons. In other words, pike strike just about anything. Use a wire leader if you plan to land many pike, for their sharp teeth can zip right through monofilament. Fly fishermen will find a nine-foot nine-weight rod to be adequate; tie on a yellow and black Dalberg Diver and remember to bring a big net.

Northerns charge their intended victim. These predators often lie in weedbeds, ready to ambush a bullhead or perch. Anglers boat-fishing the west shoreline of Springer Lake cast spinnerbaits parallel to the weedbeds. There is no mistaking the wake a pike makes as it charges your lure. The trick is not to strike until the pike actually grabs the lure; easy to say, but a bit unnerving in practice.

Northern Pike

Fishing at Springer Lake is best in April and May, decent in summer, and good in the fall. The same holds true for Navajo and all New Mexico pike waters. The key is water temperatures; the fish are active between 40°F and 65°F. Above 65°F the angler needs to retrieve at a slower rate or use bait because the fish get sluggish in the warmer water of summer. Late afternoon catches are decent at Cochiti Lake in late spring and midfall. The Rio Grande, from Velarde north through the Rio Grande Gorge, holds pike in the slower pools and backwaters. River-fishing is best in October and November. Black Rock Lake, just outside of Zuni, is full of middle-size northerns.

PERCH

Not many anglers plan their vacations around yellow perch. These little panfish are members of the same family as the walleye. Perch have a yellowish or olive coloring and a white belly. No other freshwater fish has the gold and black stripes of the yellow perch. A half-pound per fish is about right for an adult ten-inch perch.

Perch have a habit of overpopulating the lakes where they've been stocked; our fisheries managers are quite careful about where they introduce these panfish. A good perch lake must have a healthy population of predators, like walleye or northern pike. Without the predators, you end up with a zillion perch and a lake so overgrazed that the other sportfish suffer.

Once you find a school of perch, it's usually no trouble to catch a bucket full. They travel in groups, often in deep water during the day. They eat just about anything—snails, bugs, little crayfish, minnows, and small fish. And they can be caught on just about anything, though small plastic tube jigs are a good and inexpensive tackle choice.

Perch spawn in the spring, after the walleye and northerns. The state-record perch came from Miami Lake (now private). It weighed one pound and sixteen ounces. It's interesting to note that Miami has an excellent population of northern pike. Lower Charette Lake has good perch fishing along the rock cliffs of the northern shoreline. Springer Lake was stocked with perch to provide more forage for the northern pike. Stubblefield Lake is the only other perch water in the state. There is no bag limit on perch.

CRAPPIE

Crappie are members of the sunfish family (which also includes largemouth and smallmouth bass as well as sunfish). Though both white and black crappie were stocked in New Mexico, the whites are more prevalent. Crappie have a silver sheen with an olive-green color. White crappie have seven or eight vertical black bars on their sides; blacks have black spots scattered all over their sides. Crappie are prolific spawners, and their diet consists of smaller fish and insects. Though stocked in all our major reservoirs, fishing for crappie is a boom-or-bust proposition.

Crappie populations in most lakes follow a cycle difficult to predict. For two or three years the spring fishing will be great. Everybody will be catching lots of fat ten-inch crappie. Then for a couple of years there will seem to be no fish. The cycle continues with two seasons providing tons of crappie, all five inches long; and then back-to-back years with lots of big fish. Watch the fishing reports for clues to crappie waters that are having a good year. Good spring, summer, and fall crappie fishing can invariably be found somewhere in New Mexico, but the best spots change every year.

Spring is spawning time for crappie, the best time to cash in on these shallow-water spawners. Crappie move en masse to waters three to six feet deep. The best nesting areas are used by hundreds of fish. Once you've caught a fish, cast back to the same spot and there is a good chance you can continue to take fish out of that area all afternoon. Don't give an area more than a dozen casts; if you don't get a strike, move to a different part of the shoreline.

During spawning time, crappie are programmed to move anything out of their nest. Anglers in the right spot can fish with a gold hook and catch crappie. Small crankbaits and spinnerbaits catch the larger crappie, but they also snare the submerged brush prevalent around the shallows of all good crappie waters. A lead-head jig with either yellow marabou feathers or a plastic tube jig is an inexpensive way to catch these panfish.

During summer and fall the crappie are in loose schools, in five to fifteen feet of water, and normally around submerged trees and brush. Winter finds them deeper; twenty to forty feet is typical. Minnows fished at night under the glare of a Coleman lantern is a time-tested way to catch crappie. Jigging with minnows or small lures is effective when the fish are deep. Light tackle is the rule, and a one-pound fish is exceptional. The state record weighed four pound and nine ounces, and was caught from the Black River on a minnow.

Conchas and Abiquiu are the best-known New Mexico crappie waters, but all our warmwater reservoirs can have exceptional spring crappie fishing. As mentioned earlier, it depends on what part of the cycle your favorite lake is experiencing. Boom or bust is the rule with crappie populations. Here, in alphabetical order, are New Mexico's crappie waters: Abiquiu,

Crappie

Bernardo, Bill Evans, Bosque de Apache, Caballo, Cochiti, Conchas, Elephant Butte, Green Meadow, Lake Sumner, Municipal Lake, Navajo, Ojo
Caliente Lake, Santa Rosa, and Ute.

CATFISH

Catfish are easily distinguished by their whiskers and by their lack of
scales. These are the biggest fish in New Mexico. The record channel catfish
weighed twenty-eight pounds and was caught at Cochiti Lake. The record
flathead catfish weighed seventy-eight pounds and was caught in Ash Canyon in Elephant Butte Lake. Flatheads are no longer stocked, but each year
many thousands of channel cats are put in New Mexico waters.

While catfish will occasionally grab a spinner lure or a crappie jig, serious
catfish angling is done with bait. Various commercially prepared stinkbaits
and chicken or beef liver are favorites for bottom-fishing. Many serious
catfish anglers use only live bait; bluegills are a legal and excellent catfish
bait.

New Mexico has good river angling for channel catfish in the Rio Grande,
from Velarde north into the Rio Grande Gorge State Park. The Gila River
also offers very good catfishing from Gila Hotsprings downstream to the
Arizona line. New Mexico's other catfish stream is the Rio Chama, between
Abiquiu Lake and El Vado Dam.

New Mexico catfish anglers looking for good lake-fishing have many
waters to choose from. Bluewater Lake offers fine midsummer catches. Ute
Lake is one of New Mexico best catfish lakes. Navajo Lake, Cochiti, Abi-
quiu, Conchas, Lake Sumner, Santa Rosa, and the Elephant Butte, Rio
Grande, Caballo complex are all good spots. The Department of Game and
Fish stocks a lot of five- to eight-inch catfish in these lakes, totaling about
a million a year. Smaller lakes, like Bear Canyon, Eunice Lake, and Jal
Lake, also get stocked.

Catching catfish is an art that requires patience, luck, and experience.
Serious fishermen say that the best time to go fishing is anytime, but catfish
seem to be more active when the sun is off the water. From dawn to 9:00
A.M. or after dark is best. Bluewater Lake seems to be an exception. During
the dog days of August fishermen catch trout at dawn and dusk, but the
best midday catches are made by anglers pursuing channel catfish. They
cast to deep water using lead sinkers because they want their crayfish baits
right on the bottom.

New Mexico
Department of Game and Fish

Statute Authority, Politics, Funding, and Activities

You can hardly go fishing in New Mexico without dealing with the New Mexico Department of Game and Fish. On federal land, state land, even on private land or on your own land, the regulations authorized by the State Game Commission and enforced by the Department of Game and Fish control are valid. The department does not control or license game and fish activities on Indian land, but Game and Fish does work with the people responsible for wildlife management on many reservation and Pueblo lands.

Section 17 of the 1978 New Mexico Statute Authority (NMSA), originally passed in 1931, reads as follows:

> 17-1-1. **DECLARATION OF POLICY.**—It is the purpose of this act and the policy of the state of New Mexico to provide an adequate and flexible system for the protection of the game and fish of New Mexico and for their use and development for public recreation and food supply and to provide for their propagation, planting, protection, regulation and conservation to the extent necessary to provide and maintain an adequate supply of game and fish within the state of New Mexico.

This policy is the basis for all operations of the New Mexico Department of Game and Fish and the State Game Commission.

The 1931 act set up a State Game Commission with members appointed by the governor and approved by the Senate. Commissioners serve a rotating five-year term, with one term ending each year. Thus, each year the governor appoints (or reappoints) a member to the State Game Commission. Members can be removed from the commission by the governor for "malfeasance or incompetence." This tactic is typically used by a new administration to clear the commission and put in place members with the new governor's point of view. The State Game Commission cannot have more than three members of one political party and its members must be appointed, one each, from the four quadrants of the state as well as one person from Bernalillo County. Commission members are not paid for their work,

Department of Game and Fish

but they do receive mileage costs and a per diem allowance. The commission, with formal advice from the department, makes all the hunting and fishing regulations. The commission hires, and can fire, the Director of the Department of Game and Fish; the Director runs the department.

This operating procedure keeps most partisan politics out of the activities of the Department of Game and Fish. The department operates as a scientific wildlife resource management organization. Politics is kept to the commission level. Individuals and organizations lobby their desires and needs with the commissioners; the commission votes, and the department deals with the results.

Chapter 17 of the 1978 NMSA states that money from hunting and fishing licenses shall not be used for any purpose other than Department of Game and Fish activities. In other words, the money you spend on your fishing license goes only to the Department of Game and Fish and not to the general fund of the state of New Mexico. By the way, it is not the commission or the department, but the legislature that sets the fees for hunting and fishing licenses. The department also receives funds from the Pittman-Robertson, Dingell-Johnson, and Wallop-Breaux programs. These are federal excise taxes on sporting goods. Every time you buy a rod, reel, boat, fishing line, firearm, motorboat fuel, or just about any other sporting good, a hidden excise tax is included in the retail price. The federal government collects this money from the manufacturers and distributes it back to the states by using a formula based on the size of the state and the number of fishing and hunting licenses sold. Fines collected in court for breaking the fishing and hunting regulations do not go to the department, but civil damages collected to pay for illegally killed game or fish do go into the Game Protection Fund, the department's "bank account."

So most of the operating expenditures (97 percent) of the Department of Game and Fish come from the sportsmen of New Mexico. However, most capital expenditures, like the millions of dollars it takes to rebuild a hatchery, come from the bonding authority of the legislature. The department has also received lump sums from the General Fund. (Eagle Nest Lake was leased by using such money.) In both cases, elected legislators introduce identical bills in both the House and Senate. The bills go through the committee process and are either killed, tabled (which effectively kills them), or passed. If the bills make it through the committees they are then passed, killed, or tabled on the floor of the House and Senate. The legislation is then signed (or not signed) by the governor. Funding is definitely a complex part of wildlife management in New Mexico.

Forecasts of the future needs of the Department of Game and Fish show an increase in expenses and a proportional decrease in funding. Income from fishing and hunting licenses will not cover the cost of managing our wildlife resource. The department is now required to take on more and more activities, yet it is still being funded solely with sportsmen's dollars. Your fishing-and-hunting-license dollars have been stretched to cover endangered species, game-depredation work, snowmobile control, campground maintenance, and law-enforcement activities. These activities are mandated by law and are important to all the people of New Mexico. Yet it is only the sportsmen, not the general public, who are paying for these activities. The Department of Game and Fish is looking at alternative funding sources to meet the varied needs of the future.

FISHERIES MANAGEMENT AND OPERATIONS

It is the job of the Department of Game and Fish to protect and manage our fisheries resource. State law mandates two purposes for this policy: to maintain an adequate supply of fish within the state, and to manage the fish for public recreation. Fishing is big business in New Mexico. Anglers in our state spend over 150 million dollars a year on this outdoor sport, and those dollars are distributed all over the state. Campgrounds, motels, bait shops, gas stations, convenience stores, marinas, sporting goods stores, restaurants, as well as many more supporting industries depend on fishing for a good portion of their business.

Where does the Department of Game and Fish get the money to do the job? Almost 8 million dollars is made on the sale of hunting and fishing licenses. The return of federal excise taxes on sporting goods—Pittman-Robertson, Wallop-Breaux, and Dingell-Johnson moneys—annually contribute another 3 million dollars to the department's bank account. All in all, the department had expenditures of about 10 million dollars in 1984–85. Direct fisheries management accounts for 18 percent of that total, about 2 million dollars. In fact, fisheries expenditures are actually higher. That 2 million dollars doesn't include crossover costs incurred in other sections of the department. The Administration, Business Management, Special Services, Public Affairs, Law Enforcement, Area Operations, and Planning departments are all involved in fisheries management. A good guess might be that the Department of Game and Fish spends about 4.5 million dollars (using figures from fiscal year 1984–85) on fisheries management.

How do they spend all of that money? About 1 million dollars is spent in operating fish hatcheries. Another 2 million is spent on payroll. You can

Department of Game and Fish

add another 1.5 million dollars for vehicles, boats, field supplies, travel, publications, and maintenance. Remember that the Department of Game and Fish is the only state agency almost totally funded by user fees. The fishermen and hunters of New Mexico pay the bills.

The Department of Game and Fish is organized with the Director at the top. Under the Director are the Division Chiefs and the Area Supervisors. The Fish Management Division is located in Santa Fe and has a Division Chief, an Assistant Division Chief for Hatchery Operations, an Assistant Division Chief for Research and Management, and a Fisheries Research Project Leader. The department has four area offices, one located in each quadrant of the state. Each area has its own Area Fisheries Manager. Area offices are located in Albuquerque, Raton, Las Cruces, and Roswell. The uniformed men and women in the white pickups who check your fishing licenses are Conservation Officers (Game Wardens). These department employees are stationed all over the state and are not Fish Management Division employees. However, Conservation Officers see many anglers and often have the latest fishing report information.

The Fish Management Division operates six hatcheries: Glenwood Hatchery, on Whitewater Creek, sixty miles north of Silver City on U.S. 180; Lisboa Springs Hatchery, on the Pecos River just north of the town of Pecos; Parkview Hatchery, by the Chama River and near Tierra Amarilla; Red River Hatchery, near Questa on the Red River; Seven Springs Hatchery, on the Rio Cebolla near Fenton Lake; and Rock Lake Hatchery, located just south of Santa Rosa. Rock Lake has the distinction of being the only hatchery raising fish other than trout or kokanee. Fifty million walleye fry are hatched each year at Rock Lake. All the hatcheries are open to the public. Red River, Lisboa Springs, and Parkview are newly rebuilt operations with visitor centers.

With over a quarter-million licensed fishermen in New Mexico, the department has a big job in managing fish for the fishermen and managing fishermen for the fish. Choices have to be made about how to allocate resources. Some fishermen want more hatchery-raised rainbows, while others want more attention paid to largemouth bass or to catch-and-release fishing. Meeting the demands of the public while balancing the realities of the resources requires knowledgeable fisheries biologists, careful planning, adequate water and money, and good luck.

Postal surveys, telephone polls, public-input meetings, and field questionnaires help in revealing the desires and needs of the angling public. Lake and stream sample netting operations and electroshocking surveys reveal the carrying capacity, chemistry, fish populations, and hydrology of the fishable waters in New Mexico. The professionals in the Fish Management Division then sharpen their pencils, crank up their computers, and carve up the resource pie: so many man-hours for the kokanee spawn project, so many man-hours for the walleye spawn project, so many catchable-size rainbow trout for Fenton Lake, and so many rainbow fingerlings for Bluewater. Do we stock more striped bass in Elephant Butte? Or put striper fry in Caballo? But will Caballo have any water in it three years from now? Or are the stripers hurting the largemouth fishing? Or are the largemouth hurting the striper fishing? Can we even get any striper fry this year? Can we put white bass in Abiquiu without hurting the crappie fishing? Should we recommend a size limit on black bass at Ute Lake, or will that type of regulation do nothing in producing more big bass? The questions are endless, the resources limited, and more and more fishermen are moving to New Mexico. It's the job of the Department of Game and Fish to balance the needs and desires of the public with the realities of the resource.

If you want your ideas to become part of the fish management process, go to the public-input meetings held every two years, just before the New Mexico Fishing Regulations are rewritten. These are formal meetings where your input is transcribed in writing and taken into consideration. Join the local Trout Unlimited Club or one of the local B.A.S.S. clubs. Volunteers from these organizations get a chance to work with the Area Fisheries Manager on projects that benefit their local fishing waters. If you have a question about a local stream or lake, you can call the Area Fisheries Manager. Be prepared to leave a message, as these people are often working in the field. You can lobby for your point of view at the monthly meetings of the State Game Commission. Since commission meetings are formal affairs, it's best to attend a couple of these meetings before you jump up and speak your piece. You can also lobby commission members by letter. The Fish Management Division in Santa Fe is only a phone call away. A letter to the Fish Management Division Chief will always result in a written reply. It is part of the job of these people to listen and respond to the citizens of New Mexico. If you are rude or impolite, they can hang up. If you have a question or suggestion, they will respond.

Boating Regulations
in New Mexico

Any vessel using a motor or sail for power must be registered. Any vessel ten feet long or longer and using a motor or sail for power must be titled. Both the registration and the titling are handled by the Boating Section, New Mexico State Park and Recreation Division.

Boats are titled at their first registration, at transfer of ownership, or upon renewal of registration. Titles are valid until change of ownership. Boat-registration certificates are good for three calendar years, and expire on December 31 of the third year. Upon change of ownership, the New Mexico State Park and Recreation Division must be notified within fifteen days and registration and title must be transferred. Proof of ownership (dealer's invoice or notarized bill of sale) must be presented for original registration or transfer of ownership. The original registration numbers issued to a specific boat will remain with the boat upon change of ownership.

Title fee for all vessels ten or more feet in length with power or sail is $10.50. Various registration fees are established as follows:

Registration Fees

Class A—under 16 feet in length $28.50
Class 1—16 feet to less than 26 feet in length $36.00
Class 2—26 feet to less than 40 feet in length $43.50
Class 3—40 feet to less than 65 feet $51.00
Vessels over 65 feet in length $66.00
Duplicate copy of registration $5.00
Special out-of-state fee (daily) $2.00
The special out-of-state daily fee is for individuals without an out-of-state registration.

The following is a partial listing of Boating Regulations that apply on all New Mexico waters:

Boating Regulations

1. A vessel's registration number must be printed on each side of the vessel in accordance with New Mexico law, and the certificate of number must be on board when the vessel is in operation.

2. All vessels operating on New Mexico waters are subject to inspection.

3. All vessels must carry proper safety equipment while in operation, including life jackets for each person on board, a paddle, a bailing bucket, rope, signaling device, fire extinguisher, and lights (if operating at night). Class A boats must have a life jacket for each person on board. Descriptions of exact requirements for safety equipment are available at state park offices.

4. Discharging any waste or refuse into the waters of New Mexico is strictly prohibited.

5. Riding the foredeck, seat backs, or gunwales of vessels is prohibited.

6. Vessels must be operated at speeds no greater than is reasonable and proper under prevailing conditions. "No wake" restrictions are strictly enforced where posted, and in such areas as launch ramps, docks, marinas, and mooring areas.

7. Anchoring, mooring, drifting, and fishing are prohibited within one hundred feet of boat ramps, marinas, and courtesy docks.

8. Overloading vessels is prohibited.

9. Rules of the road must be observed: When passing headon, keep right; from rear, pass left; at right angles, the boat on the right has the right-of-way. A vessel leaving a dock, marina, or boat ramp has the right-of-way over an approaching vessel. Boaters must stay at least 150 feet away from swimmers, water-skiers, or fishermen.

10. Operation of a vessel in a reckless or negligent manner, or while intoxicated or under the influence of any narcotic drug, barbiturate, or marijuana, is strictly prohibited.

11. Persons using canoes, rafts, inner tubes, air mattresses, rubber rafts, or similar devices are required to wear United States Coast Guard–approved life jackets.

12. The owner of a vessel is liable for any injury or damage caused by the negligent operation of his vessel.

13. All boating accidents must be reported to a local state park office or other authority within forty-eight hours of occurrence.

Individuals operating boats on Indian waters should be aware of boat-use fees and safety requirements. Get the details from the specific tribe on whose waters you will be boating.

The U.S. Army Corps of Engineers has two additional rules that apply to Abiquiu, Cochiti, Conchas, and Santa Rosa reservoirs. All boaters must heed the wind-warning lights. All people on board a Class-A vessel must wear life jackets at all times.

The Boating Section of the New Mexico State Park and Recreation Division operates a toll free number; call 1-800-874-0675.

Fishing Regulations in New Mexico; 1959

FISHING LICENSE FEES

Resident Fishing $3.50
Nonresident 5-day Fishing 3.00
Nonresident Fishing 8.00
Resident General Hunting and Fishing 9.00

FISHING LICENSE REQUIREMENTS

All persons aged 14 and over must have license in order to fish.

The following are entitled to resident license:
(a) bona fide residents;
(b) persons who have actually lived within the state for 6 months immediately preceding application for license;
(c) students attending any educational institution in the state, who have attended at least one full term next preceding application for license;
(d) members of the armed forces who are permanently assigned to military installations within the state.

IMPORTATION OF FISH

Permit must be obtained from the Director to import into the state any species of fish except those from government hatcheries.

PLACING OF FISH IN CERTAIN WATERS PROHIBITED

No person shall put or place in any of the public waters of this state any fish or spawn therefrom of any species whatsoever, without having first obtained permission from the Director of the Department of Game and Fish.

BOATS PERMITTED ON CLAYTON AND JACKSON LAKES

Only boats without motors and having a minimum length of 12 feet, minimum beam of 48 inches and a minimum depth of 18 inches are permitted. and then only on those portions of lakes not closed for waterfowl nesting and resting marked by a posted line.

MANNER OF TAKING GAME FISH:

Game fish may be taken during the open season therefor by angling only, that is, by hook and line. The line is to be attached to a rod, held in the hand or constantly attended; not exceeding one rod or one line to one person. Catfish may also be taken by trotline or set lines, as hereinafter provided.

No game fish may be taken by angling, set line or trotline when there are also employed any means which may attract or concentrate fish into a specific locality, such as chumming or the use of mechanical or electrical devices, except for unsubmerged artificial lights. Exceptions: Catfish may be taken by angling, set line or trotline, and other game fish by angling when aided by chumming, submerged artificial lights and mechanical devices which attract fish by sound in the following waters: Main stream only of the Rio Grande from Highway No. 84 bridge at Espanola to the Texas-New Mexico state line; Main stream only of Pecos River from Colonias bridge near Rowe to the Texas-New Mexico state line; Main stream only of Canadian River from Highway No. 58 bridge at Taylor Springs to the Texas-New Mexico state line; and the reservoirs which are on the above described sections of these rivers. It shall be unlawful to chum with any substance which is injurious to fish or other aquatic life.

MANNER OF TAKING NON-GAME FISH IN GAME FISH WATERS:

Non-game fish may be taken in waters containing game fish by angling, trotline, set line, spears, gigs and arrows. Spears, gigs and arrows may not be driven by means of an explosive, gas or air. The Director may, in his discretion, issue permits for the taking of non-game fish by means of nets, seines or traps; such permits shall specify methods of taking, place or places to be taken and duration of the permit. The permittee shall report monthly the numbers, species and poundage of non-game fish taken during the month next preceding.

BAIT RESTRICTIONS:

The use of game fish of any species, bullfrogs or bullfrog tadpoles, dead or alive, or any part thereof, as bait for angling, trotline or set-line fishing is prohibited. Provided that game fish raised in private hatcheries under a Class "A" Lake License (Section 53-4-6, New Mexico Statutes Annotated, 1953 Compilation) may be sold and used as bait when the person using the same has in his possession a certificate showing the place and the date of purchase.

POSSESSION AFTER CLOSED SEASON:

No game fish, as defined by statute, shall be held in possession or stored after March 31st following the open season during which such game fish were taken, unless there is first obtained a storage permit issued under authority of the Director.

TROT AND SET LINES, MANNER USED AND WATERS WHERE PERMITTED:

Catfish may be taken during day or night by the use of a trotline or set line and/or by angling, provided that not more than 25 hooks in the aggregate be used. Any kind of bait except game fish, bullfrogs or bullfrog tadpoles may be used. No person may fish with more than one trotline or set line at one time. The tying or joining together of trotlines or set lines belonging to two or more persons shall be illegal. Any person fishing with a trotline or set line shall attach thereto a tag bearing his name, address, fishing license number, date and hour the line was set. The identification tag shall be attached to the trotline in such a manner that it will be visible and above the water line. Not more than one person may attach his name to any one trot or set line. All unidentified lines are subject to seizure and confiscation by any conservation officer. Every person using a trotline or set line in fishing for catfish is hereby required personally to visit and run the line at least once every 24 hours, except when prohibited from doing so by severe weather conditions. The placing or setting of any trotline or set line within 300 feet of any diversion or storage dam is prohibited.

Trotlines or set lines may be used for taking catfish in the following waters only: In the Canadian River watershed between Sabinoso and the Texas line, and in the Canadian River proper between Sabinoso and Taylor Springs; the Mora River between Watrous and the Canadian River; in the Pecos River watershed in Guadalupe, De Baca, Chaves and Eddy Counties; in the Rio Grande watershed from the highway bridge at Bernalillo to the Texas line, except Bluewater Lake; and the Rio Grande proper from Highway 84 bridge at Espanola to Highway 44 bridge at Bernalillo; Gila River proper from the junction of main stream and east fork of Gila River to the Arizona line; in the San Francisco River downstream from Reserve to the Arizona line; in the San Juan River downstream from the Colorado state line and in ranch tanks.

BOATS AND OTHER FLOATING DEVICES PROHIBITED:

The use of boats and other floating devices for any purpose on the following lakes is prohibited: Fenton Lake in Sandoval County, Wall Lake in Catron County, Hopewell Lake in Rio Arriba County, McGaffey Lake in McKinley County and San Gregorio Lake in Rio Arriba County.

IRRIGATION, DITCHES—SCREENS REQUIRED:

It shall be the duty of the owner or owners of any canal or ditch into which any portion of the waters of any stream or lake containing game fish as defined by Section 53-2-3, New Mexico Statutes Annotated, 1953 Compilation, are diverted, for the purpose of irrigation or any other purpose which consumes such water so diverted, to install and maintain at the head of such canal or ditch a screen, a paddle wheel or wheels or other device to prevent passage of fish when required by the Director, which shall be maintained when so required during such portion of each year as such waters are diverted for irrigation or other purposes.

POLLUTING WATERS PROHIBITED:

It shall be unlawful for any person, firm or corporation to deposit, throw or in any way permit to pass into any water wherein fish are living any substance that will tend to the destruction or the driving away of any fish from such waters, or will be detrimental to the reproduction of the fish or to the reproduction and growth of natural fish food.

TAKING FISH FROM HATCHERY PROHIBITED:

No person shall take fish from the waters of any fish hatchery or rearing ponds owned and operated by the State Department of Game and Fish or the U. S. Fish and Wildlife Service, except employees of these agencies in connection with the official operation of such hatcheries and rearing ponds.

MANNER OF TAKING BULLFROGS
(Jumbo Bullfrogs) (*Rana catesbiana*):

Bullfrogs may be taken during open season by angling, spears, gigs, and arrows and only between the hours of sunrise and sunset. Only spears, gigs and arrows not driven by explosive, gas or air may be used in taking bullfrogs.

A Quick Guide to New Mexico Fishing Waters

This annotated directory began as a direct copy of the official Department of Game and Fish New Mexico Fishing Waters pamphlets. The 1977, 1982, and 1985 editions of this handout were used to create the core for this index. Once the list and descriptions were entered into a computerized data base, it became apparent that over the years mistakes, oversights, and omissions had crept into the list. This author rechecked, cross-referenced, and updated all the major, minor, and many of the tiny fishing waters for this index. The current Department of Game and Fish Fishing Waters pamphlet includes a map with all of the streams and lakes numbered and keyed to the list. Get a copy at your local New Mexico Department of Game and Fish Area Office.

ABBOTT LAKES.   Two private lakes southwest of Abbott.

ABIQUIU CREEK.   Small stream, north side of Jemez Mountains near Abiquiu. Upper portion accessible only by trail, eight miles. Rainbow trout, cutthroats.

ABIQUIU LAKE.   Combination cold- and warmwater fishery; very few rainbows, browns, and kokanee. Very good crappie, smallmouth bass, and catfish fishing. Four thousand to eight thousand acres; reservoir on Chama River; good camping and boating facilities.

ACOMITA LAKE.   On Acoma Indian Reservation. Was once about thirty acres; now drained, may be rebuilt.

AGUA CHIQUITO.   Small creek with brook trout; flows through Sacramento in Lincoln National Forest.

AGUA FRIA CREEK.   Small stream that empties into Cieneguilla Creek just above Eagle Nest Lake; private. Cutthroats.

AGUA FRIA CREEK.   Small tributary of the Mora River. Cutthroats.

AGUA NEGRA CHIQUITA.   Small stream near Santa Rosa; private.

AGUA PIEDRA CREEK.   Small tributary entering Rio Pueblo from the south, about two miles below Tres Ritos. Rainbow trout and cutthroats.

ALAMITOS CREEK.   Nice brushy little tributary to Rio Pueblo, three miles. Cutthroats.

ALAMITOS LAKE.   Small lake at head of Alamitos. Usually heavy winterkill. Cutthroats, but very little fishing.

ALBUQUERQUE BAR RIVERSIDE DRAIN.   Heads four miles south of Albuquerque, and drains a mile northeast of Isleta.

ALBUQUERQUE RIVERSIDE DRAIN.   One of the largest and best canals; heads twelve miles north of city limits and parallels the river. Warmwater species, plus winter-stocked trout.

ALBUQUERQUE RIVERSIDE DRAIN (Williams Lateral).   Tributary to Rio Grande near Old Town, Albuquerque.

ALGODONES-RIVERSIDE DRAIN.   Five miles long, located north of Bernalillo along east bank of Rio Grande. Warmwater species.

ALICE LAKE.   Near Raton; a small lake on Chicorico Creek south of Lake Maloya; four acres. Rainbow trout; stocked when water is suitable.

ALTO LAKE.   On Eagle Creek at Alto, right off pavement near Ruidoso; twenty acres. Stocked with catchable-size rainbow trout.

AMERICAN CREEK.   Small tributary of Rio las Vacas in Jemez Mountains; five miles. Cutthroats.

AMERICAN CREEK.   Small tributary of Cieneguilla Creek in Moreno Valley, south of Eagle Nest Lake; three miles; private. Cutthroats.

ANACONDA LAKE.   Ten acres near Bluewater; private. Bass, bluegill.

ANGOSTURA CREEK.   Nice brushy cutthroat stream; enters Rio Pueblo about two miles upstream from Tres Ritos.

ANIMAS CREEK.   Small, trail, northwest of Kingston. Cutthroats, rainbow trout.

ANIMAS RIVER.   Fair trout stream of large-water volume from Colorado to San Juan River at Farmington; thirty-eight miles. Stocked rainbow, wild browns, catfish.

ARMSTRONG LAKE.   Five acres on Johnson Mesa near Raton; private.

ARROYO SECO CREEK.   Very small; Pine Lodge in Capitan Mountains.

ASAAYI LAKE.   On Navajo Reservation, thirty-acre trout lake south of Crystal; permit required.

ASPEN LAKE.   On Navajo Reservation, trout lake north of S.R. 134 in Chuska Mountains; permit required.

ATRISCO RIVERSIDE DRAIN.   West of Rio Grande in Albuquerque from Highway 85 bridge, returning to river below Isleta Diversion.

AVALON LAKE.   Five miles north of Carlsbad on Pecos River, poor fishing because of irrigation drawdown, rarely at nine hundred acres. Bass, white bass, channel catfish.

BASS LAKE.   South of Santa Rosa; private. Bluegill, bass.

BATAAN LAKE.   Municipal recreation lake on Pecos in Carlsbad; forty-two acres. Bass, catfish, trout in winter.

BEAR CANYON.   Small stream east of Raton; private. Rainbow trout.

BEAR CANYON LAKE.   A two-acre lake stocked with rainbow trout; plenty of bluegill. Southwest of Mayhill.

BEAR CANYON RESERVOIR.   East of Silver City, two miles north of Mimbres; twenty-two acres. Trout, bluegill, bass, catfish, and crappie.

BEAR CREEK.   Good mountain-stream tributary to the Mora Fork of the Pecos River, reached by trail up Mora; ten miles. Mostly browns, some rainbows in lower portion.

BEAR CREEK.   Tributary to Gila River at Cliff.

BEAR LAKE.   See *Lucero Lake.*

BEAVER CREEK.   North fork of El Porvenir Creek, tributary of Gallinas River; reached by trail from El Porvenir.

BEAVER CREEK.   Small tributary to the East Fork of the Gila River. Brown trout, smallmouth bass, and catfish.

BELEN RIVERSIDE DRAIN.   A drain beginning four miles north of Las Lunas south to Belen, sixteen miles long on the west side of the Rio Grande. Warmwater species, plus winter-stocked trout.

BERLAND LAKE.   Navajo Reservation, permit required, trout lake in Chuska mountains north of S.R. 134.

BERNALILLO RIVERSIDE DRAIN.   Short drain near Algodones, east of river on Indian land.

BERNARDO WATERFOWL AREA.   Rio Grande bosque between Socorro and Albuquerque, open from April through August; best in spring. Channel catfish, bass, crappie.

BERRENDO CREEK.   Small tributary to Pecos River at Roswell, four miles of stream; private. Bass, catfish.

BIG DRY CREEK. Tributary of San Francisco River, about fifteen miles southeast of Glenwood on the road to Silver City; not stocked. Good brown and rainbow trout population in upper reaches; closed to angling upstream from Golden Link Cabin because of Gila trout.

BIG TESUQUE. Very small stream north of Santa Fe; four miles; mostly private. Browns and rainbows.

BILL EVANS LAKE. Good warmwater lake, seven miles south of Cliff, next to Gila River. Bass, crappie, catfish, bluegill, winter-stocked rainbows.

BITTER CREEK. Small tributary to Red River at the town of Red River; four miles. Good cutthroat and rainbow trout.

BITTER LAKES. A series of artificial lakes below a natural lake of the same name, about one hundred acres total; eight miles northeast of Roswell. National Wildlife Refuge; very little fishing.

BLACK CANYON. Tributary to the East Fork of the Gila River, twenty-five miles from Beaverhead, about sixty miles from Silver City; low in summer. Rainbow trout.

BLACK LAKE. Shallow lake northwest of Ocate; private. Some fishing.

BLACK LAKE. Two hundred acres, near Mosquero; private. Bluegill, catfish.

BLACK RIVER. Tributary to Pecos, two miles east of Malaga; mostly private. Good fishing from Black River Village to Blue Springs. Bass, bluegill, catfish; winter-stocked rainbow trout at Higby Hole.

BLACK ROCK LAKE. Zuñi reservation; permit required. Good pike; and stocked rainbow trout and cutthroats.

BLUE CANYON CREEK. Very small tributary of Tecolote Creek northwest of San Geronimo; by trail, five miles.

BLUE LAKE. Taos Pueblo; head of Rio Pueblo de Taos.

BLUEWATER CREEK. Empties into Bluewater Lake; seven miles. Some trout fishing, especially during spring runoff.

BLUEWATER LAKE. Large irrigation reservoir just south of I–40, west of Grants; state park, 2,350 acres. Fine rainbow trout fishing, catfish. Good summer brown trout fishery below dam.

BONITO CREEK NORTH FORK. Small stream in Lincoln National Forest above Bonito Lake; six miles. Rainbows and brookies.

BONITO CREEK SOUTH FORK. Small stream joining North Fork just above Bonito Lake; five miles. Rainbow and brook trout.

BONITO LAKE. Twelve miles from Ruidoso, sixty acres; closed to fishing in winter, very popular in summer. Good rainbow and brook trout fishing; no boats or floating devices.

BOSQUE DEL APACHE DRAIN. Located inside Federal Waterfowl Refuge south of Socorro; closed to fishing in winter. Some bass, bluegill, crappie and catfish.

BOSQUE REDONDO LAKE. Five miles south of Fort Sumner; fifteen acres. Bass, bluegill, catfish, and winter-stocked rainbow trout.

BOTTOMLESS LAKES. Six small lakes, ten miles east of Roswell; state park. Some bass, mostly winter-stocked rainbow trout.

BRANTLEY DAM RESERVOIR. On Pecos River above Carlsbad; new lake on Pecos (1988); good facilities. Walleye, bass, bluegill, catfish.

BRAZOS LAKE. Small private lake on upper Brazos River. Rainbow trout.

BRAZOS LODGE POND. Open to public. Stocked rainbows.

BRAZOS RIVER. Large, favored trout stream extending from Tierra Amarilla through a box canyon into Brazos Meadows and heading near the Colorado state line. Upper part posted private for guests of Corkins Lodge. Thirty-six miles, entirely private but some is open to public; stocked. Rainbows, cutthroats, and browns.

BRAZOS RIVER EAST FORK. Small tributary of upper Brazos; nine miles; private, good fishing. Cutthroats.

BULL CREEK. Small tributary to Cow Creek east of Pecos; ten miles. Cutthroats, browns and rainbows, maybe some brookies.

BURN LAKE. Warmwater municipal lake in Las Cruces; seven acres. Bass, catfish, bluegill, winter-stocked rainbow trout.

BURNS CANYON. Former brood pond at Parkview Hatchery near Tierra Amarilla; fifteen acres. Good rainbow trout lake.

BURRO CANYON. Small fork of Gallinas Creek; six miles. Cutthroats in upper reaches, rainbow trout in lower.

BUTLER STREET RESERVOIR. Three-acre lake within Farmington city limits. Bass, catfish.

CABALLO LAKE. Irrigation reservoir fifteen miles below Elephant Butte Dam on Rio Grande River; boating facilities and state park; water drawdowns, but 11,500 acres when full; good fishing. Largemouth, white bass, crappie, channel cats, striped bass, and walleye.

CABRESTO CREEK. Good little rainbow trout stream above Questa town; cutthroats higher up. Road follows along lower part of stream and trail to headwaters; mostly in Carson National Forest; thirteen miles.

CABRESTO CREEK LAKE FORK. Inlet and outlet for Cabresto Lake; small tributary to main Cabresto Creek; five miles. Good cutthroat and brook trout fishing.

CABRESTO LAKE. Excellent fifteen-acre high-mountain lake near Questa; decent access road. Cutthroats and brookies.

CALAVERAS CREEK. Very small stream entering Cebolla Creek, just above Seven Springs fish hatchery in the Jemez Mountains.

CALF CREEK. Small tributary of upper Gallinas River. Brown trout.

CALLEY LAKE. Small lake south of Wagon Mound; private.

CANADIAN RIVER. From Conchas Dam upstream to town of Taylor Springs; sixty miles of river with little access by car. Channel cats abundant from Conchas upstream to Sabinoso; mostly private. No public access from Conchas Dam downstream to Ute Lake; continues below Ute dam to Texas, with very little fishing.

CANJILON CREEK. Tributary of the Chama River heading at Canjilon Mountain in Carson National Forest; goes by Canjilon Lakes. Good rainbow trout and cutthroats from above the town of Canjilon to headwaters.

CANJILON LAKE. Five or six small lakes between two and six acres, about ten miles north and east of the town of Canjilon. Excellent fishing, very popular camping spot. Rainbow trout and cutthroats.

CAÑONES CREEK. Tributary entering Chama River five miles southeast of the town of Chama. Private; lower portion accessible by car, upper part by trail; ten miles. Good rainbow trout and cutthroat stream.

CAÑONES CREEK. Very small stream on north side of Jemez Mountains, eight miles southeast of Youngsville; ten miles. Beaver dams. Cutthroats, rainbow trout.

CAPULIN CREEK. Tributary of Rio Grande near Cochiti. Cutthroats.

CAPULIN CREEK. Small tributary to the Gallinas River, near the town of Gallinas. Cutthroats.

CARLSBAD MUNICIPAL LAKE. See *Municipal Lake.*

CARRIZO CREEK. On Mescalero Indian Reservation and private land near Ruidoso; feeds Ruidoso River in Ruidoso. Rainbow and brown trout.

CARRIZOZO LAKE. Warmwater, municipal recreation lake three miles southeast of Carrizozo; two acres. Catfish, winter-stocked rainbow trout.

CAVE CREEK. Extreme south fork of Panchuela Creek about four miles above Cowles, reached by trail; six miles. Cutthroats, browns.

CEBOLLA RIVER. Good small stream in Jemez Mountains from confluence with Rio las Vacas upstream to Fenton Lake and above to Seven Springs Fish Hatchery; fifteen miles. Browns, rainbows, cutthroats. Above hatchery, good but small beaver ponds; nine miles.

CEBOLLETA CREEK. Tributary to San José River north of Laguna; private. Very little fishing.

CENTER FIRE CREEK. Intermittent tributary to San Francisco River, northeast of Luna, ten miles.

CHAIN LAKES. East of Roswell, south of Bottomless Lakes; private.

CHAMA RIVER. Right below Abiquiu Dam. Catfish, some trout.

CHAMA RIVER, LOWER. From El Vado Dam down to Rio Puerco; excellent trout first few miles below dam; best access at Cooper's El Vado Ranch. Stocked rainbows and good wild browns.

CHAMA RIVER, MIDDLE. The main Chama, from the town of Chama to El Vado Lake; one of the best streams in the state; public water above El Vado Lake and just south of the town of Chama. Rainbows, cutthroats, browns; mostly private, twenty-eight miles with some big trout.

CHAMA RIVER, UPPER. The portion above the town of Chama to the Colorado border; good public stream along Sargent Wildlife Area, upper end private; six miles.

CHAMBERINO DRAIN. Canal near Las Cruces.

CHAMITA. Main west fork of Chama River, running through Sargent Wildlife Area; twelve miles. Cutthroats, rainbows, browns.

CHAPARRAL LAKE. Warmwater municipal recreation lake at Lovington; ten acres. Bass, catfish, bluegill, winter-stocked rainbow trout.

CHARETTE LAKES. Two lakes fed by Ocate Creek; excellent rainbow trout and perch in lower lake; north of Wagon Mound about thirteen miles, then twenty miles west on dirt roads; some fishing in upper lake; four hundred acres.

CHAVEZ CREEK. Largest tributary of Brazos, entering two miles up from its junction with the Chama; good stream, mostly posted.

CHERRY CREEK. Tributary to Bear Creek, and from there to Gila River above Cliff.

CHERRY VALLEY LAKE. Private shallow lake next to Mora River south of Wagon Mound. Trout.

CHICORICO CREEK. Stream out of Lake Maloya, northeast of Raton; sometimes dry, not stocked.

CHICOSA LAKE. Good forty-acre rainbow trout lake six miles north of Roy; state park.

CHIHUAHUEÑOS CREEK. Small cutthroat creek east of Youngsville on north side of Jemez Mountains; tributary to Gallinas.

CIENEGUILLA CREEK. Intermittent stream leading into Clayton Lake.

CIMARRONCITO RESERVOIR. Small trout pond near Ute Park; private.

CIMARRON RESERVOIR. Private twenty-acre trout lake near Cimarron.

CIMARRON RIVER. From Eagle Nest Lake downstream through Cimarron Canyon to Cimarron, very good for rainbows and browns; state park.

CLAYTON LAKE. Good rainbow, bluegill, catfish, bass, and walleye lake twelve miles northwest of Clayton; 170 acres; state park.

CLEAR CREEK. Small cutthroat tributary to Cimarron River.

CLEAR CREEK (Rita Presa). Small tributary to San Gregorio Lake, then to Rio de las Vacas; fishing good below lake. Cutthroats, rainbows.

COCHITI CREEK. Small cutthroat tributary to Rio Grande on east side of Jemez Mountains.

COCHITI LAKE. Thirty miles south of Santa Fe, twelve-hundred-acre reservoir on Rio Grande; good camping, some good fishing. White bass, crappie, rainbow trout, walleye, northerns, black bass, channel catfish.

COLUMBINE CREEK. Small tributary to Red River entering just above Questa; four miles. Nice fishing in beaver ponds.

COMANCHE CREEK. Small creek in Moreno Valley emptying into Eagle Nest Lake; nine miles; private.

COMANCHE CREEK. Major tributary to Costilla River on Valle Vidal; small, but lower end full of Rio Grande cutthroat hybrids.

CONCHAS LAKE. Sixteen-thousand-acre warmwater reservoir thirty-two miles northwest of Tucumcari; full-service state park and marinas. One of New Mexico's most popular lakes, with excellent angling for largemouth, smallmouth, crappie, catfish, walleye.

CONCHAS RIVER. Tributary to Conchas Lake; private. Catfish.

CONEJO CREEK. Tributary to Pecos River in De Baca County, ten miles northeast of Dunlap; private. Bass and bluegills.

COOPER CANYON CREEK. Little tributary to Iron Creek in Gila Mountains, reached by trail; two miles. Rainbow trout.

COPELAND CREEK. Very small, on north side of Capitan Mountains.

CORRALES RIVERSIDE DRAIN (Clear Ditch). Spring-fed drainage canal on west side of Rio Grande above Alameda bridge; nine miles. Stocked browns and rainbows. Good winter fishing, excellent fly-fishing.

COSTILLA RESERVOIR. On Vermejo Park property. Excellent wild trout fishing, all species; not stocked.

COSTILLA RIVER. Best cutthroat stream in the state, heads at Colorado line and flows south to Costilla Reservoir through Vermejo Ranch, then west on Carson National Forest and state public-fishing land—no bait-fishing and two-fish limit on much of the public-access land—then on private land to Rio Grande; twenty-eight miles. Some rainbows and brooks; plenty of good public fishing.

COTTONWOOD CREEK. Tributary to Pecos north of Artesia; mostly private. Some bass and catfish angling in park.

COW CREEK, LOWER. Tributary of Pecos from Lower Colonias through Vallecitos up to the falls; twenty-six miles. Browns, cutthroats, rainbows.

COW CREEK, UPPER. Heads at Elk Mountain, reached by trail; six miles. Cutthroats and rainbows.

COYOTE CREEK. Small stream heading on north side of Jemez Mountains, flowing north past Coyote, with some nice fishing toward the head; eight miles.

COYOTE CREEK. Tributary of Mora River; from Black Lake to Guadalupita paralleled by road, nine miles; stocked in state park; then small stream above Black Lake, seven miles.

CUB CREEK. Joins West Fork of Gila near Jenks Cabin Trail in Gila Wilderness Area. Browns and cutthroats.

CUTTER LAKE. Navajo Tribe water on irrigation project near Navajo Reservoir; not stocked.

DAILY CANYON. South Fork of Manuelitas Creek near Rociada. Browns.

DELAWARE CREEK. Small warmwater stream draining from Guadalupe Mountains into Pecos River; private.

DEL RIO DRAIN. Warmwater tributary to Rio Grande near Las Cruces. Bass, bluegill, and channel catfish.

DIAMOND CREEK. Tributary of the East Fork of Gila River; home to Gila trout and closed to fishing.

DOCTOR CREEK. Small stream, entering Holy Ghost Creek from south, about four miles upstream from Pecos River. Small cutthroats.

DRY CIMARRON. Flows east from eastern Colfax County to Oklahoma; some public fishing for stocked trout above Folsom, warmwater fishing below.

DULCE LAKE. Jicarilla Reservation, permit required; seventy-five acres, just off S.R. 17 near Dulce. Rainbow trout and cutthroats.

EAGLE CREEK. Small brook trout stream in Lincoln National Forest heading in White Mountains; crosses S.R. 37 at Alto and feeds Alto Lake.

EAGLE LAKES. Mescalero Reservation, permit required; camping, two little stocked trout lakes near Ski Apache.

EAGLE NEST LAKE. Excellent rainbow, cutthroat, and kokanee fishing in Moreno Valley between Taos and Cimarron. Two thousand acres; no camping, good ice-fishing.

EAGLE ROCK LAKE. A mile east of Questa beside Red River; three acres. Stocked with rainbows.

EAST DRAIN. In Doña Ana County, heads at Vado and parallels the railroad tracks; empties into Anthony Drain two miles south of Texas line.

ELEPHANT BUTTE LAKE. Forty thousand acres when full; rated as one of the ten best largemouth lakes in the United States. Irrigation reservoir with great bass fishing, smallmouth, largemouth, white and striped bass, walleye, catfish and crappie. Full-service state park, marinas, and private accommodations. Just off I–25 at Truth or Consequences.

ELK CREEK. Uppermost tributary to Cow Creek, by trail. Cutthroats.

ELLIS CREEK. Small, swift stream, north end of Sandia Mountains; reached by road from Bernalillo, two miles.

EL PASO LAKES. Private six-acre lake located east of Bloomfield.

EL PORVENIR CREEK. Small tributary of Gallinas Creek. Good fishing in beaver ponds; by trail, browns, cutthroats.

EL POSO CREEK. Fork of Canones Creek, by trail; private.

EL RITO CREEK. Heads in high country of Carson National Forest, twenty miles northwest of the town of El Rito; eighteen miles. Tributary of Chama with cutthroats, rainbows, brookies.

EL RITO LAKE. Private.

EL VADO LAKE. On Chama River fifteen miles southwest of Tierra Amarilla; full-service state park, 3,500 acres. Fine fishing for rainbows, browns, kokanee, carp.

EMBUDO CREEK. Formed by Rio Pueblo and Santa Barbara near Peñasco, to the Rio Grande at Embudo; public and private; twelve miles. Good rainbows and browns above Dixon.

ENBOM LAKE. Jicarilla Reservation, permit required. Good little trout lake twelve miles south of Dulce.

ENCANTADA LAKE (Enchanted Lake). At head of Rito Morphy by trail from Ledoux near Morphy Lake; three acres. Cutthroats.

ESCONDIDA LAKE. Four-acre lake north of Socorro about five miles. Catfish, bass, stocked with trout in winter.

ESTANCIA PARK LAKE. Winter-stocked trout pond in Estancia, for kids under twelve years old only.

EUNICE LAKE. Four-acre warmwater lake west of Eunice. Bass, catfish, bluegill, winter-stocked rainbows.

Eustace Lake

EUSTACE LAKE.   Zuñi Pueblo; permit required. Northerns, bass, catfish.

FALLS CREEK.   Tributary of Tecolote west of Mineral Hill; four miles; mostly private.

FAWN LAKES.   Two small ponds stocked with rainbows next to Red River; two miles downstream from the town of Red River.

FELIX RIVER.   Enters Pecos River near Hagerman. Some bass fishing.

FENTON LAKE.   By road twenty-one miles north of Jemez Springs, thirty acres; state park, very popular in summer. Good fishing for rainbows and some browns; ice-fishing.

FIN AND FEATHER LAKE.   Near Roswell; private. Bass, bluegill.

FRENCH LAKE.   Little irrigation reservoir near French; private.

FRESNAL CANYON CREEK.   Small stream, near Cloudcroft; private.

FRIJOLES CREEK.   Little creek through Bandelier National Monument, feeding Rio Grande; fourteen miles. Cutthroat, brook, rainbow trout.

GALESTINO No. 1 and No. 3.   Zuñi Pueblo; permit required. Stocked cutthroats and rainbows.

GALLINA CREEK.   Heads on Jemez Mountains near Gallina, flows to Chama River eighteen miles below El Vado Dam; four miles; private.

GALLINAS CREEK.   Tributary of Mimbres River near San Lorenzo.

GALLINAS RIVER.   West of Las Vegas below junction of El Porvenir Creek, good stream; mostly private. Sixteen miles upstream from Las Vegas, good public fishing, by road and trail. Rainbows, browns.

GASCON CREEK.   Above Rociada, six miles; mostly private.

GAVILAN CANYON CREEK.   Tributary to the Brazos, six miles west of Hopewell Lake; private. Cutthroat and rainbow trout.

GILA RIVER.   Lower and Middle Box, long stretch in Grant County east of Arizona line. Mostly warmwater fishing for channel catfish, smallmouth, flathead catfish, some browns; one hundred miles; winter-stocked rainbows near Cliff. Upper Box, trail only; good fishing up from Cliff or down from Gila Hot Springs. Smallmouth bass, catfish, browns.

GILA RIVER, EAST FORK.   Good fishing stream; lower end from Gila Hot Springs Road, then by trail. Catfish, smallmouth bass, some rainbow trout, upper end from Wall Lake.

GILA RIVER, MIDDLE FORK.   Largest and best trout stream in Mogollon Mountains; extends from its junction with West Fork up through scenic box canyons and meadows for many miles in the Gila Wilderness. Browns and rainbows, some smallmouth bass. By road from Silver City, by trail from Snow Lake, Beaverhead, or Willow Creek. Great pack-in fishing, thirty miles.

GILA RIVER, WEST FORK.   Similar to Middle Fork; from Cliff Dwellings to Mogollon Baldy, reached by pack-in only; good fishing; twenty-eight miles. Rainbows and browns.

GILITA CREEK.   Headwaters of Middle Fork of Gila above Willow Creek; three miles.

GLENWOOD POND.   One-acre pond stocked with rainbow trout at Glenwood Hatchery.

GOOSE CREEK.   Small, steep, and swift tributary to Red River; three miles above the town of Red River; four miles. Rainbow trout and cutthroats.

GOOSE LAKE.   At head of Goose Creek, jeep road from the town of Red River; five acres. Shallow with plenty of small trout, rainbows and cutthroats.

GREEN ACRES LAKE.   Warmwater lake in Clovis; eight acres. Bass, bluegill, yellow perch, catfish, winter-stocked rainbows.

GREEN MEADOW LAKE.   North of Hobbs, fourteen acres. Bass, channel cats, bluegill, crappie, winter-stocked rainbows.

GUADALUPE RIVER.   Formed at Porter by Cebolla and Rio las Vacas; enters Jemez River south of Jemez Springs; road access; twelve miles. Great brown trout stream, some rainbows.

GUAJE CREEK. Heads on Baca Location in Jemez Mountains, flows east to Rio Grande at Otowi; thirteen miles. Cutthroats.

HARROUN DAM LAKE. Diversion dam across Pecos River, sixteen miles below Carlsbad; usually dry.

HARROUN LAKE. Private 140-acre lake south of Malaga; fair fishing.

HEART LAKE. At head of Lake Fork of Cabresto Creek; by trail up from Cabresto Lake. Rainbows and cutthroats, when conditions are suitable.

HERON LAKE. Major recreation area, ten miles west of Tierra Amarilla; full-service state park; six thousand acres. Great kokanee, good rainbow fishing, a few big browns, lake trout.

HIDDEN LAKE. East of Santa Rosa; private. Bass.

HIDDEN LAKE. See *Lake Hazel.*

HOLLINGER CREEK. South fork of El Porvenir; good little creek, by trail from El Porvenir. Mostly cutthroats, some rainbows.

HOLY GHOST CREEK. Heads at Spirit Lake and enters Pecos River just below Terrero; good little creek, lower end by car, upper by trail. Cutthroats and stocked rainbows.

HONDO RIVER. Tributary to Rio Grande, from Taos Ski Area down to John Dunn Bridge on Rio Grande. Upper end swift with rainbows and cutthroats; lower end has good pools and good autumn brown fishing.

HONDO RIVER, SOUTH FORK. Ten miles north of Taos, swift, cold; five miles. Cutthroats.

HOPEWELL LAKE. Beautiful fourteen-acre lake between Tierra Amarilla and Tres Piedras. Brook trout and stocked rainbows.

HORSE LAKE. Jicarilla Reservation, permit required, southeast of Dulce; good trout lake but sometimes closed; dirt road.

HORSESHOE LAKE. Five-acre high-mountain timberline lake at head of East Fork of Red River; trail from Upper Red River. Cutthroats.

HORSE THIEF CREEK. High meadow creek by trail from Cowles; tributary of Panchuela Creek; three miles.

ICE POND. Little stocked pond on Rio Cebolla at Seven Springs Hatchery, north of Fenton Lake. Rainbow trout.

INDIAN CREEK. Little tributary of the Pecos from the west; seven miles. Cutthroats two miles up from confluence.

INDUSTRIAL SCHOOL LAKE. On New Mexico Boys Ranch property near Springer; three acres; restricted use.

IRON CREEK. Very small tributary of Middle Fork of Gila River by trail from Mogollon road at Willow Creek; upper end closed to fishing; five miles. Brown and Gila trout.

ISLETA DRAIN. Located on Isleta Indian Reservation along the west side of the Rio Grande.

JACK'S CREEK. Enters the Pecos a mile above Cowles and heads near Pecos Baldy; small, swift brook trout in the upper meadows, as well as cutthroats, rainbows, and browns lower down, by trail from Cowles, eight miles.

JACKSON LAKE. Sixty-acre lake ten miles northwest of Farmington. Stocked with catchable-size rainbow trout, bass, catfish, bluegill.

JAL LAKE. Warmwater municipal lake at Jal; ten acres. Bass, catfish, bluegill, winter-stocked rainbows.

JARAMILLO CREEK. West Fork of Valle Grande Creek on the Baca Location, Jemez Mountains; private; five miles.

JARITAS LAKE. On Floersheim Ranch near Springer; eight acres; private.

Jarosa Creek

JAROSA CREEK. Small fork of the main Pecos entering just above Pecos Falls in high country; two miles. Cutthroats.

JAROSA CREEK. A fork of Vallecitos Creek southwest of Hopewell Lake, by road from Tusas; eight miles. Brook, rainbow trout.

JEMEZ RESERVOIR. Flood-control reservoir on Jemez Pueblo; no public fishing.

JEMEZ RIVER. Very popular from its beginnings at Battleship Rock downstream to junction with Guadalupe River; twenty-six miles. Browns and rainbows with good fishing, especially above Jemez Springs.

JEMEZ RIVER, EAST FORK. From Battleship Rock upstream to Valle Grande; fine strip of water crossed by road at intervals; twelve miles. Rainbows and browns.

JICARILLA APACHE LAKES. See *Dulce Lake, Enbom Lake, Horse Lake, La Jara Lake, Stone Lake, and Navajo River.* Fishing permit required; good ice-fishing. Rainbows, cutthroats, and browns.

JOHN'S CREEK. Very small stream at head of Sapello Creek, by trail; three miles. Mostly cutthroats.

JOHNSON CANYON CREEK. Tributary to White Creek; both are part of the Upper West Fork of the Gila River. Browns.

JOHNSON LAKE. Little timberline lake over the ridge north of Lake Katherine, by trail eight miles from Cowles; six acres. Cutthroats.

KAISER CREEK. Tributary of Hondo River from north above Valdez. Cutthroats.

KATHERINE LAKE. See *Lake Katherine.*

LA CUEVA LAKE. Small irrigation reservoirs southeast of Mora; private.

LAGUNA LARGA. East of San Antonio Mountain, lake made by flooding natural depression; fifteen acres. Rainbow trout, depending on water level.

LAGUNA LINDA. Private ten-acre trout lake near Cleveland.

LAGUNA MADRE. One of the Maxwell lakes.

LAGUNA SALINA. North of Las Vegas near Golondrinas; private.

LAGUNITAS LAKES. Several small lakes at head of San Antonio Creek east of San Antonio Mountain; decent lake-fishing; ten acres. Brook and stocked rainbow trout.

LA JARA CREEK. Small tributary of the Valle Grande on the Baca Location, Jemez Mountains; private, three miles. Trout.

LA JARA CREEK. Very small, six miles north of Cuba. Small trout.

LA JARA LAKE. Jicarilla Reservation, permit required; fifty-six acres, good ice-fishing. Good rainbow and cutthroat fishing.

LA JOYA LAKES. Warmwater lakes on National Waterfowl Refuge twenty-one miles south of Belen off Rio Grande, open April through August; 480 acres for six lakes. Crappie, bass, carp, catfish.

LA JUNTA CREEK. North fork of Rio Pueblo, near Tres Ritos; road; good little stream; nine miles. Cutthroats.

LAKE 13. One of the Maxwell lakes. Channel catfish, rainbow trout.

LAKE ALICE. One of three small lakes at head of Las Trampas; reached by trail, four acres. Rainbow trout, cutthroats.

LAKE DAVID. A 250-acre private lake northeast of Las Vegas.

LAKE FARMINGTON. Municipal reservoir northeast of Farmington, two hundred acres when full. Bass and channel catfish, stocked rainbow trout.

LAKE FORK CREEK.   Small stream, by trail, upper reaches of Rio Hondo northeast of Taos; five miles. Cutthroats.

LAKE HAZEL (Hidden Lake).   One of three small lakes at head of Las Trampas; by trail only; four acres. Planted with cutthroats.

LAKE ISABEL.   Eight-hundred-acre lake, northeast of Las Vegas; private.

LAKE KATHERINE.   The queen of the high-mountain trout lakes, eight miles by trail from Cowles, head of Winsor Creek; twelve acres. Cutthroat and rainbow trout.

LAKE MALOYA.   Raton city reservoir, 150 acres; twelve miles northwest of Raton; state park; camping. Stocked with rainbow trout.

LAKE ROBERTS.   A beautiful lake on Sapillo Creek north of Silver City; seventy-one acres. Good rainbow trout fishing spring and fall; tough in summer.

LAKE RUTH.   One of three lakes at head of Las Trampas, by trail. Cutthroats.

LAKE SUMNER.   A 4,650-acre lake when full; irrigation reservoir, nineteen miles northwest of Fort Sumner; state park, friendly shoreline. Bass, bluegill, crappie, catfish, walleye, white bass.

LAKE VAN.   Twelve-acre lake next to Dexter National Fish Hatchery south of Roswell; city park, small fee. Bass, bluegill, winter-stocked rainbows.

LA MESA DRAIN.   West side of Rio Grande near Las Cruces, heading two miles east of San Miguel Butte.

LA MORA CREEK.   Tributary to Pecos River near Dunlap; private.

LANGSTROTH CANYON CREEK.   Tributary of White Creek in Mogollon Mountains; four miles. Some trout.

LAS TABLAS CANYON CREEK.   Small stream heading twelve miles northeast of Capitan in Capitan Mountains, emptying into Cienega del Macho Arroyo.

LAS TRAMPAS CREEK.   Heading north of Truchas Peak and flowing northwest near village of Trampas; excellent fishing in upper portion and sometimes as far down as confluence with Rio Embudo; fifteen miles. Cutthroat, rainbow trout.

LATIR CREEK, EAST.   Tributary to Costilla Creek on Rio Costilla Cooperative property; small cutthroat creek heading at Latir Lakes; eight miles; permit required.

LATIR CREEK, WEST.   Small swift stream flowing west into Rio Grande near Cerro; heads against Latir Peaks; five miles.

LATIR LAKES.   Group of nine lakes at head of East Latir Creek; by rough road and trail; twenty-five acres; permit from Rio Costilla Cooperative. Great cutthroat potential.

LEA COUNTY PARK LAKE.   Small lake; state park, in Hobbs; no fishing.

LITTLE BLUE LAKE (Baldy Blue and Bear Lakes).   Head of Midnight Creek near Latir lakes; by rough road and trail, two acres; permit from Rio Costilla Cooperative. Cutthroat fishing.

LITTLE CREEK.   Small tributary of West Fork of Gila; upper end closed to fishing; thirteen miles. Browns, Gila trout.

LITTLE RIO GRANDE, LOWER.   From its junction with Rio Pueblo de Taos, upstream to the mouth of Pot Creek, flows through Rancho de Taos; very good open stream; eight miles. Browns, rainbows, cutthroats.

LITTLE RIO GRANDE, UPPER.   From Pot Creek to its head, flows through the canyon north of U.S. Hill on road from Taos to Mora; good stream but brushy; some private; fourteen miles.

LITTLE TURKEY CREEK.   Tributary of Willow Creek (Gila); trail.

LOBO CREEK.   Small stream, flows into Hondo River from the north about two miles above Arroyo Hondo. Rainbow, cutthroat trout.

LONG CANYON.   Small, swift stream; tributary of upper Hondo, north of Taos; three miles. Browns.

LONG LAKE.   Navajo Indian reservation; permit required. Rainbows.

LOOKOUT CANYON.   Steep rough fork of Mogollon Creek heading against Mogollon Peak; by trail from Mogollon Creek; four miles.

LOS ALAMOS RESERVOIR.   Small reservoir near Las Alamos. Summer-stocked rainbows.

LOS PINOS, LOWER.   Unusually fine rainbow, brown, and cutthroat stream flowing east along Colorado state line from Toltec Gorge to Antonito; by road from U.S. 285, upper part by trail; one of the best streams in the state; public and private; seventeen miles.

LOS PINOS, UPPER.   That portion above Toltec Gorge to state line reached via Osier, Colorado; three miles. Good wild trout water.

LOST BEAR LAKE.   Small headwater lake of the Pecos River above Pecos Falls; two acres. Cutthroats.

LOST LAKE.   See *Maestas Lake.*

LOST LAKE.   At head of West Fork of Red River in high country; reached by trail only from Red River or Twining; six acres. Fine cutthroat and rainbow trout fishing.

LUCERO CREEK.   Good swift stream heading at Lucero Lake in Taos Mountains north of Taos; by trail only, except lower portion near Taos; private, on Taos Pueblo land; twelve miles.

LUCERO LAKE (Bear Lake).   On Taos Pueblo; timberline lake at head of Lucero Creek in Taos Mountains, five acres; no fishing allowed. Cutthroats.

LUJAN CREEK.   Small east fork of Mora River above Chacon; ten miles, by car; private. Some rainbow trout fishing.

LUNA CREEK.   Small west fork of Mora River above Chacon; seven miles; mostly private. Some rainbow trout fishing, some beaver dams.

MADDOX LAKE.   A good warmwater, twenty-acre lake at Maddox Generating Station. Bass, channel catfish, bullheads.

MAESTAS CREEK.   A fork of Manuelitas Creek, west of Rociada; by car; three miles. Cutthroats.

MAESTAS LAKE (Lost Lake).   At head of Maestas Creek, one mile by trail from canyon; three acres.

MANUELITAS CREEK.   Above Sapello, flows through Rociada; upper part good fishing, lower has water removed for irrigation; seventeen miles. Browns, rainbows.

MANZANARES CREEK.   Empties into Cow Creek; by car through Pecos; small high stream; three miles. Browns, rainbows.

MANZANO LAKE.   Six-acre lake in the town of Manzano, drawn low for irrigation but stocked with rainbow trout; a few miles from Manzona State Park.

MAXWELL LAKES.   A group of irrigation reservoirs in and near Maxwell National Wildlife Refuge; subject to drawdown. Catfish, walleye, bass, sunfish, rainbow trout. Lake 13, Stubblefield, and Laguna Madre.

McALLISTER LAKE.   In National Wildlife Refuge near Las Vegas; one hundred acres, closed in winter. Good rainbow trout fishing most years.

McGAFFEY LAKE.   Six miles south of Wingate Station near Gallup; fourteen acres. Good little rainbow trout lake on good gravel road.

McKENNA CREEK.   Tributary to West Fork of Gila River. Contains Gila trout and closed to fishing.

McKNIGHT CREEK.   Tributary to Mimbres River. Contains Gila trout and closed to fishing.

McMILLAN LAKE.   Flooded out by Brantley Dam Reservoir.

MEADOW CREEK.   Small stream tributary to Sapello Creek (Gila); good fishing in years of normal rainfall, seven miles. Rainbow trout.

MEDIO DIA CREEK. Small creek on south side of Jemez Mountains across ridge east of Bland; four miles.

MESCALERO APACHE LAKES. See *Ruidoso River, Eagle Lakes, Silver Lake, Mescalero Lake*. Several good trout waters; all public fishing with Mescalero fishing permit.

MESCALERO LAKE. Good one-hundred-acre stocked trout lake at Inn of the Mountain Gods; day-fishing with permit.

MIAMI LAKE. Private; west of Miami; 190 acres. Good northern pike.

MICHALLAS CANYON CREEK. Small stream on southeast side of Capitan Mountains in Upper Hondo Watershed.

MIDDLE FORK LAKE. At head of Middle Fork of Red River; by jeep from Red River; excellent high mountain lake, six acres. Rainbow and cutthroat trout.

MIDDLE FORK LAKE OF RIO LA CASA. At head of Rio La Casa in Mora County; by trail only; five acres. Good cutthroat fishing.

MIDNIGHT CREEK. Small tributary to Latir Creek; permit required from Rio Costilla Cooperative. Cutthroats.

MIMBRES RIVER. Heads in Black Range north of Mimbres; lower portion accessible by car, upper portion better fishing but reached by trail; fourteen miles. Cutthroat, rainbow trout.

MINERAL CREEK. Over ridge north of the town of Mogollon, emptying into San Francisco River near Alma; six miles. A few browns.

MOGOLLON CREEK. Good stream flowing out of the south side of Mogollon Mountains; by trail via Cliff; ten miles. Rainbow trout, browns.

MOGOLLON CREEK, WEST FORK. Swift rough water; by trail; three miles. Rainbow trout.

MONASTERY LAKE. A six-acre lake, two miles north of Pecos. Put and take; rainbow trout.

MORA PECOS RIVER. Main tributary of the Pecos joining it a mile above Terrero and heading near timberline twenty miles north. Very fine all the way; accessible by trail at its junction with the Pecos; much open water; the author's favorite trout stream. Mostly browns. Upper part reached via Cowles.

MORA RIVER. Flowing through town of Mora; very good fishing in covered areas, but heavy grazing and irrigation prevent good fishing habitat; eighteen miles; mostly private land; eventually feeds Canadian River below Watrous. Browns, rainbows; contains some channel catfish.

MORGAN LAKE. Power-plant reservoir on Navajo Reservation, four miles southwest of Fruitland; Navajo fishing permit required; 1,200 acres. Bass, bluegill, catfish.

MOSSMAN RESERVOIR. Private; near Wagon Mound. Bass, bluegill.

MORPHY LAKE (Murphy). About three miles northwest of Ledoux near Mora; beautiful fifty acres, state park; occasional drawdown. Rainbow trout.

MOUNT TAYLOR LAKE. Private; forty acres. Some trout fishing.

MUNICIPAL LAKE. On Pecos in Carlsbad; ninety-five acres. Bass, crappie, white bass, channel catfish, winter-stocked trout.

MURPHY LAKE. See *Morphy Lake*.

NABOR CREEK. Small tributary to Chamita; Sargent Wildlife Area. Cutthroats.

NABOR LAKE. Four-acre lake on Nabor Creek. Rio Grande cutthroats.

NAMBE LAKE (Nambe Falls). Sixty-acre reservoir on Nambe Indian Reservation near Española; permit required. Good day-fishing for rainbow trout and cutthroats.

NAMBE RIVER. No fishing allowed from Nambe Lake upstream to Santa Fe National Forest; fifteen miles. Good rainbow and cutthroat fishing on national forest land.

NAVAJO RESERVATION LAKES.   See *Morgan Lake, Berland Lake, Aspen Lake, Whiskey Lake, Asaayi Lake,* and *Red Lake.* Fishing permit required.

NAVAJO RESERVOIR.   Fifteen-thousand-acre combination warm- and coldwater lake loaded with sportfish; thirty-five miles east of Farmington; major recreation area, very good boat-fishing, three full-service state parks with marinas. Rainbows, browns, carp, northerns, kokanee, largemouth, channel catfish, smallmouth, crappie, bluegill.

NAVAJO RIVER.   On Jicarilla Reservation; permit required; road along river, enters and leaves state from Colorado, eight miles. Big wild browns, some rainbows.

NED HOUK LAKE.   See *Running Water Draw.*

NEGRITO CREEK.   Empties into San Francisco River near Reserve; good springs maintain flow for much of its sixteen miles. Rainbows and browns.

NEMEXAS DRAIN.   On Rio Grande above the Texas line near Anthony.

NOGAL LAKE.   No longer stocked with rainbows, stocked now with brook trout; decent fishing only in wet years; on U.S. Forest Service land near Carrizozo; forty acres.

NORTH FORK LAKE.   Small lake at head of North Fork of Rio la Casa; eight miles. Rainbows, cutthroats.

NUTRIA LAKE No. 2 and No. 4.   Zuñi Pueblo, permit required; sixty acres, scenic meadow lakes. Rainbows, cutthroats, and catfish.

NUTRIAS CREEK.   Little stream with many beaver dams heading on northwest side of Canjilon Mountain; eight miles. Cutthroat and rainbow trout.

NUTRIAS LAKES.   At head of Nutrias Creek; dirt road in; good little lakes heavily stocked, plus wild brook trout and cutthroats.

OASIS LAKE.   Small two-acre lake at Oasis State Park north of Portales. Catfish, trout in winter.

OCATE CREEK.   Little creek flowing through Ocate; fair trout fishing in upper portion; diverted below Ocate into upper Charette Lake, fifteen miles.

OJO CALIENTE LAKE.   Zuñi Pueblo lake; permit required; forty acres. Fine fishing for rainbow trout, cutthroats, and catfish.

OSHA CREEK.   Small tributary to Cow Creek. Mostly brook trout.

PACHECO LAKE.   At head of north fork of Santiago Creek in Mora County; by trail only; five acres. Rainbow trout, cutthroats.

PANCHUELA CREEK.   Large tributary of Pecos River, joining it a mile above Cowles; very good brushy stream, many beaver dams near ranger station at end of road; upper portion by trail; twelve miles. Rainbows, browns.

PANCHUELA WEST CREEK.   Headwaters of Frijoles Creek which flows to Santa Cruz Lake; by trail; five miles. Cutthroats.

PARK LAKE.   A six-acre swimming lake in Santa Rosa; no fishing.

PASAMONTE LAKE.   Private fifty acres. Bass and bluegill.

PECOS BALDY LAKE.   Fine lake at base of Pecos Baldy Mountain at head of Jack's Creek; by trail from Cowles; eight acres. Cutthroats.

PECOS RIVER.   Eddy County: good fishing for catfish, bluegill, walleye, largemouth bass, white bass; most fish confined to large pools in the river channel; water usually clear; ninety miles. Chaves County: same only not as good, 106 miles. De Baca County: limited to channel catfish in the larger permanent pools, eighty-six miles. Guadalupe County: channel catfish in the permanent pools. San Miguel County: a few trout and catfish; thirty-one miles.

PECOS RIVER.   Short stretch below Sumner Lake planted with catchable-size rainbow trout in winter.

PECOS RIVER. From the town of Pecos downstream to I–25; mostly private. Good wild trout stream.

PECOS RIVER. Upstream from the town of Pecos Terrero; a mix of public and private water, one of the best streams in the state, well-stocked, heavily fished, twenty miles of river paralleled by road.

PECOS RIVER. From Terrero to Cowles, paralleled by gravel road. Good stocked and wild trout fishing; browns and rainbows.

PECOS RIVER. Above Cowles, by trail, small stream in alternating box canyons and open meadows. Full of wild trout, browns, cutthroats, rainbows; above Pecos Falls cutthroats only in high mountain meadow.

PEÑASCO RIVER. Heads in Sacramento Mountains, flows through Mayhill, fed by springs in Elk and above. Rainbows and browns, mostly private; stocked rainbows in public water, four miles.

PERALTA CREEK. On south side of Jemez Mountains; heads northwest of Bland, empties into Rio Grande at Cochiti, upper by trail; ten miles. Cutthroats.

PERALTA DRAIN. Warmwater drain beginning below Isleta Diversion and emptying into Rio Grande on east side of river; seven miles. Trout stocked in winter.

PESCADO LAKE. Zuñi Pueblo; permit required. Largemouth bass.

PINE LODGE CREEK. North side of Capitan Mountain at village of Pine Lodge; two miles. Good trout fishing in wet years.

PIONEER CREEK. Comes into Red River from the south just below the town of Red River; five miles. Good swift little creek: cutthroat, rainbow trout.

PIONEER LAKE. At head of Pioneer Creek, reached by trail from end of road in canyon; attractive, two acres. Rainbow trout and cutthroats.

PLACER CREEK. A small stream north and west of the town of Tusas and tributary to Vallecitos; very good fishing, accessible by road; good camping at Hopewell Lake; ten miles. Browns.

POLIZA CREEK. On south side of Jemez Mountains, heading at Cerro Pelado, emptying into Jemez River at Jemez Pueblo; six miles.

POLVADERO CREEK. On Lobato Grant, south and west of Abiquiu; six miles. Cutthroats.

PONIL CREEK. Tributary to Cimarron River. Lower, good brown and rainbow trout fishing; private. Upper on Valle Vidal, cutthroats.

POT CREEK. Middle fork of Little Rio Grande; confluence short distance below U.S. Hill; twelve miles. Many beaver; fine little brown trout stream.

POWER DAM LAKE. Located on the south side of Santa Rosa; fifteen acres. Fair fishing for bluegills, bullheads, winter-stocked trout.

PRESSLEY-JACOBS LAKE. Small private lake near Gallup.

PUEBLO CREEK (Rio Pueblo). See *Rio Pueblo de Taos*.

PUYE LAKES. See *Santa Clara Fishing Lakes*.

QUEMADO LAKE. One hundred and thirty acres of excellent rainbow trout fishing about twenty-five miles south of the town of Quemado; good in spring and fall.

RAIN CREEK. Tributary of Mogollon Creek, joining it below the falls and heading between Black Mountains and Center Baldy; very swift, eight miles.

RAMAH LAKE. One hundred acres, just northeast of Ramah; was private, but is now public. Bass, bluegill, some stocked trout.

RANCHO GRANDE POND. Two-acre pond west of Reserve. Panfish, trout stocked in winter.

RAYADO CREEK. Tributary to Cimarron River; private. Cutthroats.

RED BLUFF LAKE. Mostly in Texas, on Pecos River. Good warmwater fishing, especially hybrid stripers and white bass in spring.

RED LAKE. Two-hundred-acre lake near Fort Defiance on Navajo Reservation; permit required. Bass and northern pike.

REDONDO CREEK. East fork of Sulphur Creek, which is a fork of San Antonio Creek on the Baca Location in Jemez Mountains; private.

RED RIVER. From Rio Grande through Questa to the town of Red River. Box below Red River Hatchery is part of Rio Grande Wild River Section, reached by trail; large browns and rainbows at lower end. From Questa to the town of Red River, stream is heavily stocked with rainbows; popular recreation area; twenty-eight miles.

RED RIVER, EAST FORK. Tributary to Red River, six miles south of town of Red River; lower end accessible by car. Rainbows, brooks, and cutthroats.

RED RIVER, MIDDLE FORK. See *Red River, East Fork.*

RED RIVER, UPPER. All the river above the town of Red River to junction of East Fork and Middle Fork; partly open, partly brushy, accessible by road; eight miles. Cutthroats, brooks, rainbows.

RED RIVER, WEST FORK. Small tributary about eight miles above the town of Red River, divides into additional branches which also contain cutthroat and rainbow trout; by car.

RINER LAKE. Twenty acres, in Mora County; private. Bass and bluegill.

RIO CAPULIN. North fork of Nambe Creek on west side of Pecos Mountains, reached by trail from Aspen Ranch; six miles. Cutthroats.

RIO CHIQUITO. A fork of Little Rio Grande coming out of mountains northeast of Ranchos de Taos; a few Rio Grande cutthroats in upper end, numerous browns below Borrego Crossing, reached by car from Talpa; fifteen miles.

RIO DEL MEDIO. Fine mountain stream heading on northwest side of Pecos Baldy, flowing westward eighteen miles to Santa Cruz Lake; road to lower end, upper end accessible by trail only via Borrego Ranger Station or westside trail; twenty-four miles including tributaries. Cutthroats, rainbow trout.

RIO EN MEDIO. Little stream at Aspen Ranch accessible by road from Tesuque; five miles. Rainbow trout and cutthroats.

RIO FRIJOLES. Heads high in Santa Fe Forest, empties into Rio del Medio just above Santa Cruz Lake; upper portion reached by trail from Cundiyo; good mountain creek, thirteen miles. Cutthroat, rainbow trout.

RIO FRIJOLES. Little tributary to Rio Grande at Bandelier National Monument. Plenty of small wild brook trout and rainbow trout.

RIO GRANDE (Doña Ana County). Intermittent in its flow; good catfishing in the larger holes; in the lower part of the county, water is supplied throughout the year from drainage canals, eighty-five miles.

RIO GRANDE (Sierra County). Some excellent catfish fishing both above and below Elephant Butte and Caballo lakes; below these dams good fishing for largemouth bass, northern pike, trout, walleye, white bass, and bluegill.

RIO GRANDE (Socorro County). Has good catfishing, although at times the river runs intermittently; best fishing is near the head of Elephant Butte Lake and San Acacia; ninety-one miles.

RIO GRANDE (Valencia County). Some catfish in the backwaters and below the drainage canals; twenty-eight miles.

RIO GRANDE (Bernalillo County). Fair catfish fishing as far upstream as Velarde, with some smallmouth bass in same area; sixteen miles.

RIO GRANDE (Sandoval County). Good fishing just below Cochiti Dam for trout, walleye, bass, catfish, carp; forty-four miles.

RIO GRANDE (Santa Fe County). Some catfish fishing and northern pike occasionally in section above Cochiti Lake; eighteen miles.

RIO GRANDE (from San Juan Pueblo through Velarde to Rio Grande State Park). Some catfish and smallmouth bass as far up as Velarde, with occasional trout or largemouth bass. Trout mainly sought above Velarde, although other species are present. Good pools for browns and rainbows along highway and in Rio Grande Gorge State Park. Some large northern pike also present.

RIO GRANDE (from Rio Grande State Park to Colorado state line). Reached mainly by trails near Questa, with road access at Arroyo Hondo, river is preserved under Wild and Scenic Rivers Act. Large browns and rainbows, plus northern pike.

RIO HONDO. Tributary to Pecos River near Roswell; private.

RIO HONDO. Tributary to Rio Grande near Taos. See *Hondo River.*

RIO LA CASA, LOWER. Five miles from Cleveland; six miles total. Good rainbow trout and cutthroat fishing.

RIO LA CASA, UPPER. From five miles above Cleveland to its source; three forks. Good cutthroat, some rainbow trout fishing; four miles.

RIO LAS PERCHAS. A tributary of Rio de las Vacas, east of Clear Creek; small stream, four miles. Rainbow trout, cutthroats.

RIO LAS VACAS, LOWER. From road at Telephone Canyon, in heart of Jemez Mountains, downstream to junction with the Cebolla; ten miles. Good brown and rainbow trout fishing.

RIO LAS VACAS, UPPER. From Telephone Canyon north to source in the high country of Jemez Mountains, paralleled for a distance by the Jemez Springs–Cuba road; good; six miles.

RIO NUTRITAS. A fork of San Antonio Creeek, joining it above San Antonio Ranger Station; small open stream, good fishing; nine miles.

RIO PUEBLO DE TAOS. Major tributary to Rio Grande at Rio Grande State Park; trail only for good brown trout fishing upstream to Taos in deep canyon; stocked, and auto access near Taos; then long and brushy fair-sized creek on Taos Pueblo Land (private) to source at Blue Lake; twenty-five miles. All good trout water.

RIO PUEBLO, LOWER. Meets Santa Barbara to form Embudo; paralleled by roads up to Tres Ritos; fifteen miles. Large swift stream, good fishing; mainly rainbow trout and cutthroats.

RIO PUEBLO, UPPER. From Tres Ritos to source southwest of Holman Hill against Jicarita Peak; upper end by trail, open mountain meadows, fine stream, heavily fished; seven miles. Cutthroats at headwater, rainbow trout further down.

RIO PUERCO. Heads southwest of Coyote on north side of Jemez Mountains, empties into the Chama; headwaters have nice fish; accessible by road and trail, ten miles.

RIO PUERCO, UPPER. Heads on west side of Jemez mountains a few miles northeast of Cuba; source of Rio Puerco, which empties into Rio Grande; ten miles. A few cutthroats high up, by trail only.

RIO QUEMADO. Heads at northwestern side of Truchas Peaks, flows out to forest boundary and west to Cordova and the Rio del Medio; fifteen miles. Good cutthroats high up, reached by trail from Truchas.

RIO VALDEZ. North fork of Mora Pecos River at upper end of Mora Flats; heads in high country, brush at lower end, open meadow land higher up. Mostly cutthroats and browns, a few rainbows.

RITO AZUL. Short south fork of Rito de las Chimayosos, above Beatty's Cabin in the upper Pecos country; by trail via Beatty's Cabin from Cowles, three miles.

RITO DE LAS CHIMAYOSOS. Biggest fork of Rito del Padre or Beatty's Fork of Pecos River; heads against east side of Truchas Peaks; five miles. Cutthroats.

RITO DE LAS PALOMAS. Fork of Rio las Vacas, joining near where the Cuba–Jemez Springs road crosses it; five miles. Cutthroats, rainbow trout.

RITO DE LAS SILLAS. Tributary to Rito Encino south of Youngsville; eight miles. Small stream with good cutthroat fishing; some rainbow trout in lower part.

RITO DEL MEDIO. Small swift stream flowing west from Cabresto Peak.

RITO ENCINO. Tributary to Rio Puerco at Youngsville.

RITO DE LOS ESTEROS. Small fork of Mora Pecos, emptying into it from east at lower end of Mora Flats; three miles. Browns, cutthroats.

RITO DE LOS INDIOS. North fork of San Antonio Creek on Baca Location in Jemez Mountains; private; five miles. Cutthroats.

RITO DEL OSO. A fork of the Mora Pecos, paralleled by Rociada trail; swift brushy stream; three miles. Some cutthroats.

RITO DE LOS PINOS. Little stream heading on west side of Jemez Mountains northeast of Cuba; by trail; three miles. Cutthroats.

RITO DEL PADRE. Also known as Beatty's Fork of the Pecos. Extends from Beatty's Cabin up to source at Cerro Chimayosos; good stream in deep and dark timbered canyon. Cutthroats, browns, rainbows.

RITO ESCURO. Tributary to Cave Creek in upper Pecos country; by trail from Panchuela. Cutthroats.

RITO GALLINA. Tributary to Rio del Medio from south. Cutthroats.

RITO MAESTAS. East fork of Rito del Padre in upper Pecos country.

RITO MOLINA. Tributary of Rio del Medio; by trail. Cutthroats.

RITO PACHECO. Little stream on west side of Pecos Forest between Tesuque and Aspen Ranch; road goes up this creek; three miles.

RITO PEÑAS NEGRAS. Largest fork of Rio las Vacas in heart of Jemez Mountains; heading in high meadow country, upper portion by trail only; eleven miles. Cutthroats.

RITO PERRO. Extreme east fork of Panchuela Creek; by trail from Cowles via Round Mountain and Jack's Creek; four miles.

RITO PRESA. See *Clear Creek.*

RITO PRIMERO. Tributary of Red River, flowing through Cerro; east of Highway 3, by trail only. Rainbow trout and cutthroats.

RITO SABADIOSAS. Fork of Rito del Padre above Beatty's Cabin.

RIVERSIDE LAKE. In village of Riverside near Española; private.

ROCK CREEK. Tributary to Vallecitos Creek from northeast at Vallecitos Ranch; private, ten miles north of town of Vallecitos. Rainbow trout.

RUIDOSO RIVER. The Ruidoso stream system is the principal fishing stream in the Lincoln National Forest, from Hondo up through the town of Ruidoso to Mescalero land; good small stream, mostly private; very heavily fished, popular recreation area, paralleled by paved roads; eleven miles; public access from Mescalero land downstream through Ruidoso.

RUIDOSO RIVER. Mescalero Indian lands; good fishing, permit required; heavily fished, accessible by car; seven miles.

RUIDOSO RIVER, NORTH FORK. Good stream on Mescalero Apache land; by trail only from end of road above the town of Ruidoso; six miles.

RUIDOSO RIVER, SOUTH FORK. Mescalero; fair stream; trail.

RUNNING WATER DRAW (Ned Houk Ponds).   Small reservoir in state park north of Clovis; warm-water fishing. Catfish, winter-stocked trout.

SABINAL DRAIN.   Canal about two miles southeast of Belen.

SACRAMENTO LAKE.   On Sacramento River about twenty-five miles southeast of Cloudcroft on good roads; two acres; shallow. Brook trout.

SACRAMENTO RIVER.   Feeds Sacramento Lake. Brook trout.

SAN ANTONIO RIVER.   Tributary of Los Pinos River in Carson National Forest; heading at Lagunitas lakes and flowing past San Antonio Ranger Station; fishing from station to head, especially high up where it is accessible by trail; thirty miles.

SAN ANTONIO RIVER.   West fork of Jemez River from Battleship Rock to La Cueva; swift; four miles. Browns and stocked rainbows. Above La Cueva, heads in mountain meadow country; open water; by trail or auto; twenty-nine miles. Browns.

SANCHEZ CANYON.   Very small stream in Sandoval County; by trail two miles east of Canada; four miles. Cutthroats.

SAN CRISTOBAL CREEK.   Tributary to Rio Grande north of Taos; good fishing toward the head-waters. Cutthroats.

SAN FRANCISCO RIVER.   Enters New Mexico from Arizona above the town of Luna in Catron County and flows south ninety miles to where it passes into Arizona about forty miles below the town of Glenwood. Contains small numbers of catfish, plus some rainbow trout near Luna.

SAN GREGORIO LAKE.   On Clear Creek in Jemez Mountains; road from Cuba to within a half-mile of lake; thirty-two acres. Stocked rainbow trout.

SAN JOSÉ RIVER.   In Cibola County; fishing near lava beds and on Acoma Indian Reservation; ten miles.

SAN JUAN DRAIN.   Canal three miles southeast of Belen, east of Rio Grande.

SAN JUAN RIVER, LOWER.   In San Juan County, flowing west to Arizona; one hundred miles. Some good fishing for channel catfish.

SAN JUAN RIVER, UPPER.   From Navajo Dam to Blanco; good auto access; fifteen miles. Fishing for rainbows, cutthroats, and browns all very good; best trophy trout fishing in state immediately below dam.

SAN LEONARDO CREEK.   Tributary to Las Trampas Creek from south; by trail from Las Trampas or Truchas. Cutthroats.

SAN LEONARDO LAKE.   High Pecos lake; heads on north side of Truchas Peak; trail, five acres. Cutthroats.

SAN MATEO LAKE.   Near San Mateo; seven acres, private. Rainbow trout.

SANTA BARBARA.   One of the best fishing streams; headwaters start in the high divide between Truchas Peaks and Jicarita Peak; upper portion accessible by trail from end of road above Peñasco and by trail from head of Pecos; meets Rio Pueblo to form Embudo; twenty-seven miles. Mostly wild cutthroats, stocked at campground.

SANTA CLARA CREEK.   On Santa Clara Reservation, east side of Jemez Mountains; by road from Española; private.

SANTA CLARA (PUYE) FISHING LAKES.   A series of little ponds on a small tributary to Santa Clara Creek; Santa Clara Pueblo permits sold on site; heavily stocked; beautiful family picnicking, camping, and fishing spot.

SANTA CRUZ RESERVOIR.   An irrigation reservoir impounding waters of Rio del Medio and Rio Frijoles in a deep canyon ten miles by road from Española; very popular; ninety acres. Well stocked with good-size rainbows, wild browns, suckers.

SANTA FE RESERVOIRS. At head of Santa Fe Canyon on private and Santa Fe National Forest land; by trail, good trout fishing, but no fishing or trespassing. Cutthroat and rainbow trout.

SANTA FE RIVER. Stocked in the city of Santa Fe during spring; upper end has good cutthroat fishing; accessible by trail.

SANTA FE LAKE. Head of Santa Fe River; few fish, not stocked.

SANTA ROSA CREEK. Small tributary to San Antonio Creek on Baca Location; private; seven miles.

SANTA ROSA LAKE. One thousand to fifteen thousand acres, an irrigation storage reservoir north of Santa Rosa on Pecos River. Walleye, crappie, catfish, smallmouth and largemouth bass. Fishing all good when lake has water; is subject to almost total downdraws. State park.

SANTIAGO LAKE. At head of Rito Morphy; by trail near Morphy Lake. Stocked with cutthroats.

SAPELLO CREEK. Tributary to Mora River, twenty-five miles north of Las Vegas; twenty-nine miles; lower end private. Rainbow and cutthroat trout.

SAPILLO CREEK. Tributary to Gila River, thirty miles north of Silver City; often very low; seven miles. Some rainbow trout.

SAWMILL CREEK. Extreme east fork of Red River above the town of Red River, two miles.

SAWMILL POND. In Bernalillo; small, four acres; private.

SEGAL CREEK. Southeast of Maxwell; private; four miles. Rainbow trout.

SHEEP CORRAL CREEK. North of Pinos Altos. Gila trout, but no fishing.

SHIELE LAKES. Located in Mora County; private.

SHUREE LAKES. On Valle Vidal. Three well-stocked rainbow trout lakes; some Rio Grande cutthroat hybrids.

SILVER LAKE. Heavily stocked Mescalero Apache fee-fishing lake northwest of Cloudcroft.

SILVER SPRINGS CANYON. Very small stream, northwest of Cloudcroft; private.

SIX MILE CREEK. Flows into Eagle Nest Lake from the west; private.

SIX MILE DAM LAKE. Located six miles south of Carlsbad on the Pecos River; 125 acres. Mostly catfish, some bass and bluegill.

SNOW CREEK. Little stream tributary to Middle Fork of Gila; feeds Snow Lake.

SNOW LAKE. On Snow Creek, one hundred acres; forty miles on gravel F.R. 141 from Reserve; campground; great Gila country lake. Stocked rainbow trout.

SNYDER LAKE. Twenty-acre private lake near Des Moines.

SOCORRO DRAIN. Near Socorro; warmwater fishing.

SOLDIER CREEK. Very small west tributary of Cow Creek, heading at Soldier Creek Park; four miles. Cutthroats, brookies.

SPARKS CANYON CREEK. Extreme north fork of Maestas Creek west of Rociada; very small, brushy; four miles. Cutthroats.

SPIRIT LAKE. Good shallow lake at head of Holy Ghost Creek, reached by trail up Winsor Creek from Cowles; seven acres. Rainbow and cutthroat trout.

SPRINGER LAKE. A 450-acre irrigation lake five miles from Springer. Trout, very good northern pike, catfish, perch.

SPRING RIVER. At Roswell; private. Catfish, bass, bluegill.

SPRING RIVER PARK LAKE. A small lake at Roswell, stocked with trout in winter and warmwater species at other times. Fishing only for children under twelve years of age.

SPRUCE CREEK. A tributary to Dry Creek. Contains Gila trout, no fishing.

STAR LAKE. Small lake reached by trail, high in the Taos Mountains; six acres, no trout.

STEWART LAKE. Good lake about six miles from Cowles by trail up Winsor Creek; five miles. Rainbow and cutthroat trout.

STONE LAKE. Jicarilla Reservation; permit required. Many carp and some big rainbow trout.

STORRIE RESERVOIR. Fine lake built for irrigation, twelve hundred acres maximum, but seldom full; three miles north of Las Vegas; state park. Perch, rainbows, and browns.

STUBBLEFIELD LAKE. Irrigation reservoir subject to drawdown; near Maxwell. Walleye, catfish, sunfish, bass, and stocked trout.

SULLIVAN LAKE. Near Santa Rosa; private. Bass, bluegill, crappie.

SUMNER LAKE. See *Lake Sumner.*

SWAN LAKE. Located at Clovis; closed to fishing.

SWEAZEA LAKE. Near Quemado; private; five acres. Bass and bluegill.

TAJIQUE CREEK. Little stream heading in Manzano Mountains west of Estancia; three miles. Beaver dams, occasionally stocked.

TAOS CREEK. Little tributary to Rio Pueblo de Taos, heads west of Taos along U.S. 64; twenty-five miles. Stocked rainbow trout, cutthroats high up.

TAYLOR CREEK. Feeds Wall Lake; fishing is below the lake, a four-mile stretch. Rainbow trout and smallmouth bass.

TECOLOTE RIVER. Tributary of Pecos River; public area by trail from Johnson Mesa Campground; seven miles. Trout only in upper portion above Friendly Haven Ranch.

THREE RIVERS CREEK. Tributary to Pecos River at Roswell; private.

THROTTLE RESERVOIR. Ninety acres; Raton; private. Bass, bluegill.

TIERRA AMARILLA CREEK. Little stream flowing west, past the town of Tierra Amarilla to Chama River; private. Beaver dams and cutthroats high up; rainbow trout near Chama River early in season.

TINGLEY BEACH. Small lake near zoo in Albuquerque. Catfish, sunfish, trout in winter.

TOLBY CREEK. Tributary to Cimarron River from south, enters just below Eagle Nest dam; five miles. Rainbows, browns, cutthroats.

TOLEDO CREEK. Little tributary of Upper San Antonio on Baca Location in Jemez Mountains; private; three miles.

TOME RIVERSIDE DRAIN. Heads east of the river, opposite Isleta, and empties into Lower Peralta Drain, four miles above Belen. Stocked.

TORIETTE LAKES. Located near Reserve; private.

TRAIL CANYON CREEK. Tributary to Big Dry Creek. Gila trout, closed to fishing.

TRES LAGUNAS. Two small reservoirs near Santa Rosa; open to public. Bass, catfish, and sunfish.

TRINCHERA CREEK. Small stream, flows from Johnson Mesa to Raton; private. Cutthroat, rainbow trout.

TROUT CREEK. Very small stream, feeds Sapillo Creek, twenty miles north of Silver City; inaccessible by auto; three miles.

TROUT CREEK. Feeds San Francisco at Luna. Good little wild rainbow trout creek.

TROUT SPRINGS CREEK. Fed by five springs; tributary to Gallinas River west of Las Vegas; private. Good spawning place for rainbow trout.

TRUCHAS PEAK LAKE. At head of Rito de Las Chimayosos, on east side of Truchas; four acres. Planted with cutthroats.

TRUCHAS RIVER. Small stream heading near village of Truchas; six miles. Rainbow trout.

TUCUMCARI LAKE. A lake in a shallow silted natural basin just east of Tucumcari; limited fishing.

TULAROSA CREEK. Small tributary to San Francisco River above Aragon; spring fed; three miles. Browns, rainbows.

TULAROSA CREEK. Heads on Mescalero Apache Indian Reservation, flows west to Tularosa near Highway 70; ten miles. Good rainbow and brown trout public fishing just west of reservation to Round Mountain.

TURKEY CREEK. Small tributary of Gila River on Mogollon Mountains, reached by trail from Cliff or via Sapillo Creek trail; ten miles. Rainbows, browns.

TUSAS CREEK. North fork of Vallecitos Creek west of Tres Piedras; fishing from Tusas up to source; six miles. Browns.

UTE CREEK. A small tributary flowing from east and into Costilla River at Amalia; private; two miles. Fishing limited to a few beaver ponds, cutthroat and rainbow trout.

UTE LAKE. A large impoundment on the Canadian River at Logan; over twelve thousand surface acres; full-service state park with marina. Great smallmouth bass, bluegill, large-mouth bass, crappie, walleye, white bass, catfish.

VALLE GRANDE CREEK. Head of East Fork of the Jemez on the private Baca Location, in high mountain meadow country and flows through the Valle Grande; eight miles. Cutthroats.

VALLE MEDIO FORK. Extreme north fork of Bear Creek, reached by trail over Spring Mountain; brushy; four miles. Cutthroats.

VALLE VIDAL. Large addition to Carson National Forest. See *Costilla River, Comanche Creek, Ponil Creek,* and *Shuree Lakes.*

VALLECITOS CREEK. Large tributary to Chama, from Ojo Caliente through Cañones to head near Hopewell Lake; good stream, lower end on private and public land, upper end on Carson National Forest; thirty miles. Mostly browns.

VEGA BONITO CREEK. A fork of Valle Medio Fork of Bear Creek; heads in a meadow with marshes and underground stream; reached by trail via Elk Mountain; two miles.

VERMEJO PARK LAKES. Fantastic and expensive fee trout fishing on the private Vermejo Park Ranch west of Raton; 60 miles of stream and 308 acres of lake; on east side of the divide: Vermejo River, Merritt Lake, Munn Lake, Bernal Lake, Adams Lake, Bartlett Lake, and Mary's Lake; on the west side: Costilla Reservoir, Costilla Creek, Costilla No. 1 and No. 2 (partial listing).

WALL LAKE. Seven miles south of Beaverhead in Gila National Forest; silting in, marginal fishing; beautiful setting, campground; ten acres. Stocked rainbow trout, good bullfrogging.

WALNUT CREEK. Located west of Lake Arthur on Pecos River; private; some good fishing, but a small creek; four miles. Largemouth, bluegill, catfish.

WATERBIRD LAKE. Small lake at head of Rio Pueblo de Taos; private.

WEATHERLY LAKE. Near Des Moines; private. Bass, bluegill.

WEBSTER LAKE. On Philmont Scout Ranch near Cimarron; private.

WEST DRAIN. In Doña Ana County; heads one mile east of San Miguel Butte and enters the Nemexas Drain at the Texas line; twenty-five miles.

WHEATON CREEK. Tributary to Ocate Creek north of Ocate; private.

WHISKEY LAKE. Mountain trout lake on Navajo Reservation; east of S.R. 666, south of S.R. 134. Good trout fishing.

WHITE CREEK. Very good stream in Mogollon Mountains; tributary to West Fork of Gila River, joining it at Jenks Cabin; by trail from Willow Creek; five miles. Rainbow trout.

WHITE WATER CREEK. One of the best streams in Mogollon Mountains; flowing out through Glenwood to San Francisco River. Rugged scenic county, much box canyon; road to Catwalks, then trail upstream; not stocked; eleven miles. Wild rainbows, browns, brooks.

Zuñi Reservoir

WHITE WATER CREEK, SOUTH FORK.   Rough but scenic; trail only; five miles. Brook trout.

WILLIAMS LAKE.   At head of Lake Fork of the Hondo, north of Taos; excellent high mountain lake; trail; ten acres. Stocked cutthroats.

WILLOW CREEK.   Channelized creek feeding pumped-in Colorado water to Heron Lake; private.

WILLOW CREEK.   Fairly good little tributary of Pecos River, entering one mile above Terrero; six miles. Cutthroat, rainbow trout.

WILLOW CREEK.   Headwaters of Middle Fork of Gila River, on S.R. 78; little creek, heavily fished, heavily stocked.

WILLOW CREEK.   Heads just west of the head of the Brazos, flows westward to Chama River at the town of Chama; brushy, private; seven miles. Cutthroat, rainbow trout.

WILLOW LAKE.   A private lake, 360 acres, in Eddy County near Malaga. Bass, bluegill, walleye, and catfish.

WINSOR CREEK.   Small tributary of the Pecos at Cowles, heading at Lake Katherine and Stewart Lake; very good but brushy; six miles. Cutthroat, rainbow trout.

WOLF CREEK.   Tributary of the Chama heading in Colorado, flows southwest into the Chama four miles above the town of Chama, on Lobo Lodge land; fee-fishing. Cutthroat, rainbow, and brook trout.

YESO CREEK.   Tributary of Pecos River, southeast of Fort Sumner; private.

YOUNG'S CANYON CREEK.   Small tributary to the Gallinas; private.

ZIA RESERVOIR.   Irrigation lake near Zia Pueblo, four acres; Zia permit required; off S.R. 44 north of Bernalillo. Stocked rainbows.

ZUÑI RESERVATION LAKES.   See *Black Rock Lake, Eustace Lake, Galestino, Nutria Lakes, Ojo Caliente Lakes,* and *Pescado Lake.* Permit required.

ZUÑI RESERVOIR.   See *Black Rock Lake* and *Eustace Lake.*